Chicken Soup for the Soul®

Teacher Tales

Chicken Soup for the Soul: Teacher Tales;
101 Inspirational Stories from Great Teachers and Appreciative Students
by Jack Canfield, Mark Victor Hansen, Amy Newmark
Foreword by Anthony J. Mullen, 2009 National Teacher of the Year

Published by Chicken Soup for the Soul Publishing, LLC   www.chickensoup.com

The publisher gratefully acknowledges the many publishers and individuals who
granted Chicken Soup for the Soul permission to reprint the cited material.

Cover illustration courtesy of iStockPhoto.com/procurator/© Evgeniy Ivanov. Cover photo
courtesy of iStockPhoto.com/luminis. Back cover photo courtesy of Getty Images/Mark
Wilson. Interior illustration courtesy of iStockPhoto.com/kemie

Cover and Interior Design & Layout by Pneuma Books, LLC
For more info on Pneuma Books, visit www.pneumabooks.com

Distributed to the booktrade by Simon & Schuster. SAN: 200-2442

Publisher's Cataloging-in-Publication Data
(Prepared by The Donohue Group)

Chicken soup for the soul : teacher tales : 101 inspirational stories from great
    teachers and appreciative students / [compiled by] Jack Canfield, Mark Victor
    Hansen [and] Amy Newmark ; foreword by Anthony J. Mullen.

    p. ; cm.

    ISBN: 978-1-935096-47-4

1. Teachers--United States--Literary collections. 2. Teachers--United States--
Anecdotes. 3. Teaching--United States--Literary collections. 4. Teaching--United
States--Anecdotes. 5. Students--United States--Literary collections. 6. Students--
United States--Anecdotes. 7. Teacher-student relationships--United States--Literary
collections. 8. Teacher-student relationships--United States--Anecdotes. I. Canfield,
Jack, 1944- II. Hansen, Mark Victor. III. Newmark, Amy. IV. Mullen, Anthony J.,
1960- V. Title: Teacher tales

PN6071.T3 C45 2009
810.8/0921/3711   2009942318

PRINTED IN THE UNITED STATES OF AMERICA
on acid∞free paper
16 15 14 13 12 11   04 05 06 07 08

Chicken Soup for the Soul

Teacher Tales

101 Inspirational Stories
from Great Teachers
and Appreciative Students

Jack Canfield
Mark Victor Hansen
Amy Newmark

Foreword by Anthony J. Mullen
2009 National Teacher of the Year

Chicken Soup for the Soul Publishing, LLC
Cos Cob, CT

Chicken Soup
www.chickensoup.com
of the Soul

Contents

Foreword, *Anthony J. Mullen* xi

❶
~Why We Teach~

1. Falling Down, *Anthony J. Mullen* 1
2. I'm Glad It's You and Not Me, *Jean Lamar* 4
3. I Am a Teacher, *Alice King* 7
4. Dream, Vincent, Dream, *George A. Watson* 10
5. Destined to Teach, *Karen Gill* 13
6. Echoes in the Classroom, *Susan Johnson* 16
7. A Lesson for Life, *James Edward Phillips* 21
8. Become Like Bumblebees, *Bebi Davis* 23
9. Power of the Pen, *Susan Elliott* 27
10. Music Touches the Soul, *Mark D. Teesdale* 29

❷
~First Year Tales~

11. Ooh La La, *Adrienne Townsend* 35
12. My Mia, *Stephanie Doyle* 39
13. Who Would I Do Without?,
    Richards M. Boyce as told to Suzanne M. Boyce 42
14. First Year Drama, *Robbie Iobst* 45
15. Whatever Works, *Marcia Rudoff* 50
16. My Christmas Lesson, *Anna M. Lowther* 54
17. The Fly in the Room, *Jennifer A. Haberling* 57
18. Burgers and Cries, *Sara Matson* 61
19. Teaching from Courage, *Quyen Thai* 64

❸
~Learning from the Kids~

20. Tools of the Trade, *Beth Ekre* 71
21. The Little Choir with a Big Dream, *Kay Conner Pliszka* 74
22. Life Lessons from My Students, *Susan Waggener* 78
23. Welcome to the Fourth Grade, *Jan Bono* 82
24. An Unexpected Lesson, *Michael Lampert* 85
25. Connecting, *Tania L. Harman* 88
26. The Glitter Mask, *Celeste Miller* 91
27. School Glue, *Dorothy Goff Goulet* 95
28. Recess Moment, *Jeanne Muzi* 98
29. The Unexpected Difference, *Rebecca Snyder* 101
30. The Healing Power of Children, *Tim Ramsey* 104

❹
~Great Ideas~

31. Tales from the Rappin' Mathematician, *Alex Kajitani* 109
32. Bring Me Back a Rock, *Adrienne C. Reynolds* 113
33. Growing Roots, *Kimberly A. Worthy* 119
34. Queen Act, *Janeen Lewis* 124
35. Making a Difference in Our Community,
    Sally J. Broughton 128
36. The Beatnik of Lincoln, *Rick Weber* 131
37. Real World Math, *Heather Sparks* 135
38. Eye See You, *Malinda Dunlap Fillingim* 139
39. Gifts for Jace, *Angela N. Abbott* 141

❺
~Thanks, I Needed That~

40. The Lesson, *William Bingham* 147
41. A Few Minutes of Kindness, *Steve Johnson* 151

42. Blessed to Be a Teacher, *Margaret Williams* 155
43. A Wrinkled Piece of Paper, *Deborah Wickerham* 158
44. The Power of Belief, *Paul Kuhlman* 162
45. Not Lost In Translation, *Vickie A. Mike* 166
46. Persistence Pays, *Nancy Hamilton Sturm* 169
47. Five Words, *MaryLu Hutchins* 172
48. Mary, *Christine Gleason* 175

❻

~That Was Embarrassing~

49. Roller Call, *Martha Moore* 181
50. Field Trip Fiasco, *Ron Kaiser, Jr.* 184
51. Bountiful Sharing in First Grade, *Linda A. Smerge* 188
52. The Naughty Kid, *Sarah Smiley* 191
53. Classroom Fun, *Lori Neurohr* 195
54. Crayon Crisis, *Diane M Miller* 197
55. Full of Surprises, *Blythe Turner* 200
56. Social Secretary, *Ilah Breen* 203

❼

~Touched by a Student~

57. Letters from Home, *Jenna Hallman* 209
58. Teaching the Teacher, *Lisa McCaskill* 212
59. Ashley, *Deborah Hohn Tonguis* 214
60. Step by Step, *Derek Olson* 218
61. I Wish Every Teacher a Kevonna, *Patricia L. Marini* 221
62. Special Treatment, *D. B. Zane* 225
63. Clinton, *Cindy Couchman* 228
64. Not in My Class, *Sherry Poff* 231
65. The Heart of Emily, *Stephanie Scharaga Winnick* 236

8
~The Teacher Who Changed My Life~

66. Divine Intervention, *Gloria L. Noyes* 243
67. It's a Great Day to Be Alive!, *Kate Lynn Mishara*..................247
68. The Gift of Self-Esteem, *Leanne Maule-Sims* 250
69. Words of Wisdom, *Amanda Dodson* 255
70. A Teacher's Influence, *Dan McCarthy* 258
71. A Lifelong Friendship, *Jayde Rossi*...............................262
72. Not So Accidental, *Brooke M. Businsky* 265
73. The Dunce Row, *Deb Fogg* 268

9
~Tough Kids~

74. Unforgettable, *Barbara Walton-Faria* 275
75. A Tale of Two Students, *Roy Hudson*...............................278
76. Chad's Award, *Cheryl Y. Brundage*.................................281
77. Going the Distance, *Bob Williams*.................................284
78. When Grace Steps In, *Amy Morrison*................................288
79. Angry Blue Eyes, *Sandra Picklesimer Aldrich* 291
80. Getting Away from School, *Paul Karrer*............................294
81. Becoming an Educator, *Sarah Baird* 298

10
~Reconnecting~

82. The White Car, *Sharilynn Townsend La May* 305
83. A Lesson in Friendship, *Julie Mellott George* 308
84. A Chance Encounter, *Sharon Gallagher-Fishbaugh*...................313
85. Garage Sale Revelation, *Lisa Miller Rychel* 315
86. The Treasure Chest, *Robin Sly* 317
87. Simple Pleasures, *Jean Brody*.....................................319

88. Stoop to Conquer, *Edney L. Freeman* 321
89. More than Math, *Michael Segal* 325

⑪
~Reflections on Being a Teacher~

90. Making a Difference, *Linda Heffner* 331
91. Attitude of Gratitude, *Tommie Ann Grinnell* 334
92. Secrets Students Keep, *Luajean N. Bryan* 338
93. Brand New Starts, *Diane Stark* 342
94. Springtime Memory, *Cindi Rigsbee* 346
95. Teacher's Summer List, *Kenan Bresnan* 349
96. A Simple Place, *Diana Leddy* 353
97. A Loss for Words, *Gary Rubinstein* 357
98. A Greater Purpose, *Chantelle Herchenhahn* 360
99. First Day Jitters, *Amy Benoit* 362
100. An Indian Teaches American-Style in Polynesia,
     Murali Gopal 365
101. Touching the Future, *William Thomas* 369

Meet Our Contributors 373
Meet Our Authors 392
Thank You 394
About Chicken Soup for the Soul 396

Foreword

A veteran teacher told me recently that she was considering leaving the teaching profession. "I don't wake up with the energy I once had," she sighed. "It's taking me longer to get dressed in the morning and that's not good for my students."

Sadly, this teacher is not alone. I have been meeting many teachers who are spending too much time getting dressed in the morning. Some no longer even bother to get dressed because they have left the classroom. But I had a nagging feeling that the arduous task of teaching was not the culprit responsible for sapping her morning energy.

"What's really causing you to want to leave teaching?" I asked.

She paused for a few moments before responding. "I feel that I work in a profession people no longer respect or value," she replied. "My school measures the value of everything I do around test scores. I have never seen it so bad; each week I am being told a new way in which to raise test scores. I am slowly losing my ability to both teach *and* nurture my students."

What has become of the noble profession of teaching? From the perspective of an experienced teaching professional, the state of American education has become a data-driven system concerned more with standardized test scores than the social and emotional needs of children. A profession designed to better the human condition is losing its humane characteristics.

And that is why *Chicken Soup for the Soul: Teacher Tales* is such an important and timely book. Written by and for teachers, it is a different type of book because it does not try to promote a new method of pedagogy or try to reinvent the wheel. How refreshing. This book is about the heart and soul of teaching and why we have committed our lives to helping children.

Chicken Soup for the Soul: Teacher Tales is filled with wonderful stories about teachers and children. Some of the stories will make you laugh and some of the stories will make you cry. A few will make you want to scream at an educational bureaucracy seemingly blind to the needs of children and teachers. You may get the urge to throw this book at a bureaucrat. That's okay; just don't break the book's spine.

When I was asked to write the foreword for this book, I needed to know if the book could reinvigorate teachers who are suffering from mental and physical exhaustion. Could it be used as a balm for the weary teachers I encounter while traveling across the nation? Chicken Soup for the Soul's publisher, Amy Newmark, who has personally edited this book, quickly answered my question. Amy is a soft-spoken lady but when she speaks about the welfare of teachers her voice elevates to a higher octave. Amy stressed the need for a book that can inspire novice and veteran teachers alike, a book written by classroom teachers who know how to tell a meaningful tale. I left Amy's office feeling reinvigorated and eager to share my excitement with colleagues.

The faces of my fellow 2009 State Teachers of the Year soon flooded my mind as I thought about the purpose and importance of *Chicken Soup for the Soul: Teacher Tales*. I have been a lucky and privileged teacher, and one of the greatest privileges of being named National Teacher of the Year has been meeting so many gifted colleagues. Amy and I talked about the possibility of each State Teacher of the Year submitting a story to the book. The idea had a lot of merit because these teachers represent some of the very best teachers in our country, educators who understand that what we teach is not as important as whom we teach. I proposed the idea to the 2009 State Teachers of the Year and the response was unanimous: We need this type of book! Writing a story for this book became a means for them to express their passion for teaching and restoring the value of teachers in our lives. The stories written by these teachers are included among the many wonderful stories contributed by outstanding teachers and grateful students.

Living in a fast-paced world flooded with technology has taken something away from the essential human desire to enjoy a story. And the increasing standardization and measurement of our profession has sapped us of some of our passion. The 101 stories in this inspirational book will provide every teacher some relaxation and some fresh energy. This book reminds us why we are teachers and why we love our work. And it shows us that we are indeed much appreciated.

~Anthony J. Mullen
2009 National Teacher of the Year
2009 Connecticut State Teacher of the Year

Teacher Tales

Why We Teach

*Man's mind, once stretched by a new idea,
never regains its original dimensions.*

~Oliver Wendell Holmes

Falling Down

The best teachers teach from the heart, not from the book.
~Author Unknown

Spanish Harlem is full of life on summer nights, but this young lady wanted to die. The crowd of onlookers pointed fingers at a teenage girl standing atop a fire escape rail, dangling her body over the rusty rail and throwing pieces of jewelry to the street below.

An elderly man told me that she was *loco* and would probably jump. He shrugged his shoulders and walked away. I raced up the wooden stairs of the old tenement building, hoping to quickly locate the window leading to the distraught teenager. I found the open window on the fifth floor.

I poked my head outside the window and pleaded with the girl not to jump. A mouthful of clichés was all I could offer. "You're too young to die. You're too beautiful. You have family and friends that love you."

My words only contributed to her death wish—she released one hand from the railing. I did not want to be the last face she saw before jumping off the fire escape. And I did not want to see the look on her face as she went free-falling to a dirty New York City street.

"I'm sick of all this shit and just want to fuckin' die!" she screamed at me. She tore away a pair of earrings and threw them at the growing crowd of spectators.

I was tired and unsure. My morning was spent in a college

classroom, far removed from this urban drama. I was studying to become a teacher and learning about Howard Gardner's theory of multiple intelligences. Now I was dressed in the uniform of an NYC police sergeant trying to persuade a teenager that her life was worth living. My powers of persuasion were having the same effect as Superman wearing a suit of kryptonite.

I squeezed through the small window and stood within a few feet of the jumper. "Don't get any closer," she said. Suddenly *my* clichés did not sound like trite words.

"I'm not going to get any closer to you...."

She jumped.

Call it luck or fate or divine intervention but I managed to grab hold of one of her arms as she leapt from her wrought iron perch. Her weight quickly pulled the top half of my body over the railing and I could feel my feet lifting off the grated floor. *Lord, give me strength* echoed through my mind. My partner reached out from inside the room and he grabbed the back of my belt. I could feel her arm slipping away from my hold and told him to run downstairs; he needed to be on the fire escape directly below us. Soon he was staring up at us, trying to grab hold of a pair of swinging legs.

I was attending college because I wanted to become a teacher and work with troubled teenagers, the types of young people roaming our streets like so many broken toys. I wanted to save souls and was now losing a life.

Lord, please give me strength; I need only a few more minutes of strength.

My partner managed to take hold of the girl's legs, relieving some of the stress on my back and arms. I quickly tucked my hands under her armpits and pulled her up. We each sat huffing and puffing on the old fire escape.

A few stories have fairy tale endings, but most just end. The suicidal teenager was taken to a local hospital and I returned to patrol the streets of Spanish Harlem. A few weeks later I saw her hanging out on a street corner, laughing and listening to music with friends.

I sometimes see her face in the faces of the students that I teach today. I got my wish to teach and mentor troubled teenagers. My students suffer from depression, anxiety, bipolar disorder and psychosis. Some are lonely, some are sad, some are angry, and some are frightened. But all risk falling down unless we are there to catch them.

~Anthony J. Mullen
2009 National Teacher of the Year
2009 Connecticut State Teacher of the Year
Special Education teacher, grades 9-12

I'm Glad It's You and Not Me

*Teachers who inspire realize there will always be
rocks in the road ahead of us. They will be stumbling blocks or
stepping stones; it all depends on how we use them.*
~Author Unknown

It was 2:00 AM. The moon gleamed ever so slightly through a crack in the curtains, just enough for me to glance over at my husband, sleeping like a newborn, snoring for the entire world to hear. If only I could rest so peacefully.

But I couldn't, of course. It was the beginning of another school year, and waking up hours before the alarm invariably accompanies a new school start—even after almost twenty years. My mind raced with thoughts of all the tasks I had done—"finding" filing cabinets, shelves, tables, decorating my room, planning new course syllabi, buying supplies (and praying that I would have money left to pay my bills)—and all the things I hadn't. I was starting a new curriculum, new grade-levels at a new school, and this year, I had agreed to teach all struggling students in need of critical intervention… where would I go from here? I knew what lay ahead—arduous work hours overlaid with guilt, consumed with essays that needed feedback, lesson plans desirous of best practice strategies, and ideas to try to reach even the most reluctant learner. No wonder people always acknowledge my teaching career with, "I'm glad it's you and not me." The knot in my stomach continued to tighten.

Suddenly, my already muddled mind transported me to another time and place... to my first few years of teaching.

"Peter Potter," I called from my roll, trying to stifle my laughter. "Laughlin McLaughlin?" Surely these were not real names.

"Emotionally handicapped... keep them separated from the other kids... in this portable," the Assistant Principal commanded. This was my first teaching assignment, in a field outside my scope of training (mine was English Education), obviously long before it was considered inappropriate to label kids. Even the students had names for each other. "Stank" was the one I sadly recalled, even after all this time.

And then... "the incident"—when I looked down to see an exposed body part that I did not—in any way, shape, or form—desire to see! I felt myself hyperventilating at the mere thought....

Surely this year could never be as daunting as those first few.

Later that day, I looked across my "new" classroom, into the face of Jason, whose cumulative folder I had just read. At eleven, his mother and brother were killed in an automobile accident, leaving him with physical, academic, and certainly emotional scars. I looked at another student, Robert, standing at the door; my Assistant Principal asked if I would take him, even though he was an eleventh grader in my tenth grade class. "He can't read; he'll drop out unless you can do something with him." Of course I said yes; what else could I do?

These stories merged into others across the years—Stephanie, who used writing as a catharsis to cope with the loss of her precious cancer-stricken mother; Michael, who so powerfully connected with the Greasers in *The Outsiders* because he, too, had been abandoned by his family; Jason, whose crack-addict mother was murdered in an inner-city alley; Brian, who ran away from his foster home, desperately in search of a "real" home and perhaps more importantly, in search of himself; Joey and Dave, whose hands literally shook with fear when trying to "perform" for a test. Stories of tears and sadness, yet of hope that I could somehow make a difference in spite of such brokenness.

But then there were—and are—stories of success—of Dustin, in graduate school for Electrical and Computer Engineering; of Noah, in seminary, preparing to serve God in the ministry; of Michael—the same Michael abandoned by his mother—now a teacher in an inner city school; of Willie, once a struggling reader, who went on to become the first generation college graduate in his African-American family. I thought of Emily and Andi, of Amber and Kayla and Mallory, whose love and enthusiasm for books and characters still warm my thoughts. I thought of creative lessons, Shakespeare Festivals, school plays, and after-school tutoring sessions that have filled my life day after day, year after year. I thought of the thousands of students whose lives have touched mine far more than I could have ever have touched theirs.

I broke from my reverie, a smile radiating across my face. Sadness, tears, challenges, fears—yes, teaching is filled with all of these—yet, it is undeniably also filled with laughter and smiles, hope, dreams, and rewards beyond measure.

"I'm glad it's you and not me." Those words reverberated in my mind once again. *Yeah, so am I*, I thought… *so am I.*

~Jean Lamar
2009 Florida State Teacher of the Year
English, Reading teacher, grades 9-12

I Am a Teacher

What the teacher is, is more important than what he teaches.
~Karl Menninger

Glancing into my world, the observant sees...
Students seeking guidance
A sea of eyes filled with determination, defiance, and delight
Rooms filled with distinct personalities begging to be noticed
Adolescents bombarded with issues searching for approval
Bright minds daring me to challenge them
I accept...
I am a teacher

Drifting through the halls, the intent listener will hear...
Students voicing opinions, learning how to support them
The creaking of minds opening to new concepts
Ideas being absorbed within the walls of the classroom
Discussions full of insightful comments, shouts of celebration
        for a job well done
The tones of student voices noting signs of frustration or joy
I listen...
I am a teacher

Gurgling inspiration runs deep, I feel...
The uncertainty of students venturing into adulthood

A passion for teaching each morning as I step before my
    audience
An impression that I can make a difference one baby step at a
    time
As if I can never obtain enough knowledge, I must keep
    learning
Anguish, sometimes caring more than a heart can bear
I have faith...
I am a teacher

Inhaling deeply, I sense...
The educational winds of change blowing in a continuing eddy
Swirls of standards, expectations, and objectives surrounding
    us
Frenzied collisions of assessments and potential achievements
A call for improved cooperation among students, teachers, and
    community
The future filled with possibilities
I hope...
I am a teacher

Examining within myself, I acknowledge...
A deep need to please everyone, still knowing this is not
    feasible
Empathy pouring from my heart towards students who lose
    their direction
An imbedded desire to mend hurts and create a better
    environment
A yearning to be a teacher who taps into the creative spirit
The challenge of balancing roles of mother, wife, educator,
    advisor, and coach
I am not super woman...
I am a teacher

Offering advice to prospective teachers, I recommend…
Pursuing the field of education with an open heart and mind
Exploring all the nuances of your subject area and gaining a
    strong understanding
Accepting the fact that teaching is a life choice
Remembering that your humanity makes you perfect for the
    role
Knowing that the perks are intrinsic
Nothing compares to being an influence in so many lives
You take a chance…
Be a teacher

~Alice King
2009 Wyoming State Teacher of the Year
English, Speech teacher, grades 10-12

Dream, Vincent, Dream

You can teach a student a lesson for a day; but if you can teach him to learn
by creating curiosity, he will continue the learning process as long as he lives.
~Clay P. Bedford

I have taught Spanish to thousands of students over my thirty-six years at Walpole High School in Walpole, Massachusetts. My students have ranged from the most academically gifted to the academically at-risk. There is one young man, however, who in the course of his high school career surpassed expectations of everyone in his life: his parents, his former teachers, his peers and himself. His name is Vincent Lee.

Vinnie entered my classroom as a nervous freshman on his first day of high school in September, 2005. He was enrolled in our Spanish IA course, a transition course between Spanish I and Spanish II for students who under-performed in Spanish I. In fact, Vinnie had not had a lot of success in Spanish in the middle school. His eighth grade teacher had described him as that "sad, introverted boy in the last row who always kept his head down." Vinnie often went to class unprepared and could not see the point to learning another language. And yet there were other reasons to explain this lack of motivation. Vinnie was dealing with a lot of turmoil in his life: the recent divorce of his parents, a move from a house to an apartment, and much greater responsibility at home for taking care of his younger twin brothers as his mother, now a single parent, was going to night school to earn her bachelor's degree and better her own life and that of her family.

From the very start of my course I sensed an attitude that separated Vinnie from his peers. He entered class each day, took his seat quietly and took out what he needed for the lesson. At first he was somewhat shy about answering questions in Spanish, but as the course progressed, I was able to engage him in conversations about his family, his interests and his passions. These included football, baseball and track. With time Vinnie became more willing to volunteer and even ask me questions. He seemed fascinated by the fact that my parents were from Costa Rica and that I was fluent in both English and Spanish. When he once asked how long it takes to become fluent in another language, I explained that it takes many years and that the first sign that a person has adopted the language as his own is when one dreams in that language. Contrary to what we had seen in middle school, Vinnie rarely missed a homework assignment because this meant the dreaded "red snake" stamp on his homework calendar. On those rare occasions that this happened, Vinnie would become very frustrated with himself and I had to reassure him that he still had a very good chance at getting an A- on homework for that month.

Clearly, Vinnie was beginning to view himself as a student. Furthermore, I was beginning to view him as a positive role model for the other students. He was my "go-to guy" when no one could answer a question or when I needed to pair up a struggling student with someone who was more proficient. Once spring came I recommended that he participate in the National Spanish Exam contest. Much to my surprise he decided to do so and later we found out that he had won a *certificado de mérito*. One of my proudest moments as his teacher was to call Vinnie to the stage at our annual Foreign Language Awards Night to honor him for his outstanding performance.

By the end of the year Vinnie had achieved such a high level of proficiency that I recommended him for the honors program in Spanish, quite a remarkable achievement for a student who was in "transition." In fact, this had never happened before at our high school. I remember often wondering what it was about this class that had brought out the best in this young man.

Although I never had Vinnie again in class I followed him until his graduation this past year, watching him play cornerback in the Super Bowl state football championship at Gillette Stadium, marveling at his amazing accomplishments in track (coming in 4th in the New England meet in the 100-meter race) and hearing subsequent Spanish teachers sing his praises. During his senior year Vinnie and I had several opportunities to speak about his college pursuits and future goals. In those conversations he shared with me a couple of observations that touched me deeply. First of all, he said that my class was the first class in high school where he had tasted success. He said that my enthusiasm for the Spanish language and culture had motivated him to continue with Spanish for the next three years. In his words, my class was not just a Spanish lesson, it was a Spanish experience and this had "flipped" his view of learning a language. Secondly, he confessed to me that he had recently dreamt in Spanish. He said that when he woke up that morning he thought about what I had said in class when he was a freshman and that this had made him very proud of how far he had come in his foreign language study.

Having taught Vinnie four years ago has made me reflect on the importance of connecting with kids in class and the importance of igniting that spark which will propel them down the road to academic success. It has also reminded me how success begets success and what an amazing engine this can be for anyone who makes the effort.

Like all good stories, this one has a happy ending. Vinnie graduated in the top ten percent of his class and went on to Tufts University, the first male in his family to go to college. His dream is to attend medical school, to become a doctor, and to find a cure for Crohn's disease, an ailment which has plagued him all his life. I have no doubt that "Vicente" will be successful in whatever profession he chooses and that, perhaps, someday he may even dream in Spanish once again.

~George A. Watson
2009 Massachusetts State Teacher of the Year
Spanish teacher, grades 9-12

Destined to Teach

All that I am or ever hope to be, I owe to my angel Mother.
~Abraham Lincoln

My mother made me a teacher. I don't mean that she forced me to become a teacher; in fact she was adamant that I could be anything I wanted. My mother made me a teacher because she taught me to love learning, and to love sharing. Her own father told her that there wasn't any point in a girl going to school past the eighth grade, but my mother knew better. Between her influence, and my own natural tendencies, I was destined to teach.

In addition to my mother's overriding influence, there are several other events in my life that convinced me to become a teacher. When I was little I could not pronounce the syllable "er." No one could understand me. I remember being VERY frustrated. Then, when I was four, my mother took me to meet a wonderful speech teacher named Miss Philips. Within six weeks the problem was fixed; I could say "sister" and "flower" and all of the plentiful and powerful "er" words. I learned then, in a very personal way, the tremendous power of education. My mother said, "Teaching is the world's most important job," and I knew exactly what she meant.

When I was thirteen I spent a month in Shiner's Hospital having a spinal fusion for scoliosis. I was there for two weeks before the surgery, having tests run and getting to know the other patients in the ward. The other children were wonderful, very sweet and caring. I had them sign an autograph book so I could remember them. I remember being shocked that although they were all close to my age, and very intelligent, many of them could barely write their names. My mother explained that many of them had been in and out of hospitals their entire lives and had not had a stable education. I learned then what a difference the opportunity to learn could make for a child. My mother said, "An education is the one thing no one can take away from you."

In middle school and high school I took the most difficult, most diverse classes offered to me. My classes included band, industrial arts, visual arts, creative writing, calculus and physics. Physics was hard, and it made me really think; it was wonderful! I made straight A's and graduated as valedictorian. My mother always said, "Learn every day like you are going to live forever" and, "If it's worth doing, it's worth doing right." So when I was ready to pick a career, I had a strong work ethic, a love of learning, a respect for teachers, a desire to think and help others, and the belief that education could change everyone's life for the better. I knew I had to be a teacher.

I purposefully made the choice to teach, and except for a few times during my first year, I have never regretted it. Teaching has been a wonderful career for me and I have been lucky enough to make what I feel are some important contributions to education. I am eternally grateful to the teachers and programs that helped me learn the art of teaching and I am committed to helping other teachers. As a presenter at district, state, and national meetings and as a national "Physics Teacher Resource Agent" I have had the opportunity to share ideas with teachers throughout the state and even the nation. I know that by helping, equipping, and encouraging other teachers, I am able to touch students that I will never see.

I am very proud of my work with other teachers, but I consider my first responsibility, and most important accomplishment, to be the success of my students. I love to see the light in a student's eyes when understanding dawns. I also love hearing from former students. This note came from a girl who would hardly talk above a whisper when she first started my class. "Ms. Gill, I didn't realize HOW MUCH I learned in your class. It is three years later and I am getting A's in PHY 232 without even studying!" This e-mail came from a girl who started my class with no interest in math or science: "I've officially declared my major. I declared as a Physics BS with a math minor. I am seriously considering working towards being a professor or high school teacher. I guess this just goes to show how much a class in high school can change what you want to do with your life. Thanks again!"

Throughout my teaching career I have had many students say to me, "I know why you became a physics teacher, it's because you get to play with the coolest toys!" I just smile. The "toys" are a great teaching tool. They catch students' attention, help them relax, and make them want to understand how things work. I do have to admit they are cool—but they aren't why I became a physics teacher. My mother did NOT say "Playing with toys is the world's most important job." Watching the students learn and be excited about learning, feeling like they have benefited from my planning, support, guidance and passion—those things make teaching a wonderful job. Hearing them say things like "This is cool," "Wow—this makes sense," and "Ms. Gill, you have corrupted my mind; I am seeing physics concepts everywhere," and especially having them come back to visit after they graduate—that is why I love teaching. I feel like I am making a difference in the lives of my students, and in the world, and so I will always be grateful to my mother for making me a teacher.

~Karen Gill
2009 Kentucky State Teacher of the Year
Physics teacher, grade 11

Echoes in the Classroom

*The object of teaching a child is to
enable him to get along without his teacher.*
~Elbert Hubbard

I sit here in this empty classroom in June,
desks cleared,
chairs stacked,
computers disassembled,
lamp wires wrapped like vines around their stands.
My grades are posted,
the checkout complete.
The cabinet doors are bare, naked without the student poems.
Only the photos of Earth,
Gandhi, Sojourner Truth, and Cesar Chavez remain
high above the windows
exempt from the maintenance list.
My pile of plants, poetry books, and journals
lie by the outside door, ready to return home for the summer.
The custodian and I are the only ones
left in the building.
I sit for a moment
in the stillness.
And from the carpet in the back,
up against the curtains,
a voice rises:

"Let every soldier hew him down a bough
And bear't before him…" (*Macbeth* 5.4.4-5)

And there, in the back of the room, I am certain I can see Matt, wielding his sword, cloaked in his cape, leading his army to defeat Macbeth and claim the kingdom as its rightful heir.

Matt, who had written to me in September, "I play football. I have a hard time presenting to the class. I have a hard time writing essays like getting started." Who revealed, "I need a little help writing an introduction. I would like to write my own poem." He shared that he "didn't read that good" and that his goals were "to finish a long book…" and "As a communicator my strengths are bad because I'm not that good at speaking to a big class. I think I would do better speaking to you."

Matt, who had sat with me in October, trying to find a focus for his memoir, looking for that significant moment in his trip to Mount Rushmore. Drawing the door that led out to the monument, the wooden walkway, the carvings, himself, his grandparents. Speaking from the picture to describe the size, the colors, the faces. Having the courage to return to his draft, to narrow his focus, to organize, to go small and detailed. He wrote that memoir, even though "at first I didn't even know what a memoir was." And he wrote poetry—an "I Am From" poem, a found poem, a nonsense poem, poems he became willing to share in class. He wrote to the football coach to persuade him to purchase new jerseys for the JV team. He learned to be a writer. In fact, in November he wrote, "As a writer at this time, I just love it. I find writing fascinating to do."

He read *The Kite Runner* by choice, and "learned to understand what the book means in my eyes." He became comfortable in his small group to talk about the class readings: Atticus' courage, Langston Hughes' "salvation," Sandra Cisneros' disappointment. He explained, "At the beginning of the trimester I sucked in talking with groups…. I needed to break out of my shell and just be a communicator. Now I am a great communicator. I love speaking in groups, and to you, Mrs. Johnson…."

So in February when were ready to study *Macbeth*, and we set the classroom up as a theater and Sarah brought in her collection of costumes and we pulled out our wooden swords and turned the lights down low, Matt said he wanted to take the role of Malcolm. Matt, who had been too shy to read his memoir in Author's Circle, wanted to take the role of Malcolm.

And so he became Malcolm. In our Readers' Theatre, he fled to England upon learning of the murder of his father; he urged Macduff to turn his own grief for his family's massacre to anger; he ordered his soldiers to hide themselves with boughs from Birnam Wood. Then just about the time we were nearing Act Five, Matt approached me after school, voice lowered, head bent, shoulders dropped, "Mrs. Johnson, my mother is taking me to Arizona to see my aunt next week. I'll be gone for five days." We both knew what his absence would mean: the class would finish the play without him. "I told my mother I'm Malcolm. I've read ahead and I know he's going to become king. I told her I want to be here to finish the play."

I commiserated with Matt that day, as disappointed as he that his culminating scene would pass to another student. I privately wondered if the confidence he had built might fade without the opportunity to perform his "finale." We brainstormed solutions like delaying the trip until Spring Break — but he had already tried that suggestion to no avail. I phoned his mother, but as friendly as the conversation was, she said she needed to keep her plans. Matt and I reluctantly accepted the reality and made lesson plans for his absence.

That Saturday, I saw Matt's grandmother in the checkout line at Safeway. She and I had known each other for more than twenty years — both of us educators. In fact, she had taught my son. I decided that fate must have given me this opportunity and joined her in line. After our initial, effusive hugs and hellos, I ventured my attempt."I'm sorry Matt will miss his performance in *Macbeth* next week."

"Oh, yes," she said, "he told me how much he loves being in that play."

"I sure was hoping his mother could put that trip off until Spring

Break to give him a chance to claim the crown in the final scene. He was so excited about that moment."

"Hmm. Yes, I was thinking along those same lines," she agreed.

"Well, if you can use any of your grandma influence, it would be great for Matt."

That was that. She paid the cashier, we said our goodbyes, and I loaded my groceries onto the conveyor belt.

I arrive at school early—in the quiet of the morning—that's my best time to write plans on the board, score a few papers, check my e-mail, meet with struggling students. I had not scheduled appointments the next morning. But before the rush of the bus arrival, the flood of students in the hallway, Matt appeared at the classroom door. Smiling broadly, he strode across the floor. "Well, I've got some good news! My grandfather called my mother last night and talked her into taking our trip over Spring Break!"

"That's great news, Matt! You *are* Malcolm!" And then, with a bit of a whoop, we high-fived in celebration.

Matt readied for his final scene, nervous, for he knew his lines closed the play. As Macduff entered with Macbeth's head, all shouted to Malcolm, "Hail King of Scotland!" Matt stood tall, cloaked in his cape, sword resting in triumph, Burger King crown now placed on his head. In his nervousness, he stumbled on a few of his phrases. Nevertheless, he did his best to proclaim:

> ...*Of this dead butcher and his fiendlike queen,*
> *Who, as 'tis thought, by self and violent hands*
> *Took off her life—this and what needful else*
> *That calls upon us, by the grace of Grace*
> *We will perform in measure, time, and place:*
> *So thanks for all at once and to each one,*
> *Whom we invite to see us crowned at Scone.*
> (Macbeth 5.7.69-75)

With a final flourish, the stage emptied. Matt later chided himself for stumbling over those last words, but I assured him no one else had noticed. He had portrayed the noble role nobly and discovered the strength to perform in front of his peers.

Matt wants to perform in more plays; he wants to write more and read more. "What I learned is to just break out of your surrounding and just have fun while you're at school. My strengths are just to do it and not look back on your high school career and say hey I really wish I could have had fun in all of my classes."

So
as I sit here in this empty classroom,
I am certain I hear his voice,
see his broad smile,
feel the clap of his high-five celebration.
That's him
face-to-face with the antagonist,
rising to his challenge,
voicing his convictions,
and triumphing in his hope.

~Susan Johnson
2009 Washington State Teacher of the Year
English Language Arts teacher, grades 10-12

A Lesson for Life

Learning is a treasure that will follow its owner everywhere.
~Chinese Proverb

Petrified. That's how I felt that Monday morning when my marine science students came into class and began encouraging one of their classmates to "Tell him what happened at the beach yesterday."

My marine science students benefit from the fact that, in addition to my academic teaching responsibilities, I'm also certified as an IDC Staff Instructor by the Professional Association of Diving Instructors (PADI). Because I have the greatest Principal on the planet, each of my students receives a PADI Open Water Diver certification as part of our marine science program at Marianas High School here on the island of Saipan. Once certified, my students use their new diving skills to conduct supervised underwater research projects on the coral reefs adjacent to our island.

The program is as rewarding to teach as it is for the students who take it. Many of them have found their passion for the ocean and the resources it contains and are now enrolled as marine biology and oceanography majors in colleges and universities on Guam, Hawaii, and the U.S. mainland. It is fulfilling to know that some may one day return to take an active role in the stewardship and management of our island's precious marine resources.

On this day, however, I was frozen in fear and wondering what had happened at the beach. Being islanders surrounded by water, I teach my students that the ocean is not a dangerous place, but can be very unforgiving to those who make mistakes. As such, my first thoughts were for their safety and wellbeing. I did a quick head count. They were all in class with all their parts in place. I became less afraid and more curious about what had happened. But I was wholly unprepared for the story they told.

A three-year-old playing in the water near shore had been left unattended by his older sister for a moment. In the time it took her to turn around and find him, he had drowned. Frantic family members and beachgoers rushed to help, but no one was sure what to do. One of my students was at the beach that day and rushed over to help. She had taken a CPR and first aid course that I'd taught as an after-school program seven months earlier. Remembering her training, and with the assistance of a bystander, she began providing rescue breathing and chest compressions and directed others to call 911. By the time paramedics had arrived, the child was breathing and in his mother's arms.

As teachers, we know that through our energy and effort children learn. They become interested. Some find their passions and pursue their dreams. In this way we know we have the power to change lives. I'd add that once in a while we have the power to save a life.

Words still fail to express how it feels to have been a part of such an amazing event. The feeling of being in the right place, at the right time, with the ability to teach the right skills and knowledge that empowered a student to save a life is humbling. Perhaps my student summed it up best when I asked her how it felt to have saved someone's life. "Pretty cool," she said.

I guess so.

~James Edward Phillips
2009 CCSSO State Teacher of the Year
Commonwealth of the Northern Mariana Islands
Marine Science, Physics teacher, grades 9-12

Editor's note: The Northern Marianas are a U.S. possession about 3,500 miles west of Hawaii, and about 1,600 miles south of Japan.

Become Like Bumblebees

Teaching is leaving a vestige of one self in the development of another.
And surely the student is a bank where you can deposit your most precious
treasures.
~Eugene P. Bertin

The tranquil Hawaii night was punctuated by a sad voice, "I hate saying goodbyes. Seriously man, because it makes me feel like crying." My husband Harry turned to Julian in the back of my car and said in a curious voice, "Are you okay, you drunk or what?" My husband and I were giving Julian, Jorge, and Dio a ride back to their homes in Kalihi after they had competed with students from many countries in the 2006 International Fuel Cell Competition.

Julian slowly said, "I already miss the two boys from Japan. I feel sad, just like when I was leaving China." Julian's tearful voice formed a lump in my throat. He sadly said, "When I was in China teaching English to the kids in Baojing, I got so connected to them. As I was leaving, I started crying because the children were running after the minivan waving and shouting."

Harry replied in a calm voice, "What, did you steal their stuff?" There was silence for a few seconds, and then as we finally understood Harry's joke, we laughed and laughed all the way to Kalihi.

After that night, Julian, Jorge, and Dio became the three musketeers and Harry was the master-teer.

These three boys are a part of my family. I moved to Hawaii from Guyana, South America. In Hawaii I had no *ohana* (family). For many years, life was pretty lonely but when I became a teacher I started to understand the Hawaiian saying *Ike aku, 'ike mai, kokua aku kokua mai; pela iho la ka nohana 'ohana.* Translation: Recognize others, be recognized, help others, be helped; such is a family relationship. Having no biological children, all my students became my *hanai* (adopted) children.

When I first introduced Harry to the three musketeers, I knew that my life was never going to be the same. They hit it off! Julian's imagination is wild and Harry's is wilder. Jorge and Dio are like the icing and candles on a cake because their presence ignites and enhances the whole experience, making it more memorable and beautiful. The three musketeers formed a special bond and that was the respect and love they had for each other and me. They called me Mom, which at first embarrassed me. Later, I learned to appreciate it.

These three boys came from humble backgrounds and were on free/reduced lunch at the largest public high school in Honolulu, but they became role models for each other and for many other high school students. They never stopped striving for excellence because they wanted to make me proud. They hold a special place in my heart and they remind me of what being a teacher is all about and how grateful students are for our guidance.

I had met Jorge one afternoon after school when I ran into this tiny kid with pliers and a multimeter in the hallway of the science building. I asked, "What's up with all the tools?" He said that he was working on an Invention Factor Project to make toys more electronically viable for kids with disabilities. I was impressed. I told him that if he ever wanted to work on more projects he should stop by. Jorge stopped by the very next day and has never stopped coming, even though he graduated from high school. He is a Filipino boy who started high school with many academic disadvantages. He was placed into Hale Kulia, where the students need extra help with their academics. I used his love of computers to enable him. Jorge became one of the best programmers that our school ever produced, leading our Robotics Team to second place in the Hawaii Pacific Regional. He has overcome most of his academic challenges.

I met Dio and Julian when two boys, one Filipino and one Chinese, walked into my classroom during lunch, pushing each other forward and arguing about who should go first. This was after I was named the 2005 Milken Family Foundation National Educator. They said that they were proud of me and asked if I could help them with their schoolwork.

Dio sees my husband Harry as a father figure because his dad died before he was born. The week that I was to take Dio to the International Fuel Cell Competition, I spoke with his mother. She said, "Ms. Davis, my son has never been away from me. He is my only child and all my joy; if anything happens to him, I don't know what I would do. I know that my Dio is getting older and needs to go out and experience things." I couldn't breathe because of the pain and emotion in her voice. "Dio loves you and always tells me how well you treat them. So, I trust you to take good care of my son." I still remember that feeling.

Dio and Julian were a couple of rascals and they never stopped embarrassing me in front of large groups by going on stage and shouting out, "Ms. Davis we love you, thank you, you are the best!" Dio went on to UC Davis on a Gates Scholarship, but often shows up in my classroom and surprises me by covering my eyes and making me guess who it is.

Julian's parents do not speak English and did not graduate from high school, so Julian set out to achieve what many deemed impossible at Farrington High School. This is what he said in his valedictorian speech (reprinted with permission from Julian Yuen):

> The Chinese often use the word keku. It means to overcome hardship, a trait that is used to gauge a person's inner strength. Keku includes the ability to swallow the bitterness without complaining. I truly believe each of us has had to overcome the bitterness

in our lives. Whether it was with family, friends, school, or even within ourselves, there were times where we felt like it was the end. But something inside kept us going; that burning desire telling us that this is not the end, and that we must keep fighting. Ms. Davis, thank you for helping me overcome the adversities in my life, giving me so many opportunities, and now I'm off to MIT and tomorrow, NASA, all because you had the belief that I could really accomplish something in life....

A wise Chinese boy once said, "Think like a bumblebee. Do as a bumblebee." Because, according to science, because of the size, weight, and shape of the bumblebee's body, it should be scientifically impossible for it to fly. But as we can all see, these little bees continue to buzz around, flapping their little wings throughout the world. No one told the bumblebee that it's not supposed to fly; but they don't know that so they continue to fly anyway, regardless of what science may say. So remember, as we embark on our journey to success, society may stereotype us because of where we are from. But like the bumblebee, we do not know of this stereotype, and instead, we choose to keep on flying, until we reach our goals, and some more. Whatever the negativity we may encounter, bring it on. Cause we're from Kalihi, and we can tackle any brick walls that come our way; because we know brick walls are there to test how badly we want something; and believe me, we all want it real bad.

As a teacher I know that feeling; I hate saying goodbye to my students but I love to see them become like bumblebees.

~Bebi Davis
2009 Hawaii State Teacher of the Year
2009 Pacific Teacher of the Year
Physics, Chemistry, grades 9-12

Power of the Pen

It doesn't matter. You can still fly,
there's other ways to get around it to get to your dream.
~Kathy Ronci

In the late 1990s, a family visited the public elementary school where I taught deaf students. They said they would be moving to the district and planned to enroll their deaf daughter as a first grader. They were upset that their child's kindergarten teacher cautioned them not to have high hopes for her academically. Based upon assessment results, the teacher painted a bleak picture for their little girl's future. Standing behind them was Katherine, a beautiful five-year-old with long shiny brown hair and dark flashing eyes. The whole time her parents were there she didn't make a sound or use sign language, even when her parents prompted her.

After a few weeks with Katherine, I discovered I was dealing with a very bright, very strong-willed child. Although I was able to engage her in a variety of learning activities, writing was a constant struggle. I tried all kinds of trickery to interest her in writing. Every time the pencils came out, she would shut down and refuse to participate.

One day Katherine got off her bus and stood in front of the school wailing. The staff members present did not know enough sign language to ask her why she was crying. Finally they whisked her into the office where they handed her a pen and notepad. Katherine wrote: "PAC BAK." Immediately the office staff realized she left her backpack on the bus. They summoned the bus back to school and soon Katherine was reunited with her backpack.

That day Katherine discovered the power of the pen. From then on she had a new appreciation for writing. She is a young woman now and has become an excellent writer, public speaker and student leader. During her senior year in high school Kathy became the Douglas County Rodeo Queen and the following year she enrolled at the University of Northern Colorado determined to become a teacher. In the summer of 2008 I traveled to the National Association of the Deaf Conference in New Orleans and watched her perform competitively as Miss Deaf Colorado. Kathy keeps in touch and I especially treasure her e-mails with term papers attached. This young lady wields a very powerful pen!

P.S. Although she allows me to share this story, she rolls those big brown eyes every time I tell it.

~Susan Elliott
2009 Colorado State Teacher of the Year
2009 National Teacher of the Year Finalist
English, Social Studies teacher, grades 9-12

Music Touches the Soul

Music is the universal language of mankind.
~Henry Wadsworth Longfellow

As educators, we often never know the extent of the impact we have on our students. It is always wonderful to have former students visit us and share the successes they have encountered. And those glorious moments, when we can instantly see the impact we have on a student, fuel us to continue making connections hoping to make a difference in the life of every child.

A music teacher for twenty-seven years, I have always known that music touches the soul. It can break through all kinds of barriers to reach students in a very special way. It can be the means for each child to find their light.

I would like to share a story where music broke through a physical barrier and made a connection with a young student. For a few years I was blessed with the opportunity to teach pre-school handicapped students one afternoon a week. One of my most memorable students was a young girl I will call Vanessa. Vanessa was five years old, had difficulty walking, and could not speak. We mostly sat on the floor for our music lessons and Vanessa liked to sit on my lap. One of her favorite songs was "John the Rabbit." It was a call and response song where I sang the call and the students clapped two times while singing the repeating phrase, "Oh, yes!" Vanessa liked to put her hands together with mine and clap with me. We probably performed that song during every class, Vanessa and I clapping together. She never said or sang a word.

One day late in the school year, when the song was finished, Vanessa turned around, looked me dead in the eye, clapped her tiny hands two times and said the words "Oh, yes!" I opened my mouth in awe and for that moment I was the one who could not speak. When my heart finally started beating again, I looked over at the homeroom teacher to find her also speechless. Through music, we had made an awesome connection.

Several years later, I passed Vanessa on the street in town. I stopped my car and waved to say hello. She waved back with a big smile on her face and then clapped her hands two times, mimicking the song we had performed so many times in our music class. This precious little girl, through her connection with music, left an impression on me that will last forever. Every child has the ability to learn and grow. It is up to us as educators to discover the way to reach each and every one of our students. We all must find each child's light.

~Mark D. Teesdale
2009 Delaware State Teacher of the Year
Music teacher, grades 4-5

Teacher Tales

First Year Tales

The great majority of men are bundles of beginnings.

~Ralph Waldo Emerson

Ooh La La

You will do foolish things, but do them with enthusiasm.
~Colette

My principal came by my room that morning while I was still hanging a few last-minute posters on my walls, and the minute she walked in to wish me luck, I felt extremely unprepared. As she walked out of my classroom, I looked at the clock and realized that in fifteen minutes the first class of my teaching career was about to walk in my door. Freaking out just a little bit, I looked down at what I was wearing and immediately hated it. My outfit consisted of a plain white top with black pants and heels. As a person who loves fashion, I felt plain, but I figured I should be conservative on the first day, since I wanted my high school students to take me seriously.

It hit me that I would only be about six or seven years older than them and I freaked out even more. I reminded myself that I had been preparing for weeks; not only that, I had been preparing for years. I graduated from TCU with not only my bachelor's degree in Secondary Social Studies Education but I also graduated with my master's degree in Secondary Education. It was time and I was ready. So why were my hands shaking and my forehead drenched in sweat?

The day went by in a blur. With my freshman classes, I think they were just as nervous as I was. It was their first day in high school and sensing their apprehension eased my own. My sophomores, on the other hand, were all excited to see each other after the summer break and seemed very curious about who this new teacher was. Since the students all seemed to like my activities well enough that first day, it made the rest of our time together enjoyable.

My entire first year went by in a blur. By spring break, I was ready for summer. My first year of teaching was exhausting and consisted of a number of triumphs and some failures. I experienced happy moments with my students and instances where I wanted to cry. However, I never cried in front of them. I was determined to stand strong in front of these high school kids.

One time I wanted to cry from embarrassment because of a video I had shown in class. It had been one of those mornings, and I needed something for my first and fifth period World Geography students to keep them at the same pace as my other classes. We were studying Western Europe and I had traveled to Paris a few summers before, so I went into our school library's video closet and checked out a Globe Trekker episode on Paris. As I watched the video, I composed questions for the students to answer. The students watched the portion of the video that I had planned, and answered the questions I had prepared, but I had miscalculated and we still had fifteen minutes left in class. I figured I would just let them keep watching the video.

It was a Globe Trekker episode for goodness sake—how bad could it be? Well… it turned out to be a little inappropriate when the guide in the video visited the Moulin Rouge. I began to feel uneasy but I reminded myself that Globe Trekker episodes air on network television and teachers across the country use the videos in their Geography classes. Nevertheless, I moved a little closer to the computer… just in case. Sure enough, for a good three seconds there was a shot of a topless Moulin Rouge dancer. I swear it was the longest three seconds of my life.

It was one of those moments when your brain goes faster than your body. I knew I needed to turn off the video and turn it off fast, but my hands fumbled as some of the students, mostly boys, laughed and told me to leave it on. It was a good thing the room was dark or they would have seen my face turn as red as the skirt on the Moulin Rouge dancer!

I thought for sure this was going to be the end of my teaching career. There I was, a new teacher, and my students saw a topless girl dancing on a big screen! Yes, a big screen. My first year took place pre-Smart Board when I hooked my personal laptop up to a projector to play videos.

For the rest of the day, I had students walking into my classroom saying things like "I heard we get to watch a cool video today, Ms. Townsend," and "I can't wait to see this video I have been hearing about all day!" I could not stop thinking about what had happened, replaying the class period over and over in my mind. Of course, I did not show that video the rest of the day despite the complaints that first period was able to see it and the rest of my classes were not. I thought I would never recover from the embarrassment.

Looking back on that day, I laugh about it. I learned my lesson. I no longer show a video in my classroom that I have not watched all the way through. I told few people at the time because I was so embarrassed and afraid for my job! The teachers I did share this with thought it was hilarious and recounted their own classroom mistakes and the lessons they learned. Now I can file this away as a valuable lesson to share with new teachers.

~Adrienne Townsend

"The residents are referred to as 'Parisians', Trevor — not 'Parisites.'"

My Mia

The dream begins with a teacher who believes in you,
who tugs and pushes and leads you to the next plateau,
sometimes poking you with a sharp stick called "truth."
~Dan Rather

As a beginning teacher, I was faced with a lot of challenges, but the one that grabbed most of my time was about forty inches tall with her head down, chin against her chest, looking out at the world from the tops of her eyes with a scowl on her face and fists balled up. She was ready to take on any and all comers. To beat all, she was repeating third grade.

I quickly learned one child had the power to disrupt and destroy my classroom, and worse, she had the power to derail my career even before it got started! I really wanted to know what made her tick so I asked around and heard some incredible stories about the "little tornado" who left destruction in her wake. About the only positive information came from the reading specialist, who insisted she could learn.

I now had an idea. I contacted her father and proposed keeping his daughter after school for tutoring. To say he was disillusioned and fed up with the school system was an understatement. A review of her cumulative file pretty much explained his attitude; he gave me a deadline of November to make progress with Mia.

The first day I kept her, we talked about how she felt about school. Mia had had very negative experiences in school and it colored her outlook on almost everything else in her life. When I drew her out about things she enjoyed, I got somewhere. She liked to shop and she loved Dairy Queen Blizzards. Now that I had a carrot, it was time to set goals. I am not ashamed to admit I used good old-fashioned bribery, but the way I looked at it, it was an investment. My plan went beyond academics because this child had the social skills of a street thug. On the long list were common courtesy, table manners, and learning how to respond respectfully in unfamiliar situations.

Initially, I absolutely had to negotiate the bumpy highway of her behavior because it was a huge barrier to academic success. There was no end goal. Rather, I kept tacking on a succession of steps that would lead Mia to becoming a cooperative member of my class.

As she mastered each incremental goal, we celebrated at Dairy Queen. Sometimes it went well. Sometimes I cried myself to sleep. But I refused to give up on her—or myself. By November, I'd built a firm foundation with Mia and our relationship began to flourish. Mia's father saw an unbelievable change in his child.

As a first year teacher, living on my own and putting in long hours, cooking was not an option. At least twice a week I would eat at K&W Cafeteria, where I struck up a conversation with Ms. Bea, who served the side dishes. She called me "Sugar" and asked about my day as she dished my mashed potatoes. One frustrating day, I told her about Mia—the Mia who did not value school, who disrupted class, who hated everything and everybody. Ms. Bea, a wise woman, advised me to bring Mia in to see her during the dinner rush.

We arrived at K&W the next evening and near the end of the serving line, we encountered Ms. Bea, who looked at Mia, and said, "Help you?"

Mia spat out her order. Ms. Bea said, "No, I heard about you. I heard a lot about you. Do you want to be me one day?"

Mia was stunned. "Uh, no."

"Then you need to start doing in school what you're supposed to do because people like me never had that chance. So don't waste it." With that she served up Mia's vegetables and I gave Ms. Bea a secret wink. It was the first time that I ever saw Mia speechless.

Our dinner conversation went well beyond manners that night. I never wanted her to forget the wisdom of Ms. Bea, but Mia wasn't the only one who learned something that night. I learned the truth behind the African proverb "It takes a village to raise a child." From then on, whenever Mia needed a booster dose, we had a code term—"Ms. Bea."

The end of third grade was remarkable for two things. I had survived both my rookie year and Mia. Furthermore, she had passed two of her standardized tests with flying colors and she was close to reading on grade level. I assisted in selecting her fourth grade teacher and we had an agreement for Mia to continue being mentored.

By fifth grade, Mia had it together academically and our time together focused on monitoring and maintaining progress while attending hockey games, eating out and shopping. Her social skills had improved dramatically and her ability to deal with people she did not like was becoming more consistent. And that was when *the big change* occurred.

Not only would Mia be moving to middle school, but so was I. Both of us would face new challenges and I knew that dealing with new kids from four other schools was going to test Mia's patience. Would she maintain the determination to continue her academic growth or would her anger kick in and cause her to fall in with a crowd that would allow her to follow the path of least resistance?

Once again, I tinkered with her schedule and aligned her with teachers who were willing to reinforce the positive growth. She transitioned extremely well and I felt confident that seventh grade would be another success story.

During seventh grade, Mia's family moved and I lost touch with her until a chance encounter with a high school teacher who'd heard all about me from Mia. The lessons learned had served Mia well. She'll be serving as a co-op in her senior year, and is on track to enter nursing school after graduation. I'm thinking we need to celebrate where it began—with green beans and mashed potatoes and Ms. Bea.

~Stephanie Doyle
2009 Virginia State Teacher of the Year
History teacher, grade 6

Who Would I Do Without?

Children are one third of our population and all of our future.
~Select Panel for the Promotion of Child Health, 1981

It had been a busy summer, and now it was turning into an even busier fall. The school was humming with activity as the teachers readied their rooms for the start of classes. As their principal I was energized by their contagious enthusiasm, but I wanted to do more. Everywhere I went I asked the same question, "How are you doing?" And everywhere I went I received the same answer: "Just fine."

There was only one person who I didn't quite believe. It was her first year of teaching, but that had nothing to do with my doubts. Her room was inviting. She seemed well-prepared. On the outside everything seemed just fine, but there was something in her eyes that made me ask that question again and again.

Then came Wednesday.

"How are you doing?" I asked. "Mr. Boyce, I think I'm going to make it," she said.

It was lunch time and the work room was full of teachers and noise, but the voices became quiet as the young teacher continued.

"Monday night, after our open house, I just didn't think I could do it. There were so many parents and children, and I felt so overwhelmed that I drove to see my folks. I told them I didn't think I could do it, and they said I had to try.

"The next morning school started. I thought I was ready, but there were so many of them and their needs were so different. I just didn't know how I could manage. I drove back to my parents, and we talked for a long time.

"I told them if I just had fewer kids I thought I could handle it. So they asked me which children I would get rid of. And you know, Mr. Boyce, I couldn't decide. I'd only had them for one day, but I couldn't think of a single child I could do without.

"They're mine, Mr. Boyce. I can't do without any of them. I don't know how, but I'm just going to do the best I can and I really think I'm going to make it."

There wasn't a dry eye in the room when I replied, "I think you are, too."

~Richards M. Boyce as told to Suzanne M. Boyce

Reprinted by permission of Off the Mark
and Mark Parisi ©2007

First Year Drama

Mistakes are the usual bridge between inexperience and wisdom.
~Phyllis Theroux, Night Lights

My teaching career lasted nineteen glorious years—actually eighteen glorious years and one year of stupid mistakes. It all started with me sitting in the principal's office, desperate for a job.

"You teach English, Robbie?" He was a short, stocky man with kind eyes, but was obviously tired.

"English is what I want to teach. I have an education degree with minors in English and speech."

He made little noises, as if he were trying to keep himself awake as he read my application and résumé. My eyes skimmed his office looking for a distraction to the war zone of nerves inside my brain.

"Is that *Family Feud*?"

A framed picture of five men lined up at the game show hung on his wall.

"Yes, my brothers and I were on the show."

"Did you win?"

"No, but we had a great time."

My nerves retreated behind friendly lines, and I began talking about TV. Soon we were laughing like old friends.

"You know what, Robbie? We're also looking for a drama teacher. I see that one of your minors was in speech. Drama and speech are really similar, right? Would you be interested in teaching drama as well as English?"

I'd never taken a drama class in my life, but I smelled employment.

I had three classes that year. First, an English class made up of twenty-seven juniors and seniors, mostly boys, who'd failed English at least once. And after lunch I taught a beginning drama class and then advanced drama.

I entered my first English class determined to be Sidney Poitier in *To Sir, with Love*. I was going to take my downtrodden ghetto rebels and turn them into citizens with hearts and dreams.

Contrary to the plan, my students were suburban and affluent. Most of them owned either a Porsche or a BMW. But still I had a mission. First battle: to win them over. Easy. I would use one of my greatest assets. I would smile and inspire them.

I walked into Room 219 and smiled widely. With a West Texan accent, my sweet-as-pecan-pie self drawled, "Hi, ya'll. My name is Miss Floyd and we're going to have so much fun."

Swift, knowing glances were exchanged between classmates and my fate was sealed within the first ten minutes.

That year in Room 219 was bumpy. I didn't know how to discipline. They didn't know how to behave. Occasionally, one of the worst of the lot, David, would somehow get into the classroom and set our clock ahead ten minutes. I lived and died by that clock, so when it said time for class to end, I trusted it. More than once, I let the class out to roam the grounds before lunch.

In my attempt to build a curriculum for these students who had failed English in the past, I decided to teach a unit on living life in the real world. This had absolutely nothing to do with English, but I was changing their lives, not just making sure they knew grammar. In that unit, I decided that I would teach salad making. When Poitier did this in *To Sir, with Love* it was a great success. But my galloping gourmet lecture in 219 didn't go so well. The students thought I was joking. Make a salad? You want to teach us California rich kids how to make a salad? My lesson only lasted fifteen minutes.

"Um, okay everybody. Study hall."

This was my answer to any class that went short. It was also my answer to any class for which I wasn't prepared.

One day, I'd planned to start reading a book. But when I arrived on campus, I found that copies of the book hadn't arrived yet.

Study hall.

I guess I might have earned a couple of extra points if I'd actually made sure they studied. But they weren't the studying kind. In fact, not studying had landed them in my class to begin with, so I let them sit around and talk.

We were having study hall when a woman I'll call Mrs. Pritchett, the curriculum development director, walked in and sat down.

"Can I help you, Mrs. Pritchett?"

"Do you have lesson plans?" Her request came through her nose. Her lips barely moved.

"Sure." I found them for her. "But the books didn't come in."

"So what are you doing?" I wondered if it hurt when she spoke. "I'll observe from here."

I was placed on scholastic probation after that. The good news was that they assigned a mentor to me who actually gave me ideas for curriculum. The bad news was that I'd already established myself as a too-lenient teacher who really didn't know a lot about teaching.

Drama was difficult, but got better with time. I bought a book on how to teach it, which I kept with me always. I faked it when I could and asked for help when I really needed it. I'm happy to say our first play was a big hit. After I had one under my belt, I fell into a rhythm of joy and work and relief. We would stay after class for rehearsals, and we naturally became quite close.

They called me Mom (even though I was only twenty-six), and we laughed about everything. Unfortunately, my inexperience got the better of me again. The rules about student/teacher relationships had been laid out to me clearly. But I began spending a lot of time with the kids outside of school and even went to a movie—which was strictly forbidden—with two senior boys from my advanced drama class.

I ended up on probation for the second time that year. Even so, my principal offered me the drama position again for the following year, but only if I'd also teach music.

What? Music?

I declined and left the school. Later, I'd see him almost yearly at countywide school functions. "Hey Debbie," he'd always say. "How you doing?"

I never corrected him. It comforted me to think that that awful first-year teacher was named Debbie and not Robbie.

Fourteen years after my first year as a teacher, sweet poetic justice with a splash of irony visited me. During teacher orientation, one of the rookie teachers came up to me. He was tall and in his early thirties.

"Hello. I don't know if you remember me, but my name is David. I think I owe you an apology."

At first, I didn't recognize him, but as he explained, a bell went off.

David had been one of my English students that first year. Indeed, he was the ringleader behind the clock re-setting.

"David, it's okay. I made so many mistakes that year. I learned the hard way. So you're a teacher? How long?"

"This is my first year."

It was a wonderful moment and I laughed out loud.

"Oh David, God is going to get you back big time."

~Robbie Iobst

"Not everyone gets a chance to write their wrongs."

Whatever Works

Good instincts usually tell you what to do
long before your head has figured it out.
~Michael Burke

"Billy Wagner's father will be here at 10 AM. He wishes to speak with you," the note in my teacher's box read. I felt the color draining from my face and tried to keep my hands from shaking. I knew I was in trouble.

I was thrilled when I landed a teaching position in my new hometown's high school. The school district had a reputation of hiring only experienced teachers and I was just beginning my career. An exception had been made in my case because this was a pilot program and even the principal didn't know if it would work. (Experienced teachers probably knew to get more details about the plan and turned the position down.)

At the time, Millard High School included the seventh through twelfth grades. Each of the four elementary schools that fed into it had graduating sixth graders who, for one reason or another, would need a more sheltered environment to progress in such a large institution. Eager to teach so close to home and for such a fine school, I oozed confidence and enthusiasm for the opportunity to be a part of this pilot program, even if I had no clue about how to run it.

When I received my class rosters I was delighted—the enrollments were extremely small. My largest class had thirteen pupils. This was an unbelievable number for a public school. It should have tipped me off that my task would not be as simple as I imagined. I assumed my students would be behind in their skills and a little remediation delivered with large doses of encouragement would solve their problems. Five minutes into the first day of school, I realized things were a lot more complicated.

All of the students were in my room for more than one subject and operating at different levels because of different handicaps. For some it was intellect, for others the problems were emotional. Two were new to the country and needed to learn English. Some were late bloomers, who with a little more maturity would eventually catch up with their peers.

And then there was Billy. Skinny, sensitive Billy. Billy the outsider. Unlike others who knew at least someone else in the room from their elementary school days, Billy didn't. He was easily upset and cried a lot. He cried if he had answers marked wrong on his paper, he cried if I called on him and he didn't want to answer, he cried if classmates tried to joke with him. I was embarrassed to see a twelve-year-old boy crying like that. I didn't know what to do, so I left him to it.

There was no way I could teach a lock-step lesson with this group. Their ability levels were too diverse. We did some things together, but I had to give a lot of time to individualized instruction. I tried, with fingers crossed, to have meaningful assignments for the others to do while I worked with a single student. This didn't always make for a quiet, orderly classroom. Free-wheeling and chaotic would be a more accurate description.

Strange things happened. While I was working with Sally, Kanzo, who entered the class knowing only the alphabet and how to count to one hundred in English, was somehow able to help Danny with his math. Danny had no trouble understanding him. Mickey, Steve and Bobby began grouping together to do their work. Some might call it cheating; I preferred to see it as collaborating.

In spite of my constant fear that at any moment the principal might come into my room to complain about the noise and be horrified by my lack of control, things began to settle down. It was still noisy and a bit too social, but Wally, the withdrawn one, had begun to interact with Sally, who sat in front of him. It was a start, even if it was only with one other person. Helge now spoke in full English sentences, if you ignored the mangled syntax. Mickey's compositions had stretched from one paragraph to a full page, even if the spelling and punctuation remained abysmal. Mess-producing Myra was finally picking up after herself, and Billy had stopped crying.

Small victories. Where was the accelerated academic growth? When was I going to set stricter standards and get these youngsters up to grade level? When was I going to take control and have them acting like high school students? I wanted to, but I felt in over my head. I just didn't know how. Was it any wonder that Mr. Wagner wanted to talk to me about his son Billy's progress? How long before a mob of parents appeared, demanding to know what was going on in my classroom?

Ten o'clock was the start of my student-free period. I rushed to the faculty ladies' room a few minutes before, sick to my stomach with dread. I splashed water on my face, applied fresh lipstick and tried to smile a brave smile into the mirror. I needed time to calm down, but the meeting with Mr. Wagner couldn't be put off. I hoped he'd be late.

I found him already in my room, seated behind a student desk too small for his stocky build. I greeted him cheerfully and we shook hands. I slid into the seat next to him and steeled myself for what was to come.

"I won't take too much of your time," he said, "but I wanted you to know how much my wife and I appreciate what you have done for our son. Billy has absolutely blossomed this year. Do you know he used to cry and have stomachaches when he had to go to school? If we asked him about his school day, he'd clam up on us. Now all he talks about is school! I don't know how you did it, but our son is a happy boy again. My wife and I are so grateful; I had to come here to thank you personally." He stood up and straightened his suit coat. "Now I'd better get back to my office so we can both get some work done," he said.

I remained in my seat, stunned. He didn't know how I did it, but he was grateful for the change in his son! I didn't know how I did it either, but Mr. Wagner's comments gave me the confidence to continue with my classes the way they were. I stopped thinking I needed to get tough, be strict and concentrate solely on the academics. Billy and his father had taught me that my free-wheeling classroom, born of my inexperience, was giving a troubled young adolescent room to gain the self-confidence he needed to be able to concentrate on schoolwork. I learned from Billy that there is more to a student than the amount of English one can stuff into his head.

Over the years, I encountered other students who made me realize why I became a teacher, but Billy Wagner was the first, and the one for whom I am most grateful. When Billy went on to college, I felt as successful as he did.

~Marcia Rudoff

16

My Christmas Lesson

Christmas is not as much about opening our presents as opening our hearts.
~Janice Maeditere

I t was the last day before Christmas vacation and the last day of my student teaching assignment. I'd spent three months with a wonderful mentor and a great group of fifth-graders. Walking through the door I knew this day was both an end and a beginning. No longer a student teacher, I would become a teacher in my own right. But this would be my last day with these children I already considered "mine." It went by so quickly, and I wasn't ready to leave them behind.

I would have less than an hour before my class rushed off for lunch. The afternoon was set aside for the Christmas party. I wanted my final lesson to resonate within the children, to linger in their minds and inspire them. I'd struggled for days preparing it, honing each word with surgical precision until it was perfect.

Teachers are supposed to touch young lives and change them for the better; at least that was my philosophy. I wanted to make a difference not only in the children today, but one that would continue on and revive my hometown. Once a thriving community, it suffered economic collapse when the mills closed more than twenty years ago. No longer called the Steel Valley, the area was now known as the Rust Belt.

Many families moved away, as had mine. But I came back home to complete my student teaching assignment, hoping to show this new generation the value of education. More than half the children came from families where college was the exception. For generations the graduating class went straight from commencement into the mill. The median income plummeted when it shut down, and poverty had become a way of life. I knew I could make a difference. My lesson, the last before Christmas vacation, would be impossible to forget.

I was almost to my classroom when another teacher asked me to stay with her class for a few minutes. I smiled and nodded, struggling to hide my rising irritation. After all, there was so little time in the first place. She must know how important this day was. My lesson was planned out, timed with absolute precision. How could I sacrifice even a minute when each word was crucial? I grumbled a silent prayer, asking God to help me squeeze it all in.

A few minutes stretched into fifteen before she came back, apologized and rushed me across the hall. I opened the door and twenty-nine children shouted "Surprise!"

There were new decorations added to the holiday ones from the day before. Over the chalkboard was a banner with "Congratulations!" printed across it. Every child had signed and decorated it. I was swept up in a tangle of arms and led to a table heaped with gifts. Before long I could barely see over the holiday towels, mugs, candles, perfume, candy and jewelry.

Awed by the outpouring of love, I took time opening each gift and thanked each giver. By the time I'd opened the last gift on the table it was almost lunchtime. The room was a little quieter now and I realized that I'd received a gift from all but one of the children. It was so much more than I could ever have expected.

I looked around the room. Most of the children were grouped in twos and threes, talking and working on holiday puzzles as they waited for the bell. Joey sat alone, but that wasn't unusual. He was only in the room for morning attendance and lunch, spending the rest of the day in a Special Education class.

I barely knew him, but his ill-fitting clothes and bony frame marked him as one of the poorest of the poor. He hunched over a piece of paper, his tiny nub of pencil flitting across it. His hand darted into his pocket and pulled out a crumpled dollar. He smoothed the bill, laid it on the paper and folded the paper into an envelope around it. He ran to the supply basket, dashed back and sealed the paper envelope with a gold star.

The students stood at the door, ready for lunch. Instead of his usual place at the front of the line, Joey hung back and sidled over toward me when the bell rang. He ducked his head, scuffed his foot and held out the envelope.

"Merry Christmas! You're the best teacher I've ever had." His cheeks flushed above a smile wider than seemed possible.

I seldom find myself with nothing to say, but I was speechless. I couldn't take his only dollar! I paused a moment too long, and his smile began to fade. Three words jumped into my mind: the widow's mite. God blessed her small offering, knowing it was all she had. How could I hurt Joey's feelings by refusing his gift?

"Thank you, Joey. I'm really going to miss you." I opened the envelope. Inside, sketched in pencil, was a Christmas tree, with a star on top.

"This is beautiful! I didn't know you were such an artist." I tucked the dollar in my pocket and put the picture on top of the other cards. The room was empty. Joey would be at the end of the lunch line.

"Would you have lunch with me, since this is my last day? We can bring our trays up here."

"You mean I can have a teacher's lunch?" Wide-eyed, he grinned again.

"Of course. My treat. We can even have pizza if you want." I took him to the back of the kitchen, where teachers get adult-sized meals. We went back to the classroom and he showed me a notebook full of sketches. Most were trucks, cars or planes drawn with amazing detail.

Soon the other students returned. The rest of the day was spent eating cookies and playing games. When the final bell rang I hugged each child. And as for that final, oh so important, lesson I had planned? I never taught it. I learned one instead.

~Anna M. Lowther

17

The Fly in the Room

There can never be enough said of the virtues,
dangers, the power of a shared laugh.
~Françoise Sagan

I had officially spent only two days preparing for my first day as a teacher in a classroom of my design—lining up desks, decorating bulletin boards, planning engaging discussions and selecting life-changing literature. Don't get me wrong—I had been preparing for this moment for years, arguably most of my life, but securing a teaching position just two days before school began didn't give me leisurely time to reflect on the enormous decisions before me.

I jumped in, frantically pouring ideas into that first week of lessons, trying to remember all I had learned from my college professors, mentors and experiences, first as a teacher assistant and later as a student teacher. I was determined to make that first week perfect—perfectly mapped out and designed, perfectly paced, perfectly organized. While I didn't sleep much the two nights before the first day, I was ready for those high-schoolers who would spend the year in my class, studying American literature, applying larger themes to their lives, learning from the experiences of the authors we were to study. Well, that's what I thought anyway.

They would later become one of my most memorable groups, maybe partly because they were my first, but also certainly because of their lively personalities and willingness to let me, a first year teacher, into their minds and lives. But that first day, I wasn't prepared for how all of their faces seemed to run together. As I facilitated a discussion about a poem we had read, I struggled to remember names, even of those students who eagerly participated. The quieter ones were even more of a challenge. John, Jana, Jory, Janelle, Julia, Jim, Jada, Jason, Jennifer, Jake, Joey, Jackie, Jared… they all ran together, tumbled over one another, mixed and blended until I couldn't keep any of them straight.

By fifth hour, I was still running on adrenaline but near exhaustion when Jeremy lost his patience with my forgetfulness. With his hand raised, he made eye contact with me and knew right away that I couldn't recall his name, even though I had spoken it at least four times that hour. Being a good sport, he helped me out by joking: "My name is JEHOVAH," he boomed in a sinister voice I will never forget, his warm smile lighting up the row, belying the menacing tone of his joke. "No really, it's Jeremy," he reminded me. "It's gotta be hard to remember all these names." That sealed the deal—I would never forget Jeremy's name again, even now, some fifteen years later.

As the discussion flowed into small group work, I wandered through the clusters of students, listening to their ideas bounce from agreement to disagreement to intense conversation. I watched Jeremy and his group point back to the poem and then connect it to their own lives. As I sat on the windowsill watching, I was secretly celebrating a successful first day—almost perfect. At one point, Kathy and Sara rushed over, serious looks in their eyes, pleading, "Can we see you in the hall, Mrs. Haberling?" I glanced at the rest of their group, still huddled over desks, just in time to see the concern flash over their faces. *This must be serious*, I thought.

This was it—the moment I had been preparing for. You see, I had plans early in my college career. Like most high school students at that time, I entered college intent on figuring out what I wanted to do. After dabbling in art, I found my niche in the field of social sciences and decided to get a degree in psychology, then go on to become a counselor. My plan was to help adolescents, and in that decision, I had no idea that I would really fall in love with teaching students. Here was my chance to combine my two loves—right here with Kathy and Sara. They must have a problem I could help them solve!

As we stepped into the hall, their eyes locked and I could see the concern exchanged between them. They turned to me, nervously glancing from feet to eyes to feet, and began. "Um…" Kathy stammered. "We just wanted to tell you something kinda… embarrassing."

Wow, I thought, *could they have already gotten that far in the discussion that they were dealing with some real life issues?* I didn't expect such depth on the first day, but I would later learn that much of the joy in teaching is not about what I expect or plan for.

"Uh, we noticed something that… well, we think you should know," Sara continued, only making eye contact with her flip flops.

Kathy's words tumbled out, and I could suddenly understand why they were so uncomfortable. "Mrs. Haberling, your fly is open and it has been all hour."

My eyes must have told quite a story that moment as the day replayed through my head—the busyness of the first day, no break for lunch, no trips to the bathroom, no mirror checks… it had probably been like that since I left home that early morning! As I glanced through the window to the rest of my class, I could see that the news had obviously spread—everyone was watching to see how I would respond. My cheeks burned. I struggled to compose a coherent response before I gave in and burst out laughing, relieving the girls. As I walked back into class, Jeremy was the first to greet me with a round of applause.

At times like that, laughter is the only appropriate response—laughter at myself and my mistakes. On that first day of school, the one I had prepared for so carefully, I learned a lesson that would serve me throughout my teaching career. It's best if the students I spend the year with see me as a fallible human being, who sometimes forgets to zip. It's best if kids see me make mistakes and laugh at myself. It's best if I listen carefully to the many things my students teach me, through what they say and what they don't say. It's best if my students sometimes know more than I do, and it's best if I let them see that I, too, am still discovering. I was glad that Jeremy, Kathy and Sara took the time to teach me a lesson on that very first day. It didn't need to be my version of perfect to be wonderful. Without the fly in the room, I might have given myself too much credit for the successes and beat myself up too hard over the stumbles. Instead, three freshmen reminded me that when all else fails, I need to remember to laugh at myself.

~Jennifer A. Haberling
2009 Michigan State Teacher of the Year
English teacher, grade 7

18

Burgers and Cries

Success seems to be largely a matter of hanging on after others have let go.
~William Feather

"Od, please don't let anything happen today that I can't handle."

This was my daily prayer during my first year of teaching. My school was a twenty-five-minute commute from home, and I spent every one of those minutes worrying about what the next six hours would bring.

Landing the job was a happy surprise. Just out of college, I had spent a summer studying in Mexico and returned home in late August, certain I'd missed my chance of finding a teaching position. Then I learned of an opening for a fifth grade teacher at a local Spanish immersion school. The day after arriving home, I interviewed. The next day I signed a contract. And four days later, school started.

While other teachers had spent weeks planning and preparing, I had only a few days. It was a tough way to start, and things didn't get any easier. Some of the kids in my room had real problems. One girl had been molested by her mother's boyfriend. A boy had just finished treatment for Hodgkin's disease. Another girl lived above a bar. One night, she told me, there had been shooting in the street below and the family all got down on the floor to avoid being hit by a stray bullet.

And then there was my "girl gang," a clique of three feisty ten-year-olds. Jasmine, the sharp-tongued leader, brimmed with attitude.

Burly Lonette carried a chip on her shoulder, evidenced in the fist-fights she started on the playground. And Lakeisha was a master at the art of smacking her lips and rolling her eyes toward heaven when I said something she didn't like.

Even though some of my students came from stable homes, the ones who didn't affected the whole class. Most of all, they affected me. I didn't know how to handle the blatant disrespect, the trash talk, or the "he said-she said" conflicts that took hours to unravel. It seemed like these kids needed a social worker—or at least a teacher with more mettle than I. In desperation I clamped down, handing out consequences for even minor infractions. But it didn't help; acting like a drill sergeant just fostered resentment. I felt like I was failing.

Morale fell and tension grew; I soon hated going to work, just as many of the kids seemed to hate being at school. My prayers became more fervent: Help me. Show me what to do. I feel like quitting. Then God gave me an idea. There was a Burger King across the street from the school. What if I took my students out to eat? Maybe that would build the trust and goodwill that our classroom lacked.

So the next day I made an announcement.

"Every Friday from now on, I'm going to take one student to lunch at Burger King."

"Great," someone muttered, "I'll bet she only chooses the good kids."

Ignoring the comment, I said, "Every week, I'll randomly draw a name. By the end of the year, everyone will have had a turn."

Students sat up with interest as I picked the first name. I got the feeling that many of them didn't go out to eat very often—even to a fast food place. Maybe this was a good idea. After the first outing, I was sure of it. If nothing else, it had been fun, and everyone—me included—needed some fun in life.

The months went on. Every Friday, the chosen student and I chatted over hamburgers, fries, and Cokes. Sometimes, the student was one who had been particularly difficult that week, but that didn't matter. I never discussed behavior during those lunches, choosing instead to focus on family, hobbies, and friends.

Perhaps the student whose turn I most dreaded was Jasmine's. I had made some inroads with the other members of the "gang," but not with her. She scowled at me when I smiled, made snide comments under her breath, and once, when I ordered her to the detention room, delivered a speech so venomous that after she left I put my head down on my desk and sobbed. She really seemed to hate me, to the extent that when her name was chosen, I wondered if she would refuse to go.

She didn't. That Friday, the two of us walked across the street together, ordered our meals, and had a pleasant conversation. It was as if, for that half hour, she had called a truce.

I wish I could say things changed with her after that, but they didn't. In fact, not much changed with many of my students. I was too young, too green, and too unsure of myself to do all the good I meant to. But at the same time, I'm glad for what I did do. Maybe that trip to Burger King meant something to the kid whose mom yelled at him that morning, or the kid who usually ate alone, or the kid whose family couldn't afford to buy him a two-dollar kid's meal. I hope it did. Looking back now, eighteen years later, I'm pleased that I tried.

~Sara Matson

19

Teaching from Courage

*You block your dream when you allow your
fear to grow bigger than your faith.*
~Mary Manin Morrissey

Sixteen kindergarten students scampered in at a quarter past
eight. Their little eyes stared up at me. "Substitute teacher," I
heard them whisper.

After their little backpacks were neatly put away, they started
doing something that wasn't in the substitute plan. They opened their
folders and began reciting their spelling. Mothers and fathers were
sitting at the short tables, helping their children learn their spelling
lists, and I felt like an outsider, which I was.

Suddenly, it was five to nine and it was time to gather on the
carpet. But the parents didn't move and the kids remained at their
desks, their lips moving quietly. Big heads and little heads, focused
on a small piece of paper that was obstructing the flow of my day.

I was only a novice teacher then, and I didn't really understand
the concept of being flexible. All I knew was that I had to follow the
daily plan. Then I looked across to the other classroom (we were in
a shared space), and I saw that the teacher next door was already
taking attendance. I was supposed to be doing that too.

Suddenly I was compelled to have the whole class on the carpet;
I needed them in a neat small square where I could see them. Years
later, I learned that gathering the children on the floor was a great way
to control the classroom when everything was out of control—gather

and focus. The difference was, this class wasn't out of control; and it just felt that way to me.

After five long minutes, I had most of the children sitting quietly on the carpet. Except one.

A mother with scraggly brown hair was still working with her daughter.

I approached the wooden table, very aware that the rest of the kids were sitting down waiting for me, feeling that at any moment they would start scrambling around looking for things to do. With a burning face, I spoke to the woman.

"She has to go. I'm sorry," I said as my face flushed red again. I was upset that they were affecting my progress.

"She has to finish her spelling," said the woman, with her hand on the child's green spelling book.

"Well I'm sorry, but I was instructed to have her on the floor at this time," I said, feeling apologetic and upset at the same time.

The child stopped practicing her spelling and looked up at me, her eyes mirroring the accusation in her mother's eyes.

Unsure, I finally told the mother to continue. I felt my authority vanish. I felt unsettled.

"It's too late now," the mother declared. "You've upset her and she doesn't want to spell anymore." I was scared. Her lips were down-turned and her tired eyes darted accusations at me. I felt like I failed. I didn't want to upset her, but somehow I did.

She walked out the glass double doors, the sun illuminating her outline as she left. I was left with her daughter. Part of me wanted to go after her, persuade her that I did the right thing. I wanted to show her the plan, see... the plan proves me right.

Instead I said, "Go and sit down Stephanie." I half expected her to refuse. Luckily she went calmly to join the other kids.

The day went by quickly. Reading, writing, lunch, math and recesses came and went... but I felt uneasy.

I spent the day treating her daughter like china. "Stephanie, how are you feeling?" or "Stephanie, what would you like to do now?" Of course the girl loved the extra attention that I was giving her.

As it approached three o'clock, I kept thinking about how afraid I was of doing the wrong thing. I was afraid of not following the plans properly, I was afraid that I was going to look bad in front of the other teacher. Now I was afraid that I might have upset a parent.

Finally, I realized that being scared wasn't helping me, and I decided to ask myself what I would I do if I wasn't afraid. The answer came to me instantly.

That afternoon, as I was bidding the children goodbye, I approached Stephanie's mother with my heart pounding again.

"Mrs. Cosmos, I would like to speak to you," I said looking her straight in the eye.

Her face was stiff and she had her hands on Stephanie's shoulders.

"I'm sorry for what happened this morning," I said, my face flushed again, but this time with relief.

"I know that all you want is the best for your child, and I should have listened to that," I said, and I realized that I believed what I was saying.

In that moment, the woman in front of me transformed, her shoulders sagged and she looked at me earnestly.

"You have no idea what I have to go through. I have six children and I try so hard to come in and help." Suddenly, it all made sense: the desperate need to finish her daughter's spelling, the abrupt change of her mood when I asked her to stop. As a mother, she worked so hard to be there with her daughter each morning, and although it strained her to do it, she did it anyway.

"I'm sorry," she continued. "I know it must be hard if you don't know the school and if the instructions aren't complete."

I stopped breathing, because in less than a minute this mother was telling me her problems when before she could hardly talk to me.

I realized that teaching was not just about getting the lesson plan right, but it was about making a difference to the people I would be working with, and that included both the students and the parents.

Most importantly, I realized that if my teaching was guided by my fear, I would also impart a sense of fear to my students. Once I realized that, I suddenly saw the children and parents for what they were: human beings, with hopes, dreams and hearts that wanted to achieve many things in their lives. Like every human, I recognized that they might have fears of their own... just as that mother did. So I made a choice that day. I chose to stop listening to my fear, and to teach with courage and love. And by making that choice, I had the privilege to make a difference to these precious people, simply by being a teacher.

So these days, the classes I teach usually go as planned, but when they don't, I understand that it's still okay.

~Quyen Thai

Chapter
3

Teacher Tales

Learning from the Kids

I am learning all the time. The tombstone will be my diploma.

~Eartha Kitt

Tools of the Trade

Words can sometimes, in moments of grace, attain the quality of deeds.
~Elie Wiesel

There are days when I find it necessary to step outside my classroom and check to be sure that my name is still in the TEACHER space over my door. Sometimes I feel that I am a student in my classroom rather than the teacher.

My sixth grade students were seated in a large circle on the floor of our classroom. Each student held a different tool in his or her hand. Some were common tools—a hammer, a wrench, a flashlight, a screwdriver—and others were unfamiliar tools to the students—a copper pipe cutter, an awl, a chalk line. The lesson had gone perfectly. The students discussed how words are like tools—they have the ability to build or to destroy, and they discovered how the right tool used at the right time for the right job can yield great results. The sixth graders freely shared personal stories of how they had experienced someone's words used as a tool, to wound or to heal, and some even bravely shared how they had personally used their words at times as tools to hurt or to help others.

I watched and listened with a sense of satisfaction—the students were engaged, attentive, and enjoying the lesson. They got it! It was one of those times when I sat back and reveled in the magic of being a teacher—to have the opportunity to watch young people discover a greater truth about life, about each other, and about themselves.

A few days later, one of my students, Laura, had an unexpected and uncharacteristic outburst of disruptive defiance in class. She refused to work with her group. I was aware from reading Laura's file that she had struggled with defiant behavior in previous years, but we had developed a good rapport and she was always a respectful, thoughtful, and positive contributor to our class. Her behavior caught me off guard. I asked her to excuse herself and told her I would visit with her in our next door team center in just a minute. She refused to leave and sat silently glaring at me from the back of the room. I rather firmly told her she needed to excuse herself—this was NOT optional. She knew I meant it. She marched from the back of the room to our classroom door—huffing and shooting me an angry look, then proceeded to slam the door as she left for the team meeting room.

I continued our lesson and when the students were working together in their groups, I motioned to my aide that I was going to step out to visit with Laura. I gently closed our classroom door behind me, then marched the five steps next door to our meeting room where Laura was seated. In an unexpected and uncharacteristic gesture of frustration, I slammed the meeting room door behind me. As I stood over her, I began to express how disrespectful and uncalled-for her behavior had been to our class. Her defiance had triggered a wave of out-of-character anger in me and I was sharp in my tone and harsh with my words.

Without looking at me, she absorbed the brunt of my anger with a rigid and steely exterior. When I paused for her response, she slowly turned and smugly stated, "You're using your tool against me."

I was speechless. There are times as a teacher when you are at a critical crossroads with a student and the road you choose will make all the difference. Although part of me resented that she was continuing to be so defiant—even in her brilliant rebuke—I paused to reflect on a quote that is posted on our team center wall: "THINK! What is the right thing to do, and do that." The truth of Laura's words and our team center's quote penetrated my conscience like a sharp scalpel.

I knew at that moment the right thing to do was to humbly bend my knee, kneel down next to her chair, and softly say, "You're right, Laura, you are so right. I have used my words unwisely and unkindly. Will you forgive me?" I paused and waited silently next to her chair and gently put my hand on her arm to reassure her of my sincerity. Her defiance slowly melted away. She turned and looked me in the eye and simply said, "Yes, I forgive you, Mrs. Ekre. I'm sorry, too." We continued to visit a bit longer and shared a few laughs and a couple of tears. Eventually, we walked back into the classroom together.

For the rest of the day and the rest of the year, Laura never had another outburst. At the end of the year, she wrote me a beautiful letter about how she loved being in my class and that some of the most important lessons she learned, she learned in Room 25. Attached to the note was a small key—a tool, she said, for a language arts teacher who taught her how important words can be. It serves as my reminder of a lesson I taught as a teacher but one I really learned from my student.

~Beth Ekre
2009 North Dakota State Teacher of the Year
Social Studies, Language Arts teacher, grade 6

The Little Choir with a Big Dream

The greatest dreams are always unrealistic.
~Will Smith

"What will we be singing for contest this year?" a student from my high school choir asked eagerly.

I dreaded this moment. "I was thinking," I said, "maybe we'll skip the contest and just work hard on the concerts this year."

"NO!" the kids protested.

"We've got to go to contest!"

"In Class A."

"It's tradition!"

This was true. Award plaques lined the front wall of the music room from the past successes of large, talented classes. But a swing in educational policies, with an emphasis on academics, had reduced my choir to a mere thirty-two students. My section leaders had graduated or been forced to drop music classes, leaving me with young, inexperienced kids who couldn't read music, couldn't hold their parts, and could sing only a simple melody.

"Maybe we could enter Class B this year," I suggested, knowing even that would be a near-impossible mission.

"No!" the kids screamed. "Class A!"

I shook my head. "Class A is extremely difficult."

"We can do it!" they shouted. "We can do it!"

"I'll have to think about it," I said, hoping their enthusiasm would die off in a couple of weeks.

But that didn't happen. If anything, the class became more adamant. Every day they begged, they pleaded, they insisted. Because I had to protect their self-esteem I couldn't tell them they weren't good enough. My efforts to thwart their eagerness, by showing them a difficult piece of music from the contest list, simply ended with, "It's okay, Mrs. Pliszka, we'll get it."

I struggled to make a decision. If I crushed their hope, would I crush their spirit? On the other hand, if we entered Class A, would they be humiliated by the judges' comments?

I remembered one of my college professors saying, "Every child will learn if the teacher is willing to put forth twice as much effort as the student." I wasn't afraid of hard work, and I enjoyed a challenge. But I wasn't a miracle worker. And so I pondered this dilemma.

Finally one morning I stomped into class. "Look at the clock!" I demanded. "We've wasted two full minutes because some of you don't have your music ready. If we are entering the contest in Class A..." The rest of my sentence was lost in shrieks of delight and applause.

"From now on," I continued when the noise subsided, "you will find the day's lesson plan on the board. Be in your seats with your music folders on the desk when the bell rings and sit at attention, ready for warm-ups the instant I'm ready to begin. When I'm working with one section, there will be no talking from the others. You will listen, and you will learn. You will work harder than you've ever worked in any class before. And if one of these rules is broken, we will not go to the contest. Does everyone agree to this?"

I was certain they would fail to keep this contract, and no one would have to be embarrassed. But as the weeks progressed the kids remained focused. They followed the rules with no complaints and seemed to thrive on the discipline demanded of them.

Each morning they vocalized, worked on sight-reading, learned musical terms, practiced tempo and signature changes, rehearsed concert music, and went over and over the three contest numbers.

I was amazed at the driving force that kept pushing them on. They reminded me of "The Little Engine that Could," saying, "I think I can... I think I can... I know I can...." They advanced to two part harmony, to three, to four, to six, and finally to eight parts. Their progress was so remarkable even I began believing in their dream.

Seven months into the school year, when the contest day finally arrived, the kids felt ready to take on the world! One of the students was unable to get off work, one was ill, and one had moved away. So our little group numbered twenty-nine. They warmed up, listened to my pep talk, and made their way to the performance area.

Their eyes opened wide when the Madison choir marched in seventy-five members strong. Their jaws dropped when 125 students from King, the specialty school for the college bound, entered the room. Two private schools came with fifty members each, then Marshall with sixty; and finally, forty-five members from the elite Milwaukee School of the Arts.

As my choir mounted the risers, I looked at the three judges and remembered how improbable this scenario had seemed at the beginning of the school year.

"Smile!" I mouthed. They looked confident. I took a deep breath, and we began.

They performed masterfully. We finished our three songs, and I wanted to scream at the top of my lungs, "YOU DID IT!" But the most difficult task remained — sight-reading. We were given a short time to look over a new score. Nothing was to be sung by me or played by the pianist. The choir was allowed to hear only their starting tones, and I could direct. But they were basically on their own.

It seemed such a short time ago they could sing only a familiar melody in unison. Now they were singing four parts to a score they'd never seen or heard, without accompaniment, and doing it well. My heart swelled with pride for this little group as they executed their dream with the same spunk they had shown from day one.

After all the choirs had performed, we waited in our assigned room for the results. "The other groups were so large and so good. What chance do we have against them?" one of my students asked.

"Size doesn't matter. And you weren't competing against them," I replied, "only proving you can handle Class A." Having said that, I wished it were true. But I knew it was a competition in everyone's heart—all choirs hoping to be the best. How could size not be a factor? Could we possibly have sounded as full and rich as the larger groups?

While we waited for the judges' scores, the kids gazed at the clock, went for snacks, gazed at the clock, drew on the chalkboard, gazed at the clock....

Two very long hours later the results were posted. I stood frozen, staring at the list in disbelief. There was our name at the very top: a First Place award with the highest marks of all.

"We did it!" I gulped, scarcely breathing.

All around kids were squealing and embracing. Warm tears wet my cheeks as the memory of persistent young voices echoed in my head: "We can do it!" "In Class A." "We'll get it!"

My thoughts were jolted as a sudden rush of students nearly smothered me in hugs. And I was surrounded by kids who had a dream—kids who refused to give up—kids who taught me to never doubt the possibility of success for any student or any class ever again. I was surrounded by the little choir that COULD!

~Kay Conner Pliszka

Life Lessons
from My Students

Who dares to teach must never cease to learn.

~John Cotton Dana

It is a humbling experience when teachers are the ones who are also learning in their very own classroom. After high school and college, it might seem as if the days of tests and homework are over; however, when 150 students enter those classroom doors, teachers quickly realize that life tests and life homework come right along with the students.

As an educator, I have discovered that the life lessons that students bring with them to school are the ones that I truly need to learn.

I learn about commitment from my students who catch the 6:30 AM community bus because no family member will give them a ride to school.

I learn about perseverance from my student with special needs who is included in my geometry class and comes to tutoring every single morning, and Saturday, because he desperately wants to earn "proficient" on the end of course exam and succeed like his peers.

I learn about strength from my student who has lost both parents and is now watching his last living relative die of cancer, yet still manages to come to school and focus on his classes.

I learn about patience from my student who can only do her

homework in morning tutoring because she has to take care of her siblings from the moment the 3:30 bell rings until 10:30 at night.

I learn about compassion from my student who wears the same clothes two days in a row because he tried to stop his mom's boyfriend from hitting her. They decided to put him out, and he had to sleep in a car.

All of these qualities that I have learned from my students have added up to a philosophy that has shaken my world, transformed my thinking, and has urgently called me to teach every single moment for these students, because they all deserve a future, no matter their circumstances.

This ambitious task of using every single teaching moment to the fullest is not an adventure for the teacher. Instead, it is an adventure for the very life, soul, and purpose of the student.

One story that describes this awesome responsibility starts with a second year sophomore student. Every day, he would come into my Geometry Investigations class, sit in the very back, and avoid eye contact. When I would ask the class questions, I could hear a deep voice coming from his direction saying the correct answer every single time. I immediately began to investigate and found that he had high standardized test scores but his report card and placement in school did not match his state performances. I knew something had to change.

Through our school mentoring program, I asked him if he would like to be a part of a support team that was specifically designed to help him graduate on time with his classmates. This program would require him to come in early every single morning for tutoring and for completing assignments, not just in my class but in all seven classes, and to spend lunchtime not with his friends, but in my classroom studying.

Even after hearing all of the stipulations, he was willing to work diligently in order to change his status from a second year sophomore to a true senior. This extensive two-year endeavor required me to visit all of his classroom teachers, help him complete every assignment, provide him materials to finish projects, and constantly remind him that success could be achieved if he stayed on this path. I challenged him every day, and during his senior year he was able to make the Honor Roll, see his name in the local newspaper, and for the very first time, have his great-grandfather drive to school to pick up his report card.

On a personal note, this student had been living with his great-grandfather instead of living with his mother, her boyfriend, and six siblings. The concept of family had not been demonstrated in his life. However, at school, the mentoring program provided him with a team that focused on his academic needs as well as celebrated his successes. The idea of family, where he was cared for and was seen as important, was able to become a reality.

Unfortunately, during his senior year, his great-grandfather passed away and he had to move back in with his mother, her boyfriend, and his siblings. His grades began to fall drastically, and his newly positive view of life began to wilt. But because of the relationship and the bond that was established over the past two years through the mentoring program, I was able to keep him focused on what he *could* control to achieve his goal, rather than the numerous obstacles around him that he could *not* control.

He showed determination and perseverance, and he became a senior with his original class and had the opportunity to graduate with his friends. Sadly, when graduation day approached, he told me that he would not attend the graduation ceremony because no family member would be there to see him walk across the stage to receive his diploma. I told him that he was wrong; because on that day, I would be there as well as his six other teachers who had the unbelievable opportunity to see him transform into a student of self-worth, diligence, and potential.

I can still remember the smile on his face as he walked across that stage to receive his diploma. I still think to myself, what if that moment had never happened? What if his answers were not heard, his story not known, his chance for success not taken? What if the lessons he was trying to teach me were not learned?

The life tests and the life homework that continue to be piled on my desk are definitely a collection of knowledge that has the power to make an everlasting difference in the lives of so many students. Their voices want to be heard and their gifts want to be celebrated. I have learned that lessons are not always meant to be for students. As a teacher, I look forward every year to the lessons my students bring to the classroom, because I know these lives are ready to be changed.

~Susan Waggener
2009 Arkansas State Teacher of the Year
Math, Business Education teacher, grades 10-12

Welcome to the Fourth Grade

A child can ask questions that a wise man cannot answer.
~Author Unknown

"Good morning," I greeted each student at the door. "Please put your coats and lunch bags in the closet and sit at the desk where you find your name tag."

The children came in quietly and sat expectantly, almost reverently, their hands folded on the desk in front of them. They stole looks around the classroom, searching for familiar faces. Some of the more daring ones peeked inside the textbooks piled on the desktops; most of them didn't.

One brave soul raised his hand to ask if he could sharpen his new pencils. I smiled and nodded. As he left his seat and approached the wall-mounted sharpener, several classmates scrambled after him, whispering excitedly. This was the big time; this was the intermediate elementary school; this was fourth grade.

By nine o'clock, twenty-four scrubbed and shining faces filled the room. "How many of you like to listen to long, boring lectures about school rules?" I began.

The question was of course rhetorical; the students sat stunned. Facial expressions reflected uncertainty. One boy openly groaned and dramatically flopped his head down upon his arms folded on the desk.

After checking the seating chart, I addressed the theatrically despondent boy by name. "What's the matter, Josh? Don't you like long, boring lectures?"

"Well," he began, "since you asked... I like a whole lot of other things a whole lot better."

A born diplomat. "Just between you and me," I said, lowering my voice to a stage whisper, "I'm not too crazy about them either, so I figure if we hurry up and get this business stuff out of the way we can start having fun."

He returned my smile while the class expelled a collective sigh of relief.

By day's end my throat felt as raw as a freshly scraped knee. The majority of students wore glazed expressions. Information overload, I thought. Time to wrap it up.

"By now," I said, mustering what energy I had left, "you probably realize that I don't believe there's any such thing as a 'dumb question.' So if there's anything you want to know, about today or about the rest of the school year, please feel free to ask."

Not a single hand went up. I wondered if this was because I had explained everything so very well, or, more likely, because they were fearful of sounding foolish in front of their new classmates.

"You know," I continued, "even grown-ups are sometimes afraid to ask questions. Sometimes grown-ups think they should already know the answers, just because they're older than kids. But I'll tell you a little secret: Even grown-ups don't know everything."

The child who'd admitted he didn't especially like lectures raised his hand.

"Yes, Josh? Do you have a question?"

"Well," he began, "it's more of an observation, really."

"Okay, go on."

"I know what you're trying to do."

My silence and raised eyebrows encouraged him to expound on his idea.

"When you tell us that even grown-ups don't have all the answers," he continued, "and that sometimes grown-ups feel like they're asking dumb questions, what you're really trying to do is make us feel more comfortable."

"That's right, Josh." I nodded.

"But Ms. B.," he continued, "we already know we don't know all the answers, and now you're telling us that when we're grown-ups we still won't know all the answers." He sighed deeply. "So you're really not being very reassuring."

"Wow," I said, grinning at him, "you really followed that thought all the way through. I guess next time I'll have to try harder to put you all at ease.

Josh nodded and grinned back. "I just thought you'd want to know," he said.

The year was off to a great start.

~Jan Bono

An Unexpected Lesson

The art of teaching is the art of assisting discovery.
~Mark Van Doren

Jack had the grip of a muscle man. When he shook your hand it felt like every bone inside would break. The kids knew it too, and feared for their lives when the mood struck him to give out giant bear hugs. He spent his spare time in physics class ripping apart telephone books with his bare hands. Everything about him was strong and assured. Challenging him in physics was a constant play in kinesthetic learning.

When it came to Newton's second law, one push from Jack was all it took to get the hovercraft going at relativistic speeds, or when we karate-chopped boards, Jack led the class by breaking eight boards stacked high. Demonstrating momentum conservation was a favorite for Jack because he could crush a cinder block on my chest with a sledgehammer as I lay between beds of sharpened nails. Jack was a joy to teach because he could pretty much do anything, so I was surprised with his reaction one day when I challenged him with a lesson on pulleys.

Our topic for the week was how pulleys and ropes can be used to increase your mechanical advantage. Jack was excited because he knew it meant he would get to push and pull things. To get the point across we went outside to do a "pulley" tug of war; it was to be Jack against the entire class, with only a few pulleys to help him. The class was sure this time there was no way Jack could outgun them, but

Jack rigged up his side perfectly and to their dismay he confidently won the match.

But now it was time to get to the formality of learning and to apply what we learned through written work. Each year I end the unit with a lesson that I call "Thematic Pulleys." It is my chance to use the right and left sides of the brain together. I ask the kids to integrate art and physics into a theme using pulleys. They solve a problem of their own design, drawing it artistically on paper, yet with absolute physical accuracy. The kids come up with the most amazing drawings, some suspend spaghetti dinners with meatball pulleys on noodle ropes, or "Monopulley" game pieces with the prices of real estate representing weights, or others go for a "Beatles" theme, with records being the pulleys hanging the instruments and players of the band. The beauty of the designs are endless, entertaining and simply brilliant.

Jack sat and pondered the assignment. "Mr. Lampert," he said, "I can't draw." I was somewhat taken aback; this was the kid who I thought could do anything. This was Big Jack, self assured Jack, rip-a-telephone-book-in-half Jack. But a delicate drawing was just not his cup of tea. I assured him he could do the assignment and mused to myself, "I wonder what he will do now?" I had hit a weakness inside him, and as a teacher, I was excited to see how he would respond.

The day the assignment was due there was no Jack. Everyone turned in their work except Jack. I was curious what had happened but went home that afternoon rather tired from the week and I ended up crashing solidly on the couch, fast asleep. I awoke at dusk to a "clippity-cloppity" sound approaching down the driveway. There was a loud knock at the front door. I cracked it open slightly, quite curious about the ruckus. Suddenly a horse shoved its head right into the house! I heard a "Whoa there!" from behind the horse, and there was Jack. "Hey Lampert!" he sheepishly said, "I have something to show you. I brought you a horse to ride; mine is tied up over by the basketball hoop. Come on, saddle up!"

"Okay, this is pretty cool," I thought. I had not ridden a horse in over twenty years, so this could be fun. I got my courage up, and after Jack apologized for the mess the horse made on the driveway, we went riding a short way up the hill to his barn. As we entered, I saw hanging on the wall a whiteboard with Jack's rudimentary drawings of pulleys, ropes and various mathematical calculations. This was a good sign. He had obviously been busy doing physics today.

We dismounted and walked to the middle of the arena. There I was impressed to see what Jack had been working on. Suspended from a high girder was a strong rope winding through several pulleys; at the end was a pallet loaded with at least four hundred pounds of hay and old tractor parts. Jack said to me "Okay, Lampert, hop on!" He explained to me how he had figured out the exact lifting force needed and then, with just one arm, Jack grinned as he pulled the entire weight and me up and down with ease. "What do you say Lampert? Is that an A?" he asked in seriousness. "Jack, that's an A-plus!" I said proudly as he let me down.

I was quite taken aback by Jack's work, and as I rode home I reflected on the lesson, realizing that I had learned a lot that evening. Around me was the beauty of the horses, the open fields, the red sky and the peace of the Oregon countryside. While earlier I had mused to myself about how Jack might solve his shortcomings integrating art and physics, here Jack had clearly stepped up to the challenge. He created a masterpiece that went above and beyond the requirements for the assignment. He demonstrated that students can and will solve pretty much anything you present them. Jack was strong physically, but more importantly he was strong-willed.

~Michael Lampert
2009 Oregon State Teacher of the Year
Physics teacher, grades 9-12

25

Connecting

*The important thing is not so much that every child should be taught, as that
every child should be given the wish to learn.*
~John Lubbock

hen I entered college in the early 1980s, I had my heart
set on being a first grade teacher. I did all of my observations in others' first-grade classrooms. I student taught
first grade, and I interviewed for my first job… in a first-grade classroom. Needless to say, I was delighted when the district offered me a
job… as a fifth grade teacher in an inner-city building, considered at
the time to be one of our district's toughest assignments. It wasn't the
first-grade classroom I had hoped for, but it was MY classroom!

I was prepared for the curriculum I would teach, and even the
social issues I would encounter, but in a classroom of fifth graders,
there will always be something you're not prepared for, especially as
a first year teacher.

I navigated through my first year fairly successfully, while working to form relationships with my students in an effort to keep one
step ahead of them, which was no easy feat! There was one child in
particular, Alexander, who I just couldn't seem to connect with. He
was a special needs student who had learning disabilities in both
math and reading. He rarely bathed, his clothes were filthy, and the
other children were sometimes very cruel to him. He was a difficult
child to get to open up, but I was dogged in my efforts.

You can imagine my delight when finally, in late spring, Alexander raised his hand during math class. Not only did it go up, but it was accompanied by "Ooh, ooh, ooh," as he waved it frantically. Thrilled that Alexander was eager to participate in our discussion for the first time ever, I immediately called on him.

Well, you can imagine my surprise when he suddenly lunged into a story about his grandma, whom he was excited to tell us, had a hole in her head. You see, we were studying fractions that day, and I had just explained that a fraction is "a part of a whole." Alexander obviously didn't realize the difference between W-hole and H-ole. "Homophones," I told myself, "had better be tomorrow's English lesson!"

Acknowledging Alexander that day was exactly what he needed from me. We had suddenly bonded. Alexander felt such a connection to me after that, that he even went one step further.

I arrived at the school the following morning and was genuinely surprised to find Alexander and his grandma waiting for me. Grandma began by saying, "Alexander said he told you that I have a hole in my head." I smiled nervously and said, "Don't worry. You know kids! They have great imaginations!" Grandma replied, "You didn't believe him, did you?" "No, of course not," I stammered. Well, just that quick, Grandma proudly popped out her glass eye, revealing that she truly did have a hole in her head!

I will never forget that day, and the lessons that I learned from being Alexander's teacher. He taught me:

1. Students with learning disabilities can connect to a word or phrase, even if it is a homophone, and then just need to vocalize their thoughts.

2. I can connect with the hard-to-reach students if I allow them to speak when they are ready to.

3. The child who sits by himself, who is shunned by his peers, and who appears to be "on another planet" most days, may just be waiting for the right moment to share something with you. He is testing you to see if you really do care about him.

4. We need to look beyond the "package" that our students and

their families come wrapped in, so that we can see inside them, and find out what motivates them.

5. If a child ever again tells me about a family member with a hole in his or her head... BELIEVE HIM!

~Tania L. Harman
2009 Indiana State Teacher of the Year
Elementary teacher, grades 1-2

26

The Glitter Mask

Every artist dips his brush in his own soul,
and paints his own nature into his pictures.
~Henry Ward Beecher

I t is Tuesday, just three days before Halloween. We have been making Halloween masks in my first class of the day, and I need to quickly clear and organize feathers, sequins and glue bottles before rushing on to my next class.

Quiany sidles up to me. In the wheedling tone she uses when attempting to manipulate you into doing something "just for her" she asks, "Can I use some more glitter, Miss Miller? Can I use more sequins? Just a little more. I know you always say that with glitter, less is more. But just a little more, Miss Miller? Please?"

I say, "We'll see, Quiany. But not today. I'll be back with your class again on Thursday afternoon. We'll just have to see."

"Okay, Miss Miller. Okay."

Though I have a lot of life experience, with a family and fully developed corporate career in my past, I am a brand new teacher in a tough New York City school district and still feeling things out. I'm not sure of the right way to handle so many situations, and this is one of those.

As things turn out, I am not at work on Thursday afternoon, when I would ordinarily be teaching Quiany's class again. My first grandchild, a girl, is born Wednesday night and I spend Thursday in the hospital with Alexis and beautiful new Ruby Jane. On Friday, when I return to school, it's Halloween and our little school of students with special needs is even wilder than usual. Students are excited, and way out of control.

Since I keep some of my art materials in a cabinet in my friend Mari's room, I go there first to get myself set up for my classes. Quiany, as it happens, has been placed in Mari's classroom for the day, probably to keep her out of harm's way. Streetwise and manipulative though Quiany may be, the pre-adolescent boys in her class of complicated nine- to eleven-year-olds are leagues beyond her in that department. On the other hand, the five- and six-year-old developmentally delayed students in Mari's class, though challenging for the teachers, can be very sweet and they love Quiany a lot, and she loves them. Today, this is definitely a better place for her to be.

As soon as she sees me, Quiany comes over from the dress-up corner, where she has been playing with Starr. She is wearing a tall, pointed witch's hat covered in black sequins. In her slightly accented voice, so softly I can barely hear her, she asks, "Miss Miller, can I work on my mask? Can I use a little glitter?"

"That's okay with me today, Quiany, but let's make sure it's okay with Miss Mari."

It was.

"Okay, Quiany, I'll get your mask and some materials, and you'll be able to use a little glitter."

In a few minutes, I return with Quiany's mask and some materials she can add to her mask. I also have my toolbox, which contains, among other things, the glitter she is so focused on. But before I can get everything arranged, I hear screaming from another classroom. It is my job to check out situations like this, so I need to go see what I can do to help. I tell Quiany to start with the sequins and pipe cleaners and that I will be back shortly to help her with the glitter.

As soon as I'm able, I return to Mari's room and walk directly to Quiany. She notices me approaching and quickly hides the mask behind her back, then looks up at me sheepishly.

"What's going on, Quiany? You said you wanted to use some more glitter on your mask. Let's get to work on that."

"I used it already," she says quietly.

"Oh, really," I say, a question mark in my voice, not really sure how to handle this turn of events, "and where did you get the glitter from?"

"I went into your toolbox."

"Quiany," I say sternly, "you know that no one except me is ever allowed to go into my toolbox, for any reason."

"I know, Miss Miller," she says, sounding honestly upset despite her usual tough front, "but…"

"No buts about it, Quiany. No one. Not ever. For any reason."

For the moment, she buckles under. "Okay, Miss Miller."

I let some moments pass in silence. Then, "So… let's see it."

"Well," Quiany starts eagerly, "I know you always say less is more with glitter. But I used a little more than less…."

"Well, let me see it anyway, Quiany." My tone, I'm certain, conveys what I'm feeling, a mix of impatience and sympathy. Overall, I'm more than ready to be done with this, but somewhat surprise myself as I add, "Today is, after all, a special day. Maybe a little more than a little is okay, just for today." Nothing to be done about it now, I think. I might as well let her get out of this gracefully.

Reluctantly, she takes the mask out from behind her back and holds it out for me to see. She is right. She has definitely used a little more than a little. She has used so much, in fact, that the glitter covers all the work she had done the other day. All of the glitter colors, neatly separated in their little bottles in my toolbox, are all mixed together on her mask. None of the fabric of the mask shows through anywhere. The entire mask is glitter. Just glitter. And it is glorious.

I am at a loss for words, not sure of the appropriate teacher response to this. On the one hand, Quiany has broken several of our "art rules." On the other hand, she has created something very beautiful. To me, all of these things are important and I can't think quickly enough at the moment to determine which should have the priority.

"Quiany," I finally say, "you really did use a lot of glitter."

"Yes, Miss Miller, I know."

"And," I continue, "you do need to follow the rules. This is not the way we normally use glitter, nor can you go into my things without asking."

"I know, Miss Miller," she says, sounding quite miserable this time, and appearing to be on the verge of tears. "I know. I'm sorry. I won't do it again."

"But," I add slowly and cautiously, "your mask is very, very beautiful. Let me see it on you."

She keeps her head down and pulls the mask on, sliding the elastic of the mask up and over the black witch's hat. Taking a deep and exaggerated breath, Quiany picks her head up and looks straight at me. Her dark eyes peer anxiously from behind the magnificent mask. Her face, framed by the waves of her long, dark hair and the pointed, black hat, looks stunning. I know I will never forget how she looks at this moment.

I need to give this a lot more thought, I think to myself. Maybe less is not more all the time. Maybe Quiany, all the Quianys, know a lot more than I do about certain things.

Leaning down, not saying a word, I pull Quiany close, hugging the child she is now and the woman she will someday be.

~Celeste Miller

School Glue

What art offers is space—a certain breathing room for the spirit.
~John Updike

My classroom was a sort of "dumping ground" at one point in my career. The counselor, Mr. H., had a habit of coming to me with a timid smile and saying, "I have a kid for you who you'll just *love*. That was code for "I need to put a 'bad' kid in your class who's gotten kicked out by another teacher." I sighed and answered, "Well, alright." And thus, in walked Josh.

Some kids put up a little wall to prevent others from knowing their vulnerabilities. Josh had military-grade body armor. He was a typical, tough-acting, fourteen-year-old boy: smack in the middle of adolescence, something to prove but nothing to prove it with just yet. He didn't like school and school didn't like him.

The mention of Josh's name yielded growls and steam in three grade levels of middle-school teachers. I got him for four periods during his eighth-grade year. He was in my history class, my study hall, my "student assistant" period, and he sat in my room during another teacher's class, with whom he "didn't get along." He worked some, but mostly, he drew lots and lots of pictures. He brought with him frustration from other classes every day and would come in angry, ignore me, and get out paper. I let him draw, but I frequently complained to him that he ought to be doing work for his other teachers. He was difficult, so I just left him alone most of the time.

Pretty soon, Josh and I had come to an understanding. He held it together just enough to keep me sane. When he was finished with his work for me he would ask for paper and pencils to draw. I would reluctantly agree, as I knew it was not a battle I needed to pick during my busy day. Other teachers had complained over and over that he drew pictures in their classes, so I was reluctant to encourage him. He left a folder in my classroom with his drawings, but I never looked at it. I made it through the year, just barely, with my Josh-heavy experience.

At the end of the school year, I spoke briefly with Josh's mother. She explained that Josh's father had been deployed for over fourteen months to Iraq and was frequently in combat. I do not know how I didn't know this—no one at the school had mentioned it. I suppose there were so many deployments among our military families that it was overlooked. Josh had to help her take care of his younger brother with special needs. He hadn't had a good year at school, but he'd had an even worse year at home. The stress of the deployment had taken a toll on his family. Because Josh liked to draw, the family psychologist suggested he draw whenever he felt frustrated or angry or sad or scared. He drew all the time at home too. I felt so terrible.

Josh's mother gave me a beautiful, handmade book. It had several of the most amazing drawings I had ever seen, and a couple of photos of Josh "to remember him by," since they would be moving soon. I couldn't believe he was so talented and I had never taken a moment to notice. He had drawn me working at my desk, the view out the classroom window, the furniture in my classroom, vegetables, fruits, and many other things. Amazing.

When I asked why she had given the book to me, she explained that she knew what a difficult child he was. She told me that I was the only teacher who had not thrown his drawings away. She said Josh had actually described me to the family psychologist as the "glue" that held his world together since his dad left, and that I was the only teacher who was kind to him. Because I let him draw when he was sad or angry, he wanted me to have the book to say "thank you." She said he was too embarrassed to give me the book himself. She gave me a tearful hug, and she left. I have not seen them since. I do think about Josh lots; I have one of his pieces—a radish—framed in my kitchen.

A teacher's job is difficult. We forget sometimes, however, that day-to-day life can be far more difficult for many of our students. I try to find something special in every student, but because of Josh, I try harder with the "complicated" kids. I knew I had been kind, as difficult as it was sometimes, but I never knew I was glue—my very unintended proudest moment.

~Dorothy Goff Goulet
2009 Department of Defense State Teacher of the Year/Department of Defense Education Activity
French, Social Studies teacher, grades 9-12

Editor's note: The Department of Defense Education Activity (DoDEA) is a public school system for dependents of our nation's military members. Nearly 2 million children in military families live in the United States and on overseas military installations in twelve countries, seven U.S. states, Guam, and Puerto Rico. DoDEA employs about 12,000 educators and serves 80,000 students in nearly 200 schools.

Recess Moment

You learn something every day if you pay attention.
~Ray LeBlond

W hen you teach first grade, you spend a good deal of time developing fluency: fluency in reading, fluency in math concepts, fluency of thought in writing. Yet my most memorable lesson in fluency occurred on our school's playground and I was the learner while my student was the teacher.

It was the beginning of the school year a few years ago and I had a little boy in my class who came from a non-English speaking home. He was very quiet and incredibly shy. I wasn't sure how much he understood during the school day and I was especially concerned that he just stood by himself at recess and did not play. If I tried to talk to him, he would turn away and tightly shut his eyes to hide from me.

After a day or two of this, I decided to enlist the help of one of my outgoing and friendly little girls. I called her over and she ran to me, pigtails flying, eager to help.

I immediately launched into a long speech about what I needed from her. I asked her if she would try to get him to play, and I started babbling all these suggestions on how she could start communicating with him. I explained she could do this, she could do that, she could try this idea, she could try that idea. She touched my arm to stop my incessant talking and looked up at me in that wise and worldly way that only a six-year-old can, and said, "Don't worry. I speak Kid."

And she ran off, sun streaming through the trees, her white sneakers kicking up bits of mulch.

I stood there all alone, silently watching her. It took less than a minute for the two new friends to run off, hand in hand, happily joining a game of tag taking place all over the jungle gym.

My sweet little girl was right. I did not need to problem-solve for her. She spoke Kid fluently and accomplished what she had been charged to do.

I often think of that small moment at recess, about what I learned and how important it is for all teachers to speak Kid—big kid, little kid and middle kid. I knew my focus must be on teaching students how to think, how to approach problems, and how to figure out solutions and never take the opportunity away. We must be ready to learn from our students because those "teachable moments" during the school days are for us, the teachers, as well as our kids.

~Jeanne Muzi
2009 New Jersey State Teacher of the Year
Elementary teacher, grade 1

REHAB FOR CHILDREN
"HOOKED ON PHONICS"

The Unexpected Difference

To teach is to learn twice.
~Joseph Joubert

For a statewide teacher forum, I was asked to create a table presentation characterizing my classroom, my students, our district and community. As an avid scrapbooker, I immediately relished the idea of creating photo collages and carefully arranging artifacts and mementos that would illustrate the important work teachers do inside the world of their own classrooms.

So, for weeks, I sifted through file drawers and shoeboxes, searched in cabinets and in closets. I was hoping to find just the right prints or memorabilia that would capture the spirit and personality of my school and community—that would capture the difference I had made as a teacher. All through September, I unearthed photos of lesson activities and keepsakes I knew I had stored in a file folder in the back of one of those drawers. I asked my colleagues to help me find images or objects that would represent our most famous community members, like Mr. Rogers and Arnold Palmer, and the Pittsburgh Steelers, who hold training camp nearby. By mid-October, I had found those things. But, I had also found something unexpected, something much more dear, and very rare.

I found pictures of Gavin who gave up two weeks as a high school senior one summer to help fifth and sixth graders craft puppets out of socks at elementary drama camp. I found notes from and pictures of Calvin whom I had taught for almost six years, and remembered how he always made sure every classmate felt accepted and valued. I found a résumé written by Carrie who supported herself without the help of parents, and who despite her often late night shifts, never missed a day of class. I found a worn copy of Robert Cormier's *I Am the Cheese* that Pete proclaimed was the first book he had ever finished. I found student-questions scrawled on slips of paper and Post-it notes. I found a copy of *Macbeth* in Portuguese that belonged to an exchange student who read it first in her own language, before reading it *again* in ours, just so she could be sure she wasn't missing something important in the translation. I found Kelly and Sarah; Mark and Abby; Matt, Justin, Laura, Morgeaux, and Dave. I found Erin, Cady, Bree, and Lisa; Lindsey, Charlie, Hilary, and Kate. Amanda, Taylor, and Nenny.

I found my students.

The students who had made me laugh. The students who had moved me with their courage and compassion. The students who had challenged me to question what I knew of the world outside my own hemisphere, the students who inspired me to expect more from them and from myself.

What I found was evidence of a *real* difference. Not the difference *I* had made in *their* lives, but the difference *they* had made *in mine*. There I was, standing at my filing cabinet reviewing lessons — not those I had taught, but the many I had learned. Lessons in strength and perseverance, humility and honesty. Lessons in laughter, joy, and grace.

I came to teaching, as most teachers do, hoping to touch the hearts and minds of my students. What I never expected was how powerfully *they* would touch *mine*.

In September, my table presentation was an assignment, and I went about completing it as a professional task. In October my work became very personal, and served as a wonderful reminder of just how powerful a place a classroom can be, not just for students, but also for teachers. And, when I arrived at the forum with my presentation in tow, it wasn't a display of any difference I had made, but the difference my students had made. It didn't display lessons of my design, but my students' lessons, the ones they had taught me. I looked around at the other displays and found a similar theme. I didn't see graphs or report cards. I didn't see unit plans or portfolios. I saw stuffed animals, hats, pumpkins and patches—electronic photo albums, smiling faces, storybooks, and even fishing flies. I saw keepsakes and mementos that spoke of caring, compassion, motivation, and enthusiasm. I saw tokens of kindness and souvenirs of bravery and creativity.

I saw a real difference—the difference made by students who have walked in and out of our classrooms, in and out of our lives, in and out of our hearts.

In making lesson plans, all teachers have to ask "What will this day's lesson be?" The question begins with the students as audience, but it's a question that I now turn on myself. Today I walk through the door of my classroom ready to teach, but also eager to learn from the young people who are excited to teach me about them—their insights and interests, problems and anxieties, hopes and fears. We teachers are masters of prepared lessons, but should always appreciate that the unexpected lessons, both simple and profound, effect the most powerful difference, for they make students of us all.

~Rebecca Snyder
2009 Pennsylvania State Teacher of the Year
English teacher, grades 10-12

The Healing Power of Children

*There is a garden in every childhood, an enchanted place where colors are
brighter, the air softer, and the morning more fragrant than ever again.*
~Elizabeth Lawrence

I headed to the district office for the usual Tuesday morning leadership meeting. I had just heard about the first Twin Tower attack. Like most people across the country, I was in shock.

A television newscast in the boardroom was replaying the first plane's assault. A few minutes after my arrival, the superintendent entered and asked us all to go back to our campuses immediately and bring some semblance of calmness and order to our school community.

At my office, I summoned the counselor and together we sketched out a plan for communicating with and consoling the staff, students and parents. TVs were turned off. Teachers and I spoke only of what we knew and avoided speculation. Parents fearful of other attacks in the country were reassured. Above all, I made sure that I was in every classroom, in the cafeteria and outside at release time.

Students of every age were frightened. But it was the children who made the biggest difference overall during those first few days.

On Friday, the President ordered a moment of silence at noon across the country to honor those who had been killed in the 9/11 tragedy. This was to take place, of course, at the peak of cafeteria

104   Learning from the Kids : The Healing Power of Children

serving time with over 200 adolescents in the building. I told the aides that we would most definitely stop for a moment of respect and was rebuked: "You will never get all of these kids quiet," they said. "Watch," I replied.

At noon, I stood on the stage, took the microphone in my hand and announced the President's proclamation. Instantly the room fell silent. I had goose bumps on my arms and a lump in my throat. I thanked the kids when the minute had passed and made a statement about how fortunate we all were to be living in the U.S. The goose bumps returned as the room resounded with applause.

At dismissal time that day, we conducted a peaceful student march. Lining both sides of the main sidewalk to the parking lot were NJHS members holding American flags. One class after another walked together, some holding hands, some linked together at the elbows. Some held banners. Others sang patriotic songs. The goose bumps resurfaced. All around me were parents crying and cheering.

I truly believe in the healing power of children. They put things in perspective during that painful week and let the adults see that America still stands strong. They made me proud to be an educator as well.

So many times in my career, my students have given me strength. Often when the day has started off wrong or I'm feeling down and out, they have helped to take my mind in another, more positive direction.

They have what we, the adults in their lives, need to make sure we have daily in large amounts—the ability to "heal"—with an empathetic heart and a great sense of hope. Equipped in this manner, we can lead our students through any storm.

~Tim Ramsey

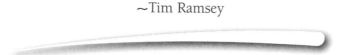

Teacher Tales

Great Ideas

If you have an apple and I have an apple and we exchange these apples then you and I will still each have one apple. But if you have an idea and I have an idea and we exchange these ideas, then each of us will have two ideas.

~George Bernard Shaw

31

Tales from the Rappin' Mathematician

Hip-hop is supposed to uplift and create,
to educate people on a larger level and to make a change.
~Doug E. Fresh

It was my first year of teaching, and I was sinking. All that preparation, all those diplomas, and I could not get my middle school students to sit down and pay attention. I felt disrespected and frustrated that I couldn't get them to remember what I had just taught the day before; yet, they could easily remember every word of the new rap song on the radio. Of course, the other problem with this was that they would come in each day singing about violence, drug use, and mistreating women, which frustrated me even more.

And then, one afternoon, it hit me. Instead of turning off their radios, I needed to offer them a different station. I went home, and made up a rap song about the math we were learning at the time (adding and subtracting decimals), called "The Itty-Bitty Dot." I practiced it all night, peppered it with clever phrases and rapped it over an authentic hip-hop beat I'd found online. I remembered my own love of rap in its cleaner youth and imagined how impressed my students would be with my "cool" factor for my way with a rhyme. Early the next morning, when my class came in, I performed it for them....

The results were disastrous. The students laughed hysterically, and I felt anything but cool—more like a complete flop. Now, not only were they not paying attention, they were laughing at me. Later that day, I trudged off to lunch like a loser from *The Gong Show*. And then it happened. As I walked by the lunch tables, the students were singing my song! The next day, they eagerly ran into my classroom, saying things like, "Mr. Kajitani, are you going to rap again? Yesterday was *the best day ever* in math class! Are you going to be on MTV?"

From that moment on, everything shifted. I had connected with my students on *their* level, using language they understood to get across what I was trying to teach. I got them laughing—it didn't matter if it was at me, because it meant they were present and comfortable (no small feat in the often dangerous neighborhood my students live in). By shifting my approach, I got them excited to come to school, to learn, and to have me as their teacher. Their behavior improved dramatically, and their test scores began to match, and then outpace, their more affluent counterparts.

I began calling myself "The Rappin' Mathematician," and started rapping about all the math concepts I was teaching, letting the wacky humor flow (realizing that "cool" really was just being myself, as we often tell our students). Unlike the songs on the radio, I used language that was positive, and included messages not only about math, but about believing in oneself, making good decisions, and the importance of school. The songs quickly became legendary throughout the school and district, and, encouraged by my fellow teachers, I recorded them onto an album (and the next year another, and a workbook the following year) so other teachers could use them in their classrooms. Now teachers throughout the United States use my songs, and I have received many e-mails and phone calls from parents and fellow educators telling me that, for the first time, their students love math.

In the end, I may never make it to MTV, but as a result of my "math rappin' epiphany" in those first desperate days of teaching, students are getting excited about learning. And that, in my book, is a much bigger success.

• • •

"No way!" erupted several teachers last November when I suggested we take our eighth graders—*all* of them, even those on academic probation—on a two-mile "walking field trip" to the California Center for the Arts to see a renowned, educational hip-hop dance troupe. "This neighborhood is too dangerous to leave the school!" one teacher said. "There's no way I'm bringing xx, he's been suspended twice for tagging the bathroom—*just imagine* what he'll do at the Arts Center!" another colleague chimed in.

That's when I made my case. Yes, our school's Latino immigrant neighborhood is "rough"—with one of the most rapidly growing poverty rates in California and a strong gang presence. And we've spent countless hours discussing how to get parents and community members to support our school, and come onto our campus. Yet we'd never spent time getting our school out into the community. Above all, as teachers in this community, we are visitors; we don't live here. If we truly want an *interconnected* community and school, which we all agree we do, we can not be afraid of taking our students into the world, *their world*, and going into it ourselves. We also can't be afraid of taking a chance on our lowest-performing students; giving them something positive (like some music education) could make a tremendous difference for them.

So, the teachers agreed to do the trip, with the entire eighth grade, and to call it, "My Neighborhood... My Hip-Hop!" We invited parents and community members, such as local police, firefighters and business owners, to chaperone. Even members of our school's office staff, normally confined behind their desks all day, excitedly volunteered to help. With our students, we examined maps of the neighborhood and discussed routes that should (and, as students pointed out, should NOT) be taken. I supervised the months of planning, but teachers, students, parents, staff and community members become engaged and empowered.

On the day of the trip, as we walked down the streets of our school's community, one student exclaimed, "Mr. Kajitani, we're getting a lot of funny looks from people in their cars—it's like they've never seen students before!" *Exactly,* I thought to myself. Students proudly pointed out their homes, or where their parents worked. They smiled and greeted people on the street. During the show, they chanted "Mission! Mission!" at the appropriate time, showing a school pride I'd never seen in three years of teaching at Mission Middle School. One normally sullen and quiet girl, who was failing her classes, danced spectacularly on the stage to the cheers of her peers; it was the first time I ever saw her smile. After the show, our parents and community volunteers, and the theater staff, all commented on how well-behaved and friendly our students were. And when we left, there was no tagging in the bathroom.

~Alex Kajitani
2009 California State Teacher of the Year
2009 National Teacher of the Year Finalist
Math teacher, grade 8

32

Bring Me Back a Rock

Man is harder than rock and more fragile than an egg.
~Yugoslav Proverb

S even years have gone by now, yet in my mind's eye I can still vividly recall every detail as if it happened yesterday. Your small round face, never quite clean enough, stringy blond bangs hanging over sad brown eyes. Clothes always wrinkled and too small on your bony shoulders, and sockless feet inside worn-out sneakers with no shoelaces. You maintained an almost invisible identity, always fearful of others who whispered as you walked by and nicknamed you "rag muffin."

Having a daughter your exact age made my heart ache for you even more. What if I couldn't afford the things for my little girl that your parents couldn't provide for you and your five brothers and sisters? I wanted to do something to help but I didn't know how or what I could do. Besides, I was just your teacher. And then from out of nowhere it hit me — that's what I can do. Along with teaching you reading and math and spelling, I'll teach you some everyday skills that might improve the quality of your life and other people's perception of you.

First I had to reverse your self-induced disappearing act and make you visible again. Others needed to see the real you, a seven-year-old boy who didn't always behave himself but who always said he was sorry when he didn't. I brought to school a grooming bag complete with soap, towel, comb, toothbrush and toothpaste and discretely sent you to the boys' room every morning to get cleaned up. I appealed to my friends who had little boys to give me their hand-me-down clothes and shoes. Sneaking crackers into your backpack for snack time and secretly paying for you to have "doubles" in the school cafeteria became everyday rituals.

Our classroom became your home away from home, your safe haven, a place where you could escape and be a child, at least for a little while. Then at 3:00 PM the dismissal bell would ring. And like the midnight gong that interrupted Cinderella's dance at the ball, I gave you a goodbye hug and smile and sent you back to your world. The world where, hopefully unlike what happened to Cinderella, I prayed you wouldn't change back into a ragamuffin.

I worried about you all the time, even on the weekends. I remember one cool, crisp North Carolina Saturday morning, right before the weather turned cold; my daughter and I went out shopping for her new winter coat. This was an annual battle we had engaged in since she was four years old. For me the perfect winter coat had to be long and wool and thick enough to shield her from the winds that got bitter cold from the months of December to March. An attached hood would also be nice, since leaving home wearing a cap didn't necessarily mean she'd come home with it.

In her eyes, the perfect winter coat had only requirement. It had to be pink. After many hours and hundreds of try-ons we finally found a coat we could both agree on. It was long, thick, hooded, and yes, it was pink.

Filled with a sense of accomplishment, all I wanted to do was pay for the coat and hurry home to curl up on the couch with a good girly movie or book. Instead, for reasons beyond my understanding, I grabbed the pink coat in one hand and my daughter's hand in the other and said, "Now we have to go to the boys department and buy a coat for Johnnie."

That's what life was like for us during the two years I was your teacher. But it was worth it. Things were definitely looking up for you. You gained weight, you smiled more and you even began to risk raising your hand in class to answer questions. You trusted me enough to know I would always lead you to the correct answer. But your trust in others was still a little shaky and it was time to fix that, especially since you would be promoted to the next grade and you weren't going to be my student next year.

I began to plan partner projects and group activities that required you to communicate with your classmates and work as a team. At first, you refused to work with anyone else but me and you even got mad at me when I insisted you work with someone else. But with a lot of time and a lot of coaxing you eventually started to relax and have trust in your peers.

That is until one cool breezy fall day in November, the last school day before the Thanksgiving holiday. The classroom buzzed with the electricity of children hardly able to contain their excitement. All they could think about were the intriguing adventures awaiting them over the holiday. By afternoon, with only one more hour of school, no one was in the mood for learning. So I ditched the video of *The First Thanksgiving*, which they had seen every November since kindergarten, and instead decided to have a sharing time where everyone got a chance to tell about their plans for the upcoming holiday.

You sat in your usual place, right next to me, and listened while your peers told about cruises to the Bahamas, trips to Disneyland and visits to Grandma in New York and other faraway places. With no one else left to share, I turned to you and asked, "Johnnie, would you like to tell us what you're doing over the Thanksgiving holiday?"

"Yes," you said proudly. "I'm going to Kernersville to visit my aunt." The words were barely out of your mouth when the class erupted with laughter. Everyone knew Kernersville, about twenty minutes outside of Winston-Salem, was nowhere special to go. You froze in embarrassment and began to retreat back inside yourself.

I rushed to your rescue, "REALLY!" I yelled out over the laughter. "Would you bring me back a-a-a rock," I stuttered. "I could really use a nice rock." The room became perfectly still with an uncomfortable silence as you silently nodded, "Yes, Mrs. Reynolds."

Thanksgiving break, like all vacations, ended much too soon. Children returned to school with stories, pictures and items to share, each child trying to outdo the other with tall tales and embellished stories. This time I knew better than to put the spotlight on you and ask you to share, but without warning you stood up and began to slowly walk to the front of the room. The shock and fear I felt for you made me hold my breath so hard, I believe my heart actually skipped a beat. For a moment you just stood there looking down at your feet and then without saying a word, you reached into your coat pocket and pulled out a rock. A rock washed and polished until it shined like a new penny, a rock just small enough for two tiny trembling hands to hold. A rock that neither you nor I could possibly know would change our hearts forever.

The entire class silently awaited my reaction. They were obviously confused and taking their cues from me on how to react. "WOW!" I said, reaching out with the kind of hands used to hold a newborn infant or something priceless and delicate. "It's absolutely perfect. This is exactly the kind of rock I was hoping for. Please tell us all about it."

Hesitantly, you began to tell about the rock—where you found it—why you chose it. With every word, your voice grew stronger and your stance grew taller. At long last, all eyes and ears belonged to you. At the conclusion of your share, classmates applauded with enthusiasm and someone yelled out, "Johnnie, YOU ROCK." I watched you like a proud mother bird watches her baby bird take flight for the very first time. I knew it was time to let you go.

Finally, you had found your wings and it was time for you to soar.

Needless to say I received many rocks that year. So many that we began a classroom rock collection. Some rocks came from volcanic mountains and underground canyons. Other rocks came from local restaurants or a relative's backyard. Every rock had a story and earned another pushpin on the map. By the end of the school year the class had collected nearly fifty rocks and had learned more about the world and themselves than any number of books could have ever taught them. Students from other classrooms came to know us as the rock experts and you, Johnnie, you were the rock master.

As fate would have it, your family moved away that summer and left no forwarding address. So I never got to see you again or say goodbye. But the rock tradition continues. Every year I tell the story of "bring me back a rock" to my new class of students. I tell them that all rocks from previous class collections are boxed up and put away except for the rock inside this clear plastic cube. This rock has a permanent place on my desk and in my heart. As I hold up the rock I explain that it may look ordinary and insignificant but it's by far the most precious rock of them all. This rock represents love, courage and acceptance of others. It is the very rock that started it all and it was given to me by someone who will always be near and dear to my heart.

Thanks Johnnie, and wherever you are, "bring me back a rock."

~Adrienne C. Reynolds

" My class brought me their Thanksgiving leftovers... part of their belief I live in the classroom and miss out on all the holidays!"

Growing Roots

Teachers who inspire know that teaching is like cultivating a garden,
and those who would have nothing to do with thorns
must never attempt to gather flowers.
~Author Unknown

E very morning, from the age of three to ten, I began my school day at Roots Activity Learning Center in Washington, D.C. by singing songs that exalted the African-American culture and spirit of goodness. In one song, we sang the words, "We are the 'Roots' of the flowers of tomorrow," and in another, we sang the words, "Responsibility, Duty to our People… goes hand in hand with freedom." During the down time of our day, my classmates and I enjoyed when our teachers pulled out the 12" vinyl record of Dr. Martin Luther King's speech, "I've Been to the Mountaintop;" and we all got choked up every time we sat to listen and learn the words to George Benson's rendition of Michael Masser's and Linda Creed's song, "The Greatest Love Of All." I still cry today when I hear:

I believe that children are our future.
Teach them well, and let them lead the way.
Show them all the beauty they possess inside.
Give them a sense of pride,
To make it easier.
Let the children's laughter remind us how we used to be.

Those various teaching methods, along with the multi-level class-room and interdisciplinary curriculum, created a challenging and safe environment for me to learn and feel loved. Those methods instilled a sense of pride within me, and they convinced me that my teachers believed in me and my promising future, as I was taught to carry the torch of the greatness of our people.

My educational experience taught me that positive interactions, cultivating meaningful relationships, building self-esteem, and instilling pride in one's heritage was vital to the learning process. These components of the learning process indirectly provided my teachers the opportunity to implement best practices that ensured that my classmates and I excelled academically.

During my matriculation at Spelman College, I read the research of Dr. Edwin Nichols, who researched why and how cultural competence in the classroom looks and works by exploring the logic systems, axiology (values) and epistemological styles of different groups. With this article, I learned the theories behind why my elementary school was so successful. I then took my personal experience, and the theories of Dr. Nichols, and applied them during my first year of teaching in Brooklyn, New York, and they worked. I have used these experiences and methodologies to guide and influence my interactions, best practices and expectations for the 1,200+ students I have had the honor to learn from, grow with and successfully teach over the last ten years.

Six years into my teaching career, I was a hired by an administrator of a start-up middle school, who understood the importance of cultural competence in the classroom, and I was thrilled. I received support for my culturally relevant, interdisciplinary curriculum ideas and pedagogical styles; I received support for cultural routines I established for the school; and the educational practice of looping was even supported. Looping, an educational practice that allows a class of students to be taught by the same teacher two or more years in a row, allowed me to forge vital relationships with my students and their parents, and to thoroughly assess, expand and address my students' academic strengths and areas of concern. I taught these 120 students two years in a row, teaching both English Language Arts and Social Studies, and we (students, parents, and myself) enjoyed those years together tremendously. We challenged each other, supported each other, expanded each other's minds, and accomplished many unfathomable goals together. We were a family, bonded through our challenges and commitment to see them through.

After developing a three-year curriculum for this group, I learned on the first day of their last year in this middle school that I would not be looping up with them. There are pros and cons to every educational model, and that year, our school decided not to loop me with my students. Though I was disappointed by this decision, I accepted and complied with our school's new approach.

Throughout the school year, I heard stories about this group; I heard they were incorrigible, and were unwilling to complete assignments and to cooperate. That was not the group I knew, respected and loved so much. They were inquisitive, in-depth, eager to learn, overachievers, funny, sensitive and perfect representations of adolescence. Their display of normal adolescent tendencies was something I nurtured, embraced, laughed at, and allowed to "remind me of how I used to be!"

At the end of this group's graduating year, my principal asked me to design a summer course for a small group of these rising ninth graders, who had received failing grades in their English and Social Studies classes that school year. These were students that I knew were capable of academic and behavioral success, so I was more than willing to develop a writing seminar course, which was designed to support those rising ninth graders for ultimate preparedness and success in high school. My ideas and plans for the course blossomed into a wide-ranging investigation of science and the environment with an emphasis on African and African-American history and the writing process.

I called the course I developed "African Knowledge and Action for Sustainable Development." Students were required to analyze ten African-American literary works, attend seven intellectually stimulating nature field trips, conduct engaging hands-on science experiments, write a standards based ELA fifteen-page research paper, design a sustainable development innovation, and defend their paper and design to a distinguished panel. Through a chronological and historical interpretation of Africans' and African Americans' knowledge, use and preservation of the earth's natural resources, students analyzed their contributions to agricultural innovations. Through the activities provided during the seven field trips, including the George Washington Carver Nature Trail at the Anacostia Museum, Rock Creek Park, NASA Goddard Center, the U.S. Botanic Gardens, the Smithsonian Museum of Natural History and more, students learned about the current greenhouse effect and its causes and effects, and were challenged as critical thinkers and scientists to devise a plan that ensures the preservation of our Earth and its natural resources for future generations—"Sustainable Development."

We met on weekdays and weekends, during the height of D.C.'s extremely hot temperatures, walking throughout neighborhoods, conducting experiments outside, taking public transportation and walking miles on some days. When students became discouraged, I called them, sent encouraging texts and went to their homes to pick them up. One student, Tony, had his aunt call me to tell me he could not join us for our Saturday field trip to the U.S. Botanic Gardens. I emphasized the importance of the field trip, and he reluctantly showed up. At the end of the trip, Tony raved about how much fun the field trip was, about how much he had learned, and the valuable ideas he gained from the experience. When I dropped him off, he said to me, "Thank you, Ms. Worthy, for refusing to let me miss this field trip."

Despite those who believed I was crazy for having such high expectations for these students, in just six weeks my summer school students accomplished these lofty goals!

That summer we had fun together; we learned about our people, our environment and ourselves. We challenged ourselves, and applied our knowledge to real-life problems. I demonstrated that teaching is not imparting knowledge to a bunch of empty vessels. Teaching is establishing relationships, instilling a sense of pride, challenging students, building on their prior knowledge, showing the usefulness of knowledge and the fun in learning, while empowering students with emotional strength, academic skills and information they need to be successful.

More importantly, that summer I reminded those rising ninth graders what they were capable of doing. I reminded them that they were NOT those failing grades they received in English and Social Studies, but that they are a part of a continuum of African and African-American genius. By believing in my students, insisting that they exceed my expectations and supporting them academically, culturally and emotionally, I actualized the words of that song my teachers at Roots required me learn, and my students learned the importance of "The Greatest Love Of All!"

~Kimberly A. Worthy
2009 Washington, D.C. State Teacher of the Year
Social Studies teacher, grade 7

34

Queen Act

Teaching should be full of ideas instead of stuffed with facts.
~Author Unknown

When I dreamed of becoming a teacher, I often thought about the impression I would make on my students. Then I started teaching and soon learned that the students were actually the ones who made an impression on me.

My first day as a teacher, I drove to school at 5 AM in my on-its-deathbed Nissan, never before having the specific swirl of emotions that were flowing through my inner core. In three hours there would be twenty fifth grade students filling the classroom that I had worked on tirelessly in the two weeks since I had been hired. That thought brought with it an emotional tsunami of panic, excitement and nausea all wrapped up in one.

I was told I had a "sweet group of kids" by their fourth grade teachers, and after making it through that first day unscathed, I found this to be true. I quickly grew to love each child in my classroom, treasuring every note, drawing, smile and hug. I told them, "You are my first class, and I don't have any children of my own yet, so you are my first kids." I was grateful for my life as a teacher.

There was just one problem. It was a struggle to keep the students' attention, a complaint I heard often from other teachers. We found it hard to compete with the endless stream of fast-paced technology that filled their lives. I worked hard to make innovative lesson plans and had structure and a discipline system that was motivated by rewards. Still, there were days I fretted about their inattention; how could I make a difference in their lives if they weren't even listening to what I was saying?

The year progressed, and we began to switch classes with the other two fifth grades. As the social studies teacher, I constantly racked my brain thinking of exciting ways to present the material. It didn't help that the whole fifth grade shared one set of ancient textbooks. It came time to teach the American Revolution and I wondered how I would connect something that happened over 200 years earlier to the students' lives. Another teacher suggested I try staging a revolution of my own, and so one Monday morning the students arrived to find me in an elegant purple dress with long white gloves and my roommate's former high school homecoming queen tiara.

I explained to the students that for a few weeks I would be "queen" of the classroom, and they would be my "colonists." I passed out five pennies to all the students each day and told them as long as they kept their pennies until the end of class, they would be rewarded. At first, they loved it when everyone got to exchange their pennies for Tootsie Rolls. As the unit progressed, I began taxing a penny to go to the restroom or sharpen a pencil at other than designated times. The tax curbed distractions because students didn't want to give up their daily reward for a few minutes of playtime in the restroom. Then, my system took a sharp turn.

"Taking care of the kingdom is quite expensive," I told the students. "I need your pennies to build a new road." I would pass out a quiz and explain that paper was costly and they would have to pay a tax. "I've decided I need a new crown and some horses," I announced to the students one day. "You will have to pay." When indignant ten- and eleven-year-old voices chorused, "That's not fair!" I mimicked King George from a *Schoolhouse Rock* video and said (in my best British accent), "I don't care!"

At times I would step aside from my queen act to give the "colonists" advice. "Think about what the early colonists did to solve their problems with the taxes. What can you do that might convince the queen to stop taxing you?" The unit took twists and turns that weren't in my lesson plans, but I let the lessons unfold without concern over everything turning out a specific way. For the first time that year, I saw students pawing through their textbooks. One student even said, "This is cool. We are learning and having fun at the same time."

Then the students led a crafty revolt against the taxes. I was frantic and sick one morning when I discovered my roommate's irreplaceable tiara was missing. Then two students returned it, confessing that they had absconded with the crown while I made copies before school. Others made signs that said "No more taxes!" and "Off with the Queen's head!" and formed a picket line in the classroom one morning. Their chants of "No more taxes!" brought other teachers and students to our door. My principal came by and said, "They will remember this for the rest of their lives."

Finally, after involving their parents and reading their textbooks, each of the three classes wrote a Declaration of Independence and each student signed it. We talked about how the original thirteen colonies had fought a long, hard war for freedom, but that the road to liberty started with a courageous declaration to be free.

Through that unit, the students taught me how to be a better teacher. I realized that if the students could see how their input influenced the class, they would be engaged. I also learned that sometimes when teachers don't think their students are listening, they really are. I know this because of what happened years later.

At the end of each school year there was an "eighth-grade walk" in which the entire school walked past all the graduating eighth graders to congratulate them. When my first-year students had their turn as eighth graders, I almost made it to the end of the line without getting emotional. And then one student said, "We were your first kids, Ms. Miracle." As I proceeded down the hall, the walls and floor became a blur, and it was hard to keep from getting completely choked up.

Later, when my first students were graduating from high school, the labor pains for my first child were starting. Those first few days that I held my newborn son in my arms, my thoughts drifted to the new graduates and my first days of teaching them, and I wondered if they remembered their "insurgence" against a new queen who was trying to get their attention.

When my son was born I resigned from my teaching job to care for him. Now almost every day I think about my students and the way they shaped me into the person and parent I have become. Sometimes I see my old students in public and am greeted with "Hey, Ms. Miracle!" even though my name changed to Mrs. Lewis years ago. Many of them tower above me, and some are preparing to graduate from college and get married. I am not sure if my principal was right; I guess I will never know if my students remember the days of our revolution. However, I am certain of one thing. The queen will never forget.

~Janeen Lewis

35

Making a Difference in Our Community

Maturity begins to grow when you can sense your concern for others outweighing your concern for yourself.
~John MacNaughton

As a teacher, it has been my goal to enable my students to become active and participating citizens in their community, the nation, and the world. Margaret Mead once said, "Never doubt that a small group of thoughtful, committed citizens can change the world. Indeed, it is the only thing that ever has." Throughout the years, my students in a K-8 rural school of about 180 have made great differences in our community. But saving lives was not really on our agenda.

In January the students asked why I was upset, so I sadly told them the story. As the wife of a Marine officer, I had moved fifteen times before settling in Bozeman. I had never had the opportunity to watch children grow up since we moved so frequently. Now that I was settled, I had watched my young neighbor change from a rambunctious eight-year-old to a sophomore in college. While we were at his parents' home for a Christmas party, there was a phone call stating that he had hit his head while ice skating; it was really nothing, but they were transporting him to the emergency room just in case. That evening he was airlifted to the nearest trauma hospital and died a few days later.

One of my sixth-grade students had been at the rink when the incident happened. The class decided to investigate head injuries. When my students became aware of the dangers of trauma to the heads of children, they did extensive research before deciding that the best solution was a helmet policy that would require all students to wear a helmet if they rode to school on a bike, skateboard, or roller blades. They chose to begin with their immediate community so they testified before the school board and got the policy passed. Then they secured a grant to purchase more than 100 helmets at a reduced rate so they could be sold for $5.00 or given free to students. They stocked the office with extra helmets and had a young man from the bicycle shop fit each helmet properly to the head of the student.

After Spring Break that year, a mother came to our class to tell the students that they had saved her daughter's life. With tears in her eyes, she said that her children had taken their bikes and new helmets to Grandma's house. While they were riding their bikes down a hill, her daughter hit a parked car. The emergency room doctor said that wearing the helmet had prevented severe brain damage or death.

In 2006, my sixth graders concluded that our greatest need was a playground for the community. They examined the problem, developed some alternative solutions, chose the best policy, and then testified before the school board. Those twenty sixth-grade students committed themselves for the next three years to make our playground a gathering place for the community and a learning center for Native American Culture. We obtained a Service Learning Grant, and we involved the community.

The result was that the students helped design and construct an eight-sided climbing structure to be used by all ages. After tightening the last bolt in the midst of a spring snowstorm, they were ready to take the next step. They selected and ordered playground equipment, and it arrived over the summer and was installed. We were able to secure another grant, which allowed them to fund their next section, two circuit courses (ages 5-12 and adult) with Native American learning stations. The Montana Conservation Corps helped us with the installation. We also completed the final phase, a running activity, right before their graduation. For their efforts these young students were awarded the Spirit of Service Award in 2008 from the Corporation for National and Community Service.

Throughout the years, my students have become problem solvers and participants in our community. In 2001, my class asked the school board to pass a policy requiring service learning to be part of the curriculum for every student in grades K-8. Little did they know what they were beginning, for the implications for our community have been astounding as our students learn and serve. Some of their accomplishments have been: getting a path along the road to school constructed, changing the lunch program, establishing a track program, introducing the concept of a four-day school week and altering the number of days we attend school, testifying in front of the city council to secure restrooms in the downtown area, asking the county commissioners to abandon a road, demonstrating the need to install early warning and safety measures at a local dam, testifying about the need for a new jail before the crime board, and persuading the school board to create a breakfast program.

Each of these ideas was selected, researched, and presented by the students. My role was that of facilitator. In September 2008, Gallatin County accepted a $267,206 grant from the Department of Homeland Security to institute the measures concerning the dam, which my students first brought to their attention in 2006. Yes, I truly believe that eleven- and twelve-year-old students can make a difference as they become empowered and engaged citizens in the community.

~Sally J. Broughton
2009 Montana State Teacher of the Year
Language Arts, Social Studies teacher, grades 6-8

36

The Beatnik of Lincoln

All the world is a laboratory to the inquiring mind.
~Martin H. Fischer

The edges of the aqua-colored notebook have eroded, exposing the hard cardboard base. The cover is wrinkled and smudged with brown markings. The binder is hideously corroded.

I open it, and my nasal passages are filled by an overpowering, musty scent — the same scent I used to notice when I looked through the Depression-era books in my grandmother's upstairs room during the 1960s. Except that this is 2009, and this book is from the 1967-68 school year at Akron Elementary in Akron, Pennsylvania.

The hand-drawn title page says ANIMALS ON OUR PLANET. Below that are drawings of a worm, a frog in mid-flight and a jellyfish with ominous-looking tentacles. The next eight pages describe and illustrate "Experiment: The Development of an Animal." They end with my impressions of the final result: "Three chicks were hatching. We were expecting more. At 1:25 PM, two chicks were walking around. They hatched on Feb. 25. The membrane stuck to one chick. The first three dozen were duds."

The next 271 pages are a mixture of information, notes and intricately colored drawings of animals — everything from a Ceratoid Angler to a Swinhoe's Pheasant. They don't look like drawings I could have made at age ten — or even now.

The notebook tells the story of a passionate, compassionate teacher who brought science alive for a student who hadn't cared whether a nautilus had tentacles or twelve-inch wings. It tells the story of a recent college graduate who dared to defy convention and conservatism. It tells the story of a grand experiment that, instead of blowing up like liquid nitrogen at room temperature—as some fellow teachers suspected it might—blossomed into an incomparably beautiful canvas of fragrant, tropical flowers that would be forever preserved.

Aaron Hostetter arrived at Akron Elementary in the fall of 1967, a twenty-three-year-old fresh out of nearby Elizabethtown College. He energetically stalked the room in his suede jacket, the tail flapping wildly behind him. He would have been unique if he had simply been the first male teacher in the school's history. But from the very beginning, everybody knew they had stumbled upon an unabashed maverick, a powerful prodigy, a true visionary. "The Beatnik of Lincoln," they had called him in his teenage years in the nearby town of Lincoln.

He didn't really teach from a textbook. He reached deep into his soul and summoned everything he could offer to ignite our imagination.

We didn't report to a classroom every morning. We enthusiastically returned to an interactive laboratory/jungle bustling with discovery and fascination. It looked like it had been designed through a collaboration of a mad scientist and the creator of The Addams Family. You'd walk in and think, "Wait a second. Where's Morticia?"

He stocked a fifty-gallon aquarium with more varieties of goldfish than we had ever seen—Black Moor, Fantail, Lionhead, Oranda, Ryukin—and we were responsible for feeding them. Next to that was an aquarium with a black snake. Geraniums were planted around the room.

In the back of the room was a piano, which he'd occasionally play for us. But to get to it, you practically had to hack your way through vegetation with a machete—it had been bookended with a massive banana tree and a four-foot Philodendron. He had wanted to major in music in college, but decided on biology. He ended up giving us both disciplines—with gusto.

In this stimulating place, our senses were heightened in ways we had never felt.

And he didn't feel like he needed to keep us confined to the room, as stimulating as it was. If the spirit moved him, we'd break from a lesson and take the classroom outside. One time he marched us outside and we had an airplane-making/throwing contest. I'm sure Mr. Hostetter threw in a lesson about aerodynamics and physics to justify the excursion and fend off the complaints of a few outraged fellow teachers—and they did complain.

That's why the students in the other fifth-grade class—taught by a veteran teacher with restraint, defined borders, and conventional wisdom—were insanely jealous of us.

"What did you do this morning?" one of them would ask me during lunch.

"We went outside and studied the movement of earthworms," I'd reply.

"You didn't!"

"Yes, we did! For two hours! *Na-na-na-na-na-na!*"

I wanted very much to please Mr. Hostetter. I wanted to do my very best because I knew he cared so passionately.

That's where that aqua-colored notebook came in. He'd use his prodigious artistic talent to draw a multitude of animals for us to study. Then he'd mimeograph the sheets, give them to us and tell us to put them in our binder. He had a master notebook that showed us exactly how it should look after we used colored pencils to depict each animal's characteristics. He'd give us one-on-one instruction, telling us the sequence in which we should apply the shadings in order to get it just right.

I was one of the students who wanted to get it just right. He'd compliment me, saying, "Ricky, I love the way you did the purple and black shading on that Blue Mud Dauber's wings!"

At the end of the year, all of us were crestfallen. We had always wanted to bust out of that school and frolic in the summer heat. Not now. We knew he had to set us loose, but the goodbyes seemed cruelly painful.

The next year, I saw Mr. Hostetter just about every day in the halls of Akron Elementary, and I remember being filled up with warmth that seemed to emanate from my very core. But in seventh grade, I was shuttled off to Ephrata Junior High School and entered the world of bus rides, locker mates and corporate, schedule-oriented education. After college, I moved away from Pennsylvania forever and had little contact with anyone from my school days.

I always wondered what happened to Mr. Hostetter, so I called Akron Elementary early in 2009. Much to my surprise, the secretary knew exactly who he was—she said he had taught there until his retirement in 2002. Much to my distress, she said he had passed away in 2006. She promised to track down some former teachers and ask them to call me.

Two days later, the phone rang. "This is Janice Hostetter, Aaron Hostetter's widow."

Over the course of the next week, we talked three times for a total of more than two hours. We laughed and we cried. She told me so many things I did not know, so many things that opened a new window into his soul.

She said that when he retired, the school constructed a wooden bench with a plaque just outside the entrance, and dedicated it to him while 200 current and former teachers and students looked on. She said that she is still working through profound stages of grief. Sometimes, on a difficult day, she will drive five miles to Akron Elementary and sit on that bench.

"Just to be close," she said.

I told her nothing would make me happier than to join her on that bench.

~Rick Weber

Real World Math

If you're going to be thinking, you may as well think big.
~Donald Trump

I t was my first year as a middle school math teacher, and in an effort to motivate and engage my students, I designed and implemented a classroom money system. Each day, students who came to class prepared earned a salary of twenty-five "royal" dollars. From the salary earned, the students paid monthly rent on their chairs and taxes on their classroom materials. My goals for the program were to help students learn the importance of financial management while also promoting positive classroom behavior.

I gave students daily opportunities to earn additional salary in the form of bonuses, such as ten dollars for catching my errors, fifty dollars for good mathematical arguments, and one hundred dollars for acing an assessment. Students deposited any money they earned in our class bank. As the banker, I maintained the accounts and notified students of dangerously low balances. After all, students knew what happened in the "real world" when you didn't have the money to pay rent, and none wanted to be evicted from his or her chair.

I explained that at the end of each quarter, after the students paid their rent, taxes and any fines, they could use discretionary money to bid on items in a class auction. Auction items varied from quarter to quarter, but typical fare included small trinkets, snacks, and school supplies.

My system worked beautifully. The students were fully engaged, especially when I began to distribute cash bonuses. I decided I could also minimize classroom disruptions if I levied fines. Students soon realized that use of inappropriate language or arriving tardy to class was not financially beneficial.

Three weeks into school Mayra met me at the door with a question.

"How much would it cost to buy my chair?"

"Buy your chair?"

"Well, if I could buy my chair, I won't have to pay you rent each month. Then I'll have more money to spend at the auction."

"That's really great thinking," I replied. "Let me think about it and I'll let you know."

I quickly calculated a reasonable purchase price and announced to the class, "If you prefer to save your money and purchase your chair, you can buy it for six hundred dollars."

Mayra's hand immediately shot up.

"So if I sit on the floor for twenty more days, I'll have enough money to buy my chair. Can I do that?"

Without fully processing the implications of her plan, I responded, "Absolutely!"

She and several of her tablemates began to gather their materials and reposition themselves on the hard, wooden floor of our class-room. I thought to myself, "This will never last. They will be back in their chairs within a few minutes."

I certainly underestimated the resolve of middle school penny pinchers. Not only did Mayra and her crew last the hour, they resumed their positions the following day, with several peers joining in. By the end of the week, almost the entire class had selected seat-ing on the floor. Each day, I stepped precariously over students to reach those who had questions. While it was slightly inconvenient for me, I reminded myself that these students were making a conscious decision to be frugal with their money.

The following Tuesday was Open House. Parent after parent flowed in to meet the teacher who was charging rent. They relayed stories of enthusiasm for the program from both their perspective and their child's. "Thank you for teaching my child the value of money!" was a common refrain. I was now more motivated than ever to continue.

Two weeks later, Mayra arrived at my door announcing, "Today, I can buy my chair!"

I looked at the handwritten ledger she excitedly held. With no direction from me, she had recorded each deposit she had made to the bank. After verifying her accounting, I announced congratulations to her. She proudly took her "purchased" seat at her assigned table.

At the end of class, Mayra approached me with another question, "Now, can I save more money and buy José's chair, and then charge him higher rent?"

I laughed. Clearly, my goal of improving financial management had been met by at least one of my students and I'm sure those skills will serve her well in the future.

~Heather Sparks
2009 Oklahoma State Teacher of the Year
Algebra, Pre-Algebra teacher, grade 8

"No, you may not 'buy a vowel'."

38

Eye See You

Vision is the art of seeing what is invisible to others.
~Jonathan Swift

I walked into a wild third-grade classroom. Music was playing loudly, children were under tables applying make-up, kids were throwing a football indoors, and students were dancing wherever they could find space. I was a mid-year replacement. The previous teacher said he could no longer manage these children and resigned without notice during the holiday break.

As soon as I walked in the room, I realized why he left.

I sat down quietly in my chair and began reading their names softly. After each name, I prayed, asking God to help me understand that child.

I then nailed a mirror to the wall next to the chalkboard and began writing my name and a reading assignment on the board.

I then asked each child to come to me, tell me their name and what they wanted to learn. It was a difficult task, because only two children there wanted to learn anything!

Rules were set, boundaries established, parents contacted. But the mirror saved the day—no, the year!

Unbeknownst to the children, the mirror allowed me to see their every move while I was writing on the board. They soon became puzzled as to how I knew who was misbehaving while I was writing on the board. When one student finally asked me, I told him I had a special teacher's eye in the back of my head that my hair covered.

At first they did not believe me. But they did begin to exhibit better behavior, especially while I wrote on the board, thinking I had magical vision.

I never told them differently. Why mess up a good thing?

~Malinda Dunlap Fillingim

39

Gifts for Jace

The giving of love is an education in itself.
~Eleanor Roosevelt

I'll never forget the day that one of my students shyly raised his hand and said that he had never received a gift. My shocked fifth-graders were discussing a reading story about a boy who was not going to be getting anything for his birthday because money was tight that year. Even though this class was very open during reading discussions, Jace's honesty surprised even me. What was even more eye-opening was the fact that this sweet, fifth-grade boy had gone ten years and never experienced the joy and surprise of receiving a present.

I searched my internal data bank for a reason that he might be saying this. Did he want attention from his peers? No, that was definitely not his style. Was he exaggerating? Again, he was not the type. Then I remembered his story. His mother was out of the picture and he lived alone with his dad. His father had a hard time holding down a job, and come to think of it, I didn't see his father at enrollment or parent-teacher conferences. Even though on the outside Jace was a bit disheveled, he always came to school with a smile and sincere enthusiasm for learning.

A couple of weeks after Jace's comment, he was absent from school. This happened to be the day I was sending home the annual note about the classroom Christmas gift exchange. Traditionally, each boy was to bring a gift for a boy in the three-dollar range and the same was true for each girl.

As we were discussing the specifics, a girl raised her hand and matter-of-factly suggested that we do away with our traditional policy, and each buy a gift for Jace instead. The enthusiasm grew as the students discussed the kinds of things they knew Jace would like, such as art supplies and Star Wars figurines. We took a quick vote and unanimously agreed to go ahead with this wonderful idea.

With great excitement, the gifts began to come in. Students with bright eyes would eagerly tell me how they found the "perfect gift" and how their parents spent more than three dollars on Jace's gift! One student bought a complete art set, knowing that Jace loved to draw. Another student found toy aliens for him, remembering a paper Jace had recently written about aliens where he surprised us all with a paper plate spaceship prop he had made. As the gifts poured in, I remember being so proud of my thoughtful, selfless students who were truly demonstrating the spirit of Christmas.

After several days of absences, you can imagine our disappointment when we learned that Jace's absences were due to the fact that he had moved away! I was sure of one thing. I couldn't let my students or Jace down.

I found my information sheet and called every number listed. Apparently, Jace's father had lost his job, causing them to relocate. No one knew where they were, and the cell phone number I had would ring with no response despite my continuous efforts. Even into our Christmas vacation, I constantly gave the phone number a shot. Finally, at 9:30 PM on Christmas Eve, I decided to try one last time. By then, I really didn't worry about calling at a late hour. I was so used to no answer that I was startled to hear a response. Amazingly, Jace answered the phone!

I explained the story to Jace and told him how his classmates really wanted to do this for him. I spoke with his father and the next thing I knew, I was driving to Jace's home.

As I drove down his road, I saw the porch light of his trailer flicking on and off signaling which home was his. I was thrilled to see Jace. It took several trips back and forth to my car to get all of the gifts inside. We filled the room with all of the carefully wrapped gifts that were especially for him. He was so surprised and grateful. I was glad that I had an unopened box of chocolates that I could give to his dad. Jace's joyful smile that evening lit up the sky like a strand of twinkle lights.

I went to sleep that night thinking about Jace and all of the fun he was going to have playing with all of his new presents during Christmas break. I thought about my thoughtful students and how excited I was to tell them all about finding Jace. With a smile of my own, I was thankful to be a part of one of the most important "lessons" of their lives.

~Angela N. Abbott

Chapter 5

Teacher Tales

Thanks, I Needed That

I am indebted to my father for living, but to my teacher for living well.

~Alexander the Great

The Lesson

Teaching is not a lost art, but the regard for it is a lost tradition.
~Jacques Barzun

On the southeast corner of Star Ridge Road and Route 6 in Brewster, New York, a rundown ATI gas station beckons travelers north and south, east and west. Two mighty interstates cross nearby and the steady drone of their traffic is a constant presence. Brewster is a small border town, lying on an imaginary divide between upstate New York and what at times seems like the rest of the world. The ATI is a catchall kind of joint, a throwback to the old garage-style coffee stops of rural America, only maybe not as picturesque. Hard to find one of these in upscale Westchester County just across the line to the south. Way too grassroots for Westchester County.

Inside, there is no place to sit, only narrow aisles and shelves crammed with everything from imported English chocolates to engine oil. You can get good, hot coffee at all hours, a fresh doughnut, or an icy beer for the road. I have two friends who work the mornings there. Gus, the owner, is a soft-spoken man from India who handles the register and makes the best fried egg sandwich in Brewster. And Page, a robust horseman in his sixties with a round, friendly face and eyes that smile at you when he speaks, greets everyone who comes through the door. That's because Page knows everyone who comes through the door.

"How are things up on that mountain?" he would inquire

loudly, referring to the small private school where I work in Kent, Connecticut. The campus occupies over seventy acres on top of one of the tallest mountains in the state.

"Just fine," was my usual reply. Only this particular Saturday morning in February things weren't really fine. I had left my house in North Salem a few miles away, at 6:45 AM in a foul mood. After a long week, the considerable demands of a boarding school had spilled over to one of those periodic weekends when you pull extra duty. And I was the Weekend Head, for godsakes, no getting out of that. A shepherd with a flock of precious, needy sheep to tend, feed, entertain, and get to bed on time. And heaven help you if you lose one. All the way to the ATI station I grumbled about this and that, the mortgage payment, the leaking ceiling in my kitchen, how little I see of my family. I mulled over my uncertain future as a teacher and questioned decisions made years before when I chose to give the profession a try, decisions which were repeatedly challenged by many close to me.

"Those who can, do, and those who can't, teach," a former acquaintance in the advertising business once snickered when told I was taking a hiatus from writing film stories and television shows to teach.

"Really?" I had answered glibly while wondering why he didn't say that to John Irving, or Gardner, Oates, and Galbraith. Or why not insult the ghosts of C. S. Lewis, Tolkien or William H. Armstrong, who wrote *Sounder* and taught at the Kent School in the valley for years? The list could go on and on. All teachers and hugely successful writers whose works have impacted generations. On second thought, the "cream-fac'd loon" had probably never heard of them.

So it was with a sense of relief that I carried my troubles into the ATI that morning to a chorus of greetings from my small fraternity. Page poured coffee in my travel cup and stood with me while I waited to pay Gus at the counter. As we chatted about the school and whose horses he was exercising that day, I noticed a man come through the door and make his way over to the coffee machine. He was older, perhaps seventy, dressed for the weather with a woolen cap pulled down onto a kind, unshaven face. When he had finished he took his place in line, listening casually to our conversation. I had just started complaining to Page about my schedule when the gentleman with the woolen cap suddenly leaned in.

"You work with kids?" he said, looking at me with deep, inquiring eyes.

"Yeah."

"You a teacher?"

"Yes."

"What do you teach?"

"English… mostly." My voice trailed away, almost apologetically. I felt slightly uncomfortable. He nodded, took a beat, then thrust out his hand.

"Thanks."

I stood there, wondering first if I had inadvertently paid for his coffee or something. Then it dawned on me. He was thanking me for what I do, for teaching. Slowly, I reached out and shook his hand but couldn't manage to say more than something muffled and indistinct. I was utterly taken back by this complete stranger. No one had ever… he slapped me on the shoulder, handed Gus four quarters, turned and walked out.

There are stretches on Route 22 where the road is a glistening ribbon in winter, especially during the peripheral hours of day. I drove north with a gray, overcast morning breaking, passing all the oncoming commuters pouring out of rural Putnam and Dutchess Counties. My lane was comparatively clear and I made good time in silence, thinking of nothing other than what was to me, at least, an extraordinary act of generosity. For the first few miles I was fine. And then, from somewhere foreign and with no warning, a rush of emotion poured through the cracks of what used to be my very formidable armor. By the time I reached the little covered bridge over the Housatonic River just south of Kent, I had to pull over to compose myself and think about the irony of what had happened that day. Of all the mornings I had stopped at the ATI for coffee on my way to school, none had been bluer than this one. And yet, in the briefest of encounters, the immense, incandescent power of a single word changed everything. It was simply meant to be, I was certain. Meant to remind me how many times in a single day I find solace in a glance, or a smile, or a casual touch. Gratitude in lilliputian portions, but always there.

I checked my watch and knew it was time to go. First class began in fifteen minutes and I didn't want to be late, even on a Saturday. As I backed my little truck out onto the road and drove across Bull's Bridge, one last revelation came to me. I knew that when my colleagues and I gather for our last faculty meeting in June and the Head of School asks each of us to recall one meaningful event that made our year, my response will be clear and succinct. I know now that for me, it will have occurred not in the halls, in the classrooms, or on the playing fields, but away from the school. Miles away in Brewster, New York, at an old gas station where the coffee is always hot, the greetings easy, and where, for a moment, all thoughts other than the brilliantly plain and simple reasons why I teach faded away.

~William Bingham

A Few Minutes of Kindness

He is rich or poor according to what he is, not according to what he has.
~Henry Ward Beecher

Teachers strive to care equally about each of the students they teach. For most of us, however, some students stand out because they have profoundly influenced our lives. Years ago, I had a young Hispanic boy in my first year chemistry class who I will never forget. Our experiences together impressed upon me the tremendous influence that just a few minutes of kindness can have on a young life.

Juan came from a very poor, single parent home. His mother was disinterested in his education and in his life in general. Throughout the year, I noticed that Juan had an unusual ability to solve equations, and to correlate abstract relationships between concepts. Juan picked up new ideas as fast as any of my other students. I was shocked when he approached me after school one day to tell me that he liked chemistry, but did not think he was smart enough to attend college. He did not feel that his mother would be interested in helping him with school. What should he do with his life?

I explained to Juan that he was one of my very best students. His face lit up with excitement, and he looked at me incredulously. I proceeded to explain to him that he could apply for scholarships, loans, and federal grants to pay for college. I continued by telling

Juan that it would be a waste of considerable talent if he did not go to college. Finally, I told Juan that I would be teaching advanced placement chemistry next year, and I was really hoping that he would take the class. Juan looked as though he would need to re-think his entire life. He told me that he would consider what I had said.

The next morning, I went out for my daily jog around the block. I was startled when Juan appeared from nowhere on my front lawn. "Hi, Mr. Johnson," Juan said cheerfully. "I have been thinking about what you told me yesterday, and I am going to take your advanced placement class. Did you know that I live just across the street?" I hadn't known that Juan was my neighbor. I invited him to jog with me, and from then on, Juan would join me before school several mornings each week for a half-hour jog. We got to know each other quite well. We were both Dallas Cowboys fans, we both liked the outdoors, and we both liked math and science. Soon, Juan was joining my family for evening games of *Monopoly*, or Hearts. When I took my own two children fishing, he tagged along and caught his first fish.

Juan was my best student that year in advanced placement chemistry. His skills and abilities continued to grow, and he never tired of mind-bending calculations or homework. His confidence increased, and he literally blossomed before my eyes. Other students wanted to be Juan's lab partner, and he developed into a popular outgoing young man.

As the end of the year approached, Juan stayed after school one day to thank me for my interest in his life. I was profoundly moved when he told me that those fifteen or twenty minutes that we had talked the previous year had changed his life. He got a 5 on the advanced placement chemistry exam and he was awarded enough scholarship assistance that he was able to attend the local university. I was very proud of him, and not surprised when he graduated with a degree in Chemical Engineering. We stayed in touch over the years, and eventually, Juan moved into the top management level of an international corporation.

I have often wondered how both of our lives would have been

different had our paths not crossed. When I thought of leaving the teaching profession for a career in medicine several years later, Juan stood out in my mind. How important had my encouragement really been to him, and to the path he would follow? The life of a teacher is often a life of poverty in the material sense. However, teachers have the unique opportunity to inspire their students to reach for the stars. What could be a more worthwhile pursuit? Who could have known the importance of fifteen minutes in the life of a young man? I was so thankful that I took the time to encourage Juan to believe in himself.

My experiences with Juan contributed to my decision to remain in the classroom. My love for my students and for the subject I teach has continued to grow over the years. I consider myself most fortunate to be a chemistry teacher, and to have been a part of so many young lives, hopes, and dreams! I may not drive the nicest car on the block, but I am very rich in the things that count the most.

~Steve Johnson
2009 Nevada State Teacher of the Year
Chemistry teacher, grades 10-12

Blessed to Be a Teacher

The greatest good you can do for another is not just to share your riches
but to reveal to him his own.
~Benjamin Disraeli

I woke up this morning at five and I thought to myself, "It's time to get up." Then, a flash of another thought ran through my mind. "No. You do not have to get up. You're retired. Go back to sleep." I cried silently.

This is the first day of school for my students and I will not be there, after 38 1/2 years of teaching. I will not help a puzzled freshman find his classroom on the opposite side of our building. I will not get hugs from my former students who are so full of energy and looking forward to their SENIOR year! This year, I have not prepared my room to give my students some things to think about as their young, open, busy, and gifted minds wander from time to time during class.

I will miss all of the wonderful, caring, and smart teachers who so graciously shared their ideas, materials, laughs, stories, and food with me. I will miss the much younger teachers who rush up and ask for books, supplies, or some kind of support from me, their Instructional Team Leader.

I will not have the rush of nervousness during the first few seconds of that first class that goes away shortly after I say something like, "Good morning! I am Mrs. Margaret Williams and I am so happy to have you, each one of you in my class. We are in an awesome school with awesome students and it is a blessing to be your teacher...."

As I turned off my light (set on a timer) to return to bed on my first morning of retirement, a warm, pleasant feeling came over me. I was thinking about my opening statement to my classes when I said that I was blessed to be their teacher. I said to myself, "You are blessed to be a teacher who is now blessed to be able to retire and work at a more relaxed pace. You can do new and special things for students and for teachers that time would not allow while you worked. No more planning, debates, meetings after meetings. No more grading papers and doing all the other work until June."

With my eyes closed and a smile on my face, I was about to return to sleep when I thought, "By helping my colleagues with their field trips, college prep activities, maybe helping new teachers and continuing to coach the Mock Trial Team, I am still blessed to be a teacher... just retired."

Being a teacher *is* a blessing, and an awesome responsibility. As I began to doze off, I remembered one of my students who came back to see me ten years after he was in my class. He told me how I had inadvertently changed his life with a few words of advice which at first I didn't even remember giving him.

Ricky often gazed out the window during one of my ninth-grade United States history classes early in my teaching career. He was quiet, and his good grades and mild manner were why I did not move him away from the seat by the window.

One day, I leaned over his shoulder and quietly asked, "What are you looking at? You gaze out of this window during every class."

He said, "I am looking at the band."

According to Ricky, I said, "If you like the band so much that you have to look at them during this class every day, I want you to go down to Mr. Overby (the band teacher/director) and tell him that I sent you. Tell him that you want to be in the band. Now turn around and finish working before the bell rings."

The next day Ricky went to Mr. Overby and told him that I had sent him and that he wanted to be in the band. He added that he did not know how to play any instrument.

When Ricky visited me ten years later, he thanked me for telling him to go to Mr. Overby because he fell in love with music and discovered that he had musical talent that had not been tapped. His musical talent resulted in him getting a scholarship to college.

Ricky was married and had a family. He played in a local band and they had "gigs" all over the St. Louis metropolitan area. According to him, music kept him occupied and out of trouble, and it gave him a chance to go to college and earn a degree that now allowed him to provide for his family. Most of all, music had brought great pleasure and satisfaction to his life.

After Ricky thanked me, I pointed out that he did all of the hard work it took to become the wonderfully talented person that he was. I did not make him walk downstairs to join the band, practice his instrument, and get the good grades that led to his college scholarship.

Ricky responded that I could have yelled at him for looking out the window, or moved him away from the window. Instead, I gave him an alternative that changed his whole life.

After he left, I thought about his words. Ricky's words changed the way I looked at teaching from that moment forward. I realized that I was teaching children with every word I said, every action I took, and with every decision I made. Most of all, I realized that this was a fact that was true whether I did things consciously or unknowingly. Ricky's story raised my teaching bar. I have shared his story with new teachers and sometimes when I make public appearances. Most of all, I have never forgotten the lesson Ricky taught me, a blessed teacher.

~Margaret Williams
2009 Missouri State Teacher of the Year
Retired Social Studies teacher, grades 9-12 /
Instructional Team Leader
Mock Trial Team Coach

A Wrinkled Piece of Paper

Teachers appreciate being appreciated,
for teacher appreciation is their highest award.
~William Prince

Over the past thirty-four years, I have been asked many questions: How old are you? What's your favorite movie? But one day, one of my fifth graders asked me, "Why did you decide to be a teacher?" That really made me think. I know that I have always wanted to be a teacher. My sister and I played school down in the basement. I even had a grade book and plan book at the age of twelve. I was serious about it.

A teacher is someone who changes or influences the lives of others. For me, Annie Sullivan, Helen Keller's teacher was this person. It was Annie's caring and determination that impressed me. I am living my dream because of her. Every day I try my hardest to reach both the deaf children and the hearing children in my inclusion classroom. I work to ensure that all of my students are accepting and appreciative of each other's differences. I want them to understand that everyone is special and that each one has something to offer to our classroom. Throughout the years, I have also worked very hard to create an atmosphere of acceptance within the entire school building.

Annie Sullivan's caring, dedication and understanding are what I have based my teaching upon. She proved that by hard work and looking at the individual child, a teacher could meet the needs of each child and help him/her achieve success. She taught me to look for new ways to meet the challenges that I am faced with each and every day. She taught me to keep trying when everything else seemed to fail. She taught me to laugh with my children, cry with them, to feel their frustrations, and to experience their joys. I knew that I could make a difference, but it would take hard work. I am a teacher, a confidence builder, a cheerleader, and a good listener. I am whatever my students need me to be.

As teachers, we strive year after year to help our students feel successful. We do the best we can to find ways to make them achieve their goals and grow as individuals. But then there comes one student that presents a challenge. A few years ago, I had that challenge. His name was David. Before school even started, his reputation had preceded him. He had moved from one intermediate school in our district into mine.

Imagine the first day of school. All the excited students walk into the room eager to start: everyone but David. He had had a hard summer. His father was in jail. This angered him because now his family was not together. His mother had to work nights, so she wasn't there in the evening and was sleeping when he woke up. During the evenings his sixteen-year-old sister was his guardian. David was a bright student. All data showed that he had the aptitude, but very little motivation.

So began my challenge to help David achieve success. I liked him immediately and saw so much potential hidden behind an angry wall he had built up around himself. But as the weeks went on, David slowly quit doing his homework and staying on task, and began to get into more trouble out on the playground. He was going downhill quickly. It was evident that he was looking for any kind of attention—even if it was negative. I also knew that he was not getting much support at home. In addition to all of that, his older brother was taken from middle school in handcuffs. If David was going to pass the fifth grade, I needed to come up with a plan. I had to look at him as an individual and find out what made him tick.

One day, David and I sat in the library and just talked. I told him that I knew that he was not an "F" student and that I was not going to let him fail. It was my job to teach him, but his job to try. We talked about home and what he did after school. He wanted to do well, but school was not a top priority. At this point in his life, he was just trying to survive emotionally. From then on David and I periodically sat in the library and just talked. He knew what I expected from him and that I respected him as a person.

We also sat with Mrs. McGonnell, our principal, and tried to find ways to help him. He knew both she and I would listen to him. We would not jump to conclusions without hearing his side of a story. Consequently, his behavior in my room improved. Unfortunately, he was still very impulsive at lunch and at recess. He would talk back to other adults. Removing him from recess did not help because he was a very active student who had trouble focusing or staying on task. Neither in-school suspension nor out-of-school suspension helped to stop his impulsiveness. We asked him why he had never talked back to the principal or myself. He said that we always took the time to listen.

One day as we were having lunch together, he told me that his goal was to pass the fifth grade and to not be suspended. He wanted to be in school. There were six weeks left to the school year. So, whenever an outside assignment was due, I would ask if he had started. If not, he and I would work together to get it done. Sometimes this was during the school day or after school. This seemed to work. David was very creative and had good ideas, but he didn't know how to share them with a group. I took special care when placing him in a group. There were students that he worked well with and they also worked with him. Earlier in the school year, no one wanted to be in a group with him. But, now they could see that he really wanted to be a part of a group. When his Nature Journal was due, I helped him choose a topic and find the resources. In reading we did a Living Wax Museum, so I made sure he had a costume for his explorer.

Finally, the last day of school arrived. David had met his goals. He had passed the fifth grade and had not been suspended. As I hugged him goodbye and told him to have a good summer, I thought that would be the last I heard from him. But during Teacher Appreciation Week, the students had written about any teacher they wanted. In my booklet, on a wrinkled up piece of paper, it read: "You never give up on me and focus on the silver lining because you know I am smart, and you always had that way of making learning fun and easy at the same time. And for that I not only appreciate you, but I admire you." — signed David.

After reading that, I sat down with tears rolling down my face. I had reached him. He knew that someone thought he could learn and that someone had listened to him. That following August, who was the first sixth grader that came back to visit? David, with a big hug. We, as teachers, never know when or how we affect our students. But it's the notes like this that make all we do worthwhile.

~Deborah Wickerham
2009 Ohio State Teacher of the Year
Elementary teacher, grade 5

44

The Power of Belief

Keep your dreams alive. Understand to achieve anything requires faith
and belief in yourself, vision, hard work, determination, and dedication.
Remember all things are possible for those who believe.
~Gail Devers, three-time Olympic Gold medalist

Teachers are constantly striving to teach our kids as much knowledge as possible. However, in the meantime, we also have the opportunity to teach them so much more. It has always been my goal, as a teacher, to get kids to believe in themselves and to understand that with hard work and a positive attitude, they can accomplish almost anything. Many times, in order for students to believe in themselves, they first must see their teachers believe in them. This belief can be very powerful, as illustrated by the following e-mail I received from a student.

Mr. Kuhlman:

I ran across your Internet site and I guess I'm just hoping
you are the right Mr. Kuhlman!
After thinking about it, I thought you might not answer my
original e-mail, if you remembered me. I was a bit of a scoundrel.
I was in your Biology, Advanced Biology, Chemistry, and Physics.
I had dyed black hair, and I guess I probably seemed a little
"Goth" looking. We were the rough crowd. I was a cheerleader for
a year but I didn't take anything seriously then.

I never had a personal conversation with you, but I think everybody knew I was into a lot of bad things. I came from a very poor family, was involved in gang activity, abused a lot of alcohol, and experimented with a lot of drugs. I got pregnant in my senior year of high school, and the superintendent asked me to leave. I ended up graduating as a home school student and I eventually married the child's father. We have three children now.

I needed to tell you that even though we never really talked, or were friends in anyway besides professional cordialities, you had a big influence on me. You expected a lot from me. No one else did. I wasn't a dumb kid, but I knew everyone thought I was a throw away. In your class, it didn't matter who I was because you treated me like everyone else. I didn't do homework for other classes, but I did the homework you assigned — because it was expected and I had been bitten by the science bug.

I spent several years after high school putting myself back together. I learned how to be responsible, confident, and respect authority. I had to learn it all the hard way! I did things like deal blackjack, and sew blankets and placemats, housekeeping, etc.

One thing I always remembered was a time when you were asking us what we wanted to do when we "grew up." When my turn came, I said I wanted to be a physicist. Everyone laughed, even me. But you didn't. You said I could be a physicist if I wanted and you were serious. It stayed with me — even when I was working to just keep my head above water.

I ended up earning a two year degree at a Community College. The science instructors there saw my interest in the sciences, and I did a lot of science-related projects. Now I am a senior at the university majoring in Biology, with a minor in Chemistry, and secondary education licensure requirements. I love teaching and I love science, and you started the fire under me to accomplish all of this. Sure, I'm not a physicist, although I've taken several Physics courses — but maybe one of my students will be. I just wanted you to know that you have made a big difference in my life by doing what you do best. Because of what you have done for me, my students will have the opportunity to become scientists and teachers, because of my own dedication to my work in education.

Even though this student never became a famous physicist, in that one instant she learned an adult believed she could be. That one minute exchange became a tipping point for this student. She later commented, "I believed you because you had a strong value system, never called in sick, were always prepared, and had strict classroom standards. You had the same high expectations for everyone. For this reason, when you said something, I took it to heart. If you saw something in me, I thought, it must be real." I received that e-mail several years ago, so this story would not be complete without an update.

Wow, I can't believe how fast time flies, I didn't realize it had been that long since I sent that e-mail to you. As a student teacher, I taught Science to high school students on the Spirit Lake Nation Reservation. The majority of my students there were living the life I had growing up: living in poverty, coming from broken homes and just trying to make it day to day, often getting in a lot of trouble along the way. I went on to earn a Masters Degree in Biology with an Educational Leadership cognate from the University of North Dakota. After graduation, I was hired as the Science Director at the Sisseton Wahpeton College. What I have found, even years later, is that your enthusiasm for science and learning was contagious, and you had passed it on to me. In turn, I have passed it on to my students as well.

Like you, I set high expectations for my students and demanded more of them, while encouraging them to set goals and dream big. A number of my former students have gone on to college and earned Bachelor's Degrees, against all odds. In fact, one student got a hold of me a month ago to let me know that she's been accepted to Law School. Like me, she started with nothing and had to fight her way through, every step of the way. While she credits me for her good work, I credit you.

My science education has really opened doors for me. As someone who feels the strong need to make a difference, and seeing the lack of American Indians within that field, I decided to pursue a law degree. In December 2008, I earned a Juris Doctorate Degree from the UND School of Law. In 2009, I was hired as an attorney for my tribe. Currently I am writing the Environmental Code for my tribe, as one has not yet been established. This Code will help my tribe gain important recognition under the EPA and guide us in regulating and managing our natural resources more effectively. Once again, thanks for thinking of me.

This story illustrates how the greatest strength of a teacher may be the ability to raise the expectations of their students and to convey a personal belief that with hard work, all students can succeed in life. The power of belief in oneself is a truly remarkable gift that should be given to all children. As teachers, we have the ability, and the responsibility, to give this gift to our students!

~Paul Kuhlman
2009 South Dakota State Teacher of the Year
Math, Science teacher, grades 7, 9-12

Not Lost In Translation

A teacher affects eternity; he can never tell where his influence stops.
~Henry Brooks Adams

As a teacher we all have those memories of students—we wonder if we were able to teach them or reach them. They pull at our heartstrings. You know, the students who run, not walk, into the room, bounce around in their seats, have a need to get out of their seats every five minutes or so, go to the pencil sharpener, throw something away, and always have an excuse to leave their seats. They don't like to do homework, and yet they love to participate because they love to talk and they love attention.

I recently received an e-mail from one such student. Paco Rodriguez-Sanchez (not his real name). My students have always selected a Spanish name for themselves. Most select just a first name. However, there are those who insist on not only a Spanish first name, but also the two Spanish last names, to be culturally appropriate.

Paco's e-mail brought back memories of one particular day and one particular class:

It is our high school's first year of block scheduling—our classes are 80 minutes long instead of the traditional 40 minutes. There are no bells to signal the beginning and ending of a lesson. On this particular day, I am to be observed by two college professors because the class I teach is a college credit course in our high school.

Of course, I am proud of the fact that the class is conducted entirely in Spanish and the students do feel comfortable expressing themselves in Spanish. They come to this Spanish class with a Spanish name they selected for themselves when they took Spanish I. Many are attached to their new name and their Spanish class identity. This class of twenty-five is a pretty typical intermediate Spanish class. There are the third who absolutely want to be there—some are even considering majoring in Spanish in college, the third who are there because their parents want them to earn the college credit, and the third who are there because this class had seats left or because their friends are taking it. There are all sorts of reasons why high school students take the classes they take.

On this day, Paco comes running through the door with a toasted cheese sandwich in hand and a bowl of sauce for dipping. "After all, Señora Mike, it is the third 80-minute block of the day and my lunch is not until next period. I'm hungry and I hope you don't mind if I just quickly eat this great toasted cheese sandwich." Because I insist on Spanish at all times, Paco has actually said in Spanish, "Señora, yo hambre y como el sandwich con queso, ¿vale?" (Translated literally, "Mrs., I hunger and I eat sandwich with cheese, okay?")

I say, "Go ahead, Paco, finish your sandwich, quickly." Paco has not yet noticed the two visiting professors who are there to observe me today. He sits down and finishes his sandwich, with three or four bites, dipping each time into the sauce. "Bueno, muy bueno," Paco says as he savors the last bite with sauce.

Paco has now noticed our two visitors. Of course, our two visitors noticed Paco the minute he ran through the door. (I am sure college professors are not used to seeing students run through a door and bounce into a seat with a toasted cheese sandwich and a bowl of sauce in hand.)

I am wondering how long Paco will stay seated.

The lesson is going along quite well, all the students are working in their groups, engaged in the assigned activity, and the professors go from group to group to interact and speak Spanish with the students. To my relief, this is going quite well.

Suddenly, Paco raises his hand. "Señora, está lloviendo en mis pantalones." ("Mrs. M. it is raining in my pants.") Now, being Paco's

Spanish teacher, I understood what he wanted; his request was not lost in translation. I know that it was his way of requesting to go to the bathroom.

You can just imagine the laughter from the other students and the chuckles from the visiting professors.

I always wondered just how much Spanish Paco learned in that class, but I know he learned more than just Spanish based on an e-mail he recently wrote to me:

> *I know I was a handful but you actually cared & were adamant about it. You knew I had potential but I messed up a lot & you never backed down.... But A HUGE THANK YOU to you Señora, everything you taught me about Spanish, my attitude & life will stick with me the rest of my days....*
>
> *Wish I could go back for a day & do it again, toasted cheese & secret sauce from the cafeteria in hand, ready for fourth period!*

You see, Paco Rodriguez-Sanchez was my student ten years ago.

~Vickie A. Mike
2009 New York State Teacher of the Year
Spanish teacher, grades 10-12

Persistence Pays

Trust your hunches.
They're usually based on facts filed away just below the conscious level.
~Joyce Brothers

As the door to my portable classroom opened, a gust of wintry air captured the papers on my desk. I looked up from grading essays to see Jessie rushing through the door, her dark hair whipping around her head. I wondered what kind of creative excuse she would offer for missing my junior honors English class earlier that day.

She hurried across the room, talking a mile a minute. "Ms. Sturm, I came to tell you why I missed class today. I really like your class; I wasn't skipping, honest. You see, Casey and me, we were worried about our friend. She said she was going to commit suicide."

Suicide? Alarm bells clanged in my head. Her friend had been talking about committing suicide? Does she realize how many teens follow through on their suicide threats? I wondered how I could intervene and help.

"When she didn't show for third hour, we were worried," Jessie continued. "We went to her house to check up on her. Honest. That's all we were doing. So since I wasn't skipping your class, can I get my make-up work? Please?"

"Jessie, this is more important than your English grade. Do you realize how serious your friend's situation might be?"

"Oh, my friend's great! Casey and me just came from her house. Can I get my work?"

Still trying to intervene, I questioned her. "Jessie, will you give me your friend's name?"

"No, I can't."

"Jessie, have you told an adult who knows your friend? What about your mom or dad or your friend's parents?"

"Oh, no, I couldn't do that. We promised we wouldn't tell. We promised! I wouldn't have told you except I need my make-up work. She won't do anything stupid. Honest."

For the next fifteen minutes I pleaded with her, whispering inaudible prayers the whole time. My heart silently screamed at me not to let her out of my room until she promised to tell a trusted adult.

"What about Mrs. Cable, the school counselor? Have you confided in her? You know she's trained to deal with potential suicides and she knows how to keep everything confidential."

Calm on the outside, I was beginning to feel desperate inside and prayed that Jessie would talk with Mrs. Cable and divulge the friend's name.

At long last Jessie relented. "Okay Ms. Sturm. Since you insist, I'll go tell Mrs. Cable, and I'll tell her my friend's name. Now can I get my make-up assignment?"

Quickly I gave her the day's work and sent her to the counselor's office.

Several days passed before Jessie popped back into my room after school to tell me what had happened. "Ms. Sturm, you'll never guess what happened at Mrs. Cable's."

"What happened, Jessie? Is your friend alright?"

"I went to the counselor's office. Thank you for making me go."

"Good for you Jessie. You did the right thing. So what happened?"

"Right away Mrs. Cable called her mom. I was so scared we'd get in trouble...."

Jessie continued her story, "Her mom went to check and then we heard her mom scream and Mrs. Cable called 911 and they went and revived my friend and took her to the hospital. Ms. Sturm, I want to thank you for saving my friend's life. The doctor said she would have died in another hour. She's out of the hospital now and getting counseling. Thank you for making me tell. You saved her life. Thank you. Thank you."

With that farewell, Jessie flew out the door, letting it bang shut. In the quiet of my empty room I shed my tears. I never learned the name of her friend, but I know she's alive today because I wouldn't give up.

~Nancy Hamilton Sturm

Five Words

We need to understand that every time an elementary school teacher
captures the imagination of a child through the arts or music or language,
this nation gets a little stronger.
~Former Secretary of Education, Richard W. Riley

When we measure success in the classroom, we think of bonds forged with families and children's increasing academic growth as measured on a regular basis. To facilitate sustained intellectual gains for our students, we strive to form ongoing two-way communication with the parents and families of our students. Research has repeatedly shown that once established, these critical relationships enable our children to become much more successful in all academic pursuits. Authentic relationships are built and nurtured when teachers and parents have the same goal and work together to motivate our children.

Parents are often as perplexed as teachers about the best way to inspire students to learn what must be taught. When parents and teachers communicate well, our adult communication makes a positive impact in the lives and learning of our children. Success is based on setting goals and working to achieve personal dreams, and as a team, parents and teachers share these values with the children to whom we are responsible.

At times, teachers are stunned to learn that no one at home is able to supply the necessary support. The responsibility for educating some young learners rests solely on the shoulders of the teacher.

Usually parents come to meetings sharing their high expectations, soaring hopes and limitless dreams for their children. For some families, keeping a roof over their heads and food on the table has to be enough and they have no aspirations beyond meeting daily needs. There is no time for "frivolous" things like storybooks.

So, it was my honor to be humbled by a compliment from one of my students. His name was Willard, and he was the seventh of eleven siblings. When he arrived in our first grade, he couldn't actually recognize his own name in print. I was dismayed and worried because this was completely atypical of my first grade students. Young children tend to master this skill set at a much earlier age. I immediately resolved to confer with his mother so that we might collaborate to help Will throughout the school year. In my first meeting with his mother, she confided that she was illiterate. Indeed, there were no readers in his immediate family. This explained why he had never heard a story read aloud to him, and it became clear to me why he certainly didn't recognize any letters of the alphabet or have any desire to make marks on paper, as his mother called them.

In all my years of teaching, I had never experienced a distressing academic situation of this nature; I wondered how this child was ever going to experience any level of success in a classroom full of twenty-five needy students. But, what his mother hadn't even considered was that this young man was able to dream. His classmates acted as role models for that little boy, and I truly believed he could learn.

Will wanted to be a member of this class, so his fellow learners and I welcomed him with open arms. Applying an enormous amount of patience, and after exertion of a great deal of pure dedicated hard work and creativity, together Will and I were able to achieve some honest-to-goodness breakthroughs. His temper tantrums subsided as he eventually began to enjoy listening to stories. Will learned to sing and dance, and he was willing to share pencils, crayons, and puzzles instead of biting other children in frustration. He stopped fighting, literally tooth and nail, for every moment of attention from me and could sometimes respond appropriately to peers as he interacted in our learning activities. It was an evolving miracle as Will learned to read on grade level and use number concepts well enough to be promoted to second grade with his newfound friends.

However, the thing I will always remember about this little blond-haired boy was the day he decided he wanted to write me a note. I don't know how or why he ever decided to thank me and in writing. I guess it was because he could. He handed me a crumpled piece of paper; I didn't even realize it contained a message. I held it for a moment. I had never seen Will volunteer to write anything, so when he said, "Aren't you gonna read it?" I was more than a little surprised. He used those marks on paper to express his thoughts in exactly five words. It said, "Mrs. Hutchins, you done good." When I was recording Will's story; my computer kept pointing out that this sentence exhibits poor grammatical skills. But at the moment I unfolded that crumpled little piece of paper, I wasn't worried about his shortcomings.

In fact, in that moment I knew the genuine definition of the word success and so did Will. It is doing the best you can with your abilities, every chance you get. Will achieved what no one else in his family had to date, and because of one little boy's determination, the doors of literacy were opened for his entire family.

When parents cannot fulfill this role of communicating high expectations, teachers step in. This is one of our strengths. We, as teachers, must refuse to fail, so therefore we refuse to accept it from our students. We teach learners to embrace literacy, numeracy, and the principles of loving kindness. Character, compassion, and ethical behavior build relationships and create feelings of belonging. Nothing is more important for school and success in life. When we make being a member of a learning community compelling enough, our students engage in learning despite the odds.

~MaryLu Hutchins
2009 West Virginia State Teacher of the Year
Elementary teacher, grade 1

48

Mary

Even hundredfold grief is divisible by love.
~Jareb Teague

I live in a border town. We are right next to Juarez, Mexico. Right now, drug cartels are trying to take control of Juarez, a city with roughly two million people. In 2008, more people were murdered in Juarez than were killed in Iraq. To put it in perspective, the drug cartels do not discriminate. If you happen to be in Mexico and you happen to be with someone the cartel doesn't want around anymore, you will be executed. Because of this, more than half the kids that attend my school know someone who has been murdered in the drug wars. One of my kids in particular, Mary, has been hit particularly hard and I would like to share her story.

November 2008—Mary was sleeping peacefully in her bed in her family's house in Mexico. The silence was broken by armed men breaking into their home looking for her father because he owed someone money. They found him in his bed and amidst the chaos, Mary and her mother pleaded with the gunmen not to take him. Her father was forced out of the house, without a shirt, hands tied behind his back, and a gun to his head. They found him the next day, decapitated.

Overnight, this beautiful, vibrant, tenacious seventeen-year-old on the cusp of graduation, shut down. She no longer smiled. She no longer spoke. Her zest for life was gone. She barely moved in class when she walked down the hall, she hung her head low. Eye contact was non-existent and she kept her hands in her sweatshirt pockets. She simply existed. She was barely hanging on to any grip of reality she had left.

In January of 2009, she sat in my class and read an essay she wrote about that night. She wrote about her dad and the gunmen, about how she was alone now, and about how her every breath was a morose tribute to the joy she once felt. She told us that she wished she was dead too. Every kid in that class cried with her.

On February 25, 2009, she gave me a card she made on a computer in another teacher's class. It said she really appreciated me and everything I did for her during "that time." As I sit here crying, and remembering this precious girl, I am perplexed why Mary thought of me during the worst time in her life. She will never go through anything more difficult than what she is dealing with now… and she thought of me.

Slowly, after that day when Mary read her essay, she started to heal. Little by little, she started to make eye contact with people around her again. At first it was just a glance. By March, I heard her beautiful laugh echo off the walls of my classroom again. Granted, the underlying innocence that was once there was gone, but this is a time to celebrate the small victories. She reluctantly went to prom, and proudly walked across the stage at graduation, but last I heard she had not returned to the house in Mexico where they once lived. A few weeks before graduation, Mary gave me another letter. She again thanked me for everything I had done, said she was still a mess on the inside and was only being strong for her mom, and said she would never forget me. What a coincidence — I will never forget her.

~Christine Gleason
2009 Texas State Teacher of the Year
English teacher, grade 12

Chapter
6

Teacher Tales

That Was Embarrassing

Humor is merely tragedy standing on its head with its pants torn.

~Irvin S. Cobb

Roller Call

The truth will set you free, but first it will make you miserable.
~James A. Garfield

I remember thinking about the slogan "Dress for Success" when I picked out the suit. It was beautiful, a black wool jacket and skirt, a creamy silk blouse. Expensive. I'd never owned clothing so nice. I even bought new shoes, not the comfy rubber soles that I normally wore to my teaching job at the high school, but pretty black heels with leather soles. I wanted to look great.

The event would be in the university ballroom, a special reception for participants considering a new graduate degree program. It was important, my first step on the journey toward an exciting future. Who knew where it might lead? Perhaps I might eventually enter the halls of the university itself as an esteemed faculty member. That could mean so many things. No more scraping gum from the bottom of desks, no more listening to "I forgot my homework," no more carrying my own soap to the shared student-faculty restrooms. I was excited.

The reception was all I expected and more. Beautiful vases of fresh-cut flowers rested on white tablecloths arrayed with delicate cake treats, bites of cheeses, crackers, and glasses of champagne. It was nothing like the receptions at my school, which featured fruit punch and plates of cookies furnished by the PTA.

I looked around the grand ballroom adorned with art in gilded frames. Soft cello music played in the background. I didn't know anyone at the reception, but it seemed that everywhere I looked, someone was looking in my direction. Many of them smiled. I remember thinking that perhaps there really was something to "dressing for success." It was one of those rare moments when I felt polished — no messy chalk marks on my hands or red ink on my fingers.

Later, when I left the reception and headed toward my car, I decided that I didn't want to go home, change into my sweats and sit around all evening grading stacks of boring high school essays. That was way too mundane. No, I'd go somewhere else, maybe to a nice coffee shop or maybe visit a small art gallery. Who knew when I'd be this dressed up again? Before backing out of my parking spot, though, I decided to check my hair and lipstick. I actually smiled into the overhead mirror. And then I froze.

A pink hair roller was just sitting there near the top of my head, a little toward the back, on the left side. The roller was totally exposed, only a small wimpy strand of hair draped lazily over it.

I thought I'd die. I thought I would never ever show my face at the university again. No wonder people were smiling. What could they say? Excuse me, you have a pink roller stuck on your head?

I sat in the car, holding that stupid roller in my fist, tears rolling down my face.

"Turn it around," I always told my students when they messed up, when they felt like quitting. "Use your mistakes," I'd tell them. "Don't let them use you."

Sorry. This was different. I felt miserable all the way home.

Zoom ahead a year or two. I'm in a classroom, not in a university, but in a public high school, a classroom of struggling kids who are used to failure. I'm trying to reach them, but it is hard. Impossible. It seems as if nothing works. Finally, in a weak moment, I find myself telling them the hair roller story. I tell them everything, every tiny humiliating bit, my tears, my shame, my vow to never show my face in a university again, the horrible aloneness I felt.

"Oh no!" one girl says. "I couldn't stand it!" Some students laugh. They can't believe I'd share such an embarrassing event. "That really happened to you, Miss?" one kid asks. "No lie?" Another student suggests I check my hair before I go anywhere. Someone else has an important question. "Did you go back to the college?"

"Yes, I did," I answer. "But I learned I didn't want to teach in a place where people might not tell you that you have a roller on your head." We all laughed at that.

The next day when I walked into the classroom, it was totally quiet except for a little giggle here and there. I looked out at the class. They were all watching me. Some were smiling. It didn't take me long to notice. Every kid, every single one, had a pink hair roller stuck on his head.

"Hey, Miss," came a voice at the back. "You ain't alone!"

Many years ago, when I was first studying to be a teacher, one of my professors said, "Before you teach me, you must reach me." Who would have known that a little pink hair roller could play such a big part!

~Martha Moore

Field Trip Fiasco

Every day may not be good, but there's something good in every day.
~Author Unknown

When I accepted the teaching position at the small private school in the Green Mountains of Vermont, I expected to be passing on my love of language to middle-school children with learning disabilities. I did not expect to be standing in a parking lot with a bleeding little girl surrounded by Vermont state troopers, hands at their holsters. But that was exactly my position at 11:25 AM one August day.

At seven years old, Sabrina was on her third set of adoptive parents when she showed up at Autumn Acres. Our little school only housed about sixty kids, but they were sixty kids who'd already seen more horrible things than most people ever see. Sabrina had it worst of all.

I wasn't with them at recess when it happened, but Sabrina managed to climb fifteen feet up a tree and then fall. When I came into work Monday morning, teachers huddled in corners, from which I could hear snatches of conversation: "... wasn't being watched... shouldn't be left alone... bit her tongue completely in half...."

Sabrina showed up for school on Friday with her jaw wired shut. They were able to re-attach the tongue, but there had been significant nerve damage, and it was questionable that she'd ever be able to speak normally again. Mr. Garrity, the principal, pulled me aside as I was warming up the van to take the kids on a field trip.

"Mr. Kaiser, we really want to get Sabrina reintegrated into the population as quickly as possible."

"Sabrina? I don't know if bringing her is a good idea. We'll be walking a couple of miles. If something should happen…"

"Look, Mr. Kaiser. Rather than punish her even more, I'd like you to take her along on the field trip today."

Of course they wanted Sabrina to go on the field trip. That way none of the administrators would have to deal with her back at the school.

I parked the raucous student-packed van in the handicapped spot at the Green Mountain Animal Sanctuary. Mrs. Bourne, the science teacher, got out of the van, and opened the back door to let the kids out to stretch their legs and eat the orange slices we'd brought for snack. The seven other teachers walked over with their lists. Each teacher would have eight students.

I heard a cough behind me, and there sat Sabrina alone in the van. I looked at my clipboard; she was not mine. Her blue eyes looked even bigger than usual, her face drawn and her jaw sticking out as if she was angry. I couldn't tell if she truly was, or if the wiring made her look so. I stepped into the van and extended my hand to her, and her big eyes became narrow slits. She shook her head vigorously. She didn't know me. To someone who'd experienced terrible things at the hands of those closest to her, a stranger must have looked like another predator. I stepped back and Sabrina extended a white, skinny arm to Mrs. Bourne.

Mrs. Bourne took her group straight to the skunk pen, outside of which was a table holding little metal cans. Each can had a perforated top, and everyone was invited to pick up a can and smell the skunk's musk. The badger pen was located near the skunk pen and the badger musk smelled like the worst armpit in the world according to one boy. He was right. I gagged after I lifted the can to my nose.

We continued on the winding tarmac to the hut housing the moles. When I stepped through the doorway I saw Sabrina standing perfectly still and staring up at a mole burrow behind the glass. Behind her was what looked like a giant captain's wheel, but with badgers and moles and skunks and mountain lions and other animals painted on it. When the wheel stopped, the animals would be lined up with either what they preyed on, or what preyed on them. But it was the wheel itself that preyed on little Sabrina, because when she took a step back, the wheel's wooden handle slammed right down on top of her head. She collapsed to her knees and I heard the haunting, muted cry of a child trying to scream through a wired jaw. Sabrina's lips were drawn back as far as they would go and her teeth were bared to expose the thin strips of metal running across her teeth, and blood seeped from between her teeth. She'd bitten her tongue stitches.

I radioed for help, and fearing she might choke on her blood, I stooped and in one motion tipped her over into my arms and stood. She immediately began kicking her feet wildly and thrashing and screaming as if she had a gag in her mouth. I began running the mile or so back to the van.

Sabrina was still kicking as I ran, and her attempts at screaming had jetted blood from between her teeth all over the right side of my head and face. Sabrina was only sixty pounds, but she began to get heavy as I plodded along, fetching strange looks from bystanders who saw a man running away with a screaming, bloody girl who sounded as if she'd been gagged.

The science teacher Catharine had heard my radio transmission and she was waiting at the van, with a little boy named Derek.

She said, "Do you want me to drive her to the hospital?"

"I can drive her. Can you just get her in the van for me? She doesn't trust me." I put Sabrina down and Catharine took both her hands and bent down, whispered something to her. Surprisingly, Sabrina stepped into the van and sat in the very back. Derek climbed in and even snapped her seatbelt on, then belted himself in too.

"Can I come?"

"Oh, um, actually that's not a bad idea, Derek." I started the van and heard movement behind me — Sabrina was trying to unbuckle her seatbelt, and Derek was holding her hands so she couldn't.

"Hip-hop!" cried Derek. "She likes hip-hop!" I tuned the radio to a rap station.

"Turn it up! Loud!" he cried. In the rearview mirror, I could see Sabrina smiling in her blood-sprayed white T-shirt, bouncing to the rhythm.

I called the school on my way to the hospital, but they gave me other instructions. Sabrina's parents did not want her brought to the small local hospital, but to Children's Hospital Boston, where she had her tongue sewed back on in the first place. I started to protest, but she did seem okay back there with Derek, so I agreed to meet Sabrina's parents in a parking lot on Main Street.

And it was there, with hip-hop music blasting, blood-covered Sabrina and Derek dancing, leaning against the driver's door myself covered with blood, that the three Vermont state police cruisers arrived and surrounded me.

They exited their vehicles and, gun hands at their hips, slowly began walking toward me. I was leaning on the car watching this unfold, thinking this was just what I needed to top off this wonderful day

"I've got a hurt kid here — I'm waiting for her parents to pick her up!" I yelled. They closed in, and I handed over my license. They seemed to think they'd caught me at something. Then I saw an older woman standing on her porch, peeking out from behind a post with a cordless phone in her hand. Of course I would probably have thought it suspicious too if I saw a man in his late twenties hanging out with a bloody little girl, having a hip-hop dance party in a parking lot. As it turned out, they thought I was a pedophile luring children with music.

When I look back at that day, my most stressful ever of teaching, what sticks in my mind is not being mistaken for a pedophile, or any animosity toward poor wounded Sabrina, but the kindness of that little boy Derek, who like so many good people who pass briefly through our lives, touched me with his goodwill and moved on before I let him know how grateful I was.

~Ron Kaiser, Jr.

Bountiful Sharing in First Grade

A good teacher is like a candle—it consumes itself to light the way for others.
~Author Unknown

As a first grade teacher who cares deeply for her students, it is important to start building a strong classroom community immediately upon beginning the school year. Acts of the teacher are taken very seriously by the students and consciously or sub-consciously calculated by them as to whether the teacher cares about them and has prepared a safe place for them during school hours. Since six-year-olds, generally, are very honest and loving toward their teacher... the love notes and drawings come quickly and continually after the first day of school. Sometimes, reciprocal acts of love toward the students are a little more intricate and messy for the teacher.

At the beginning of last year, for about a month, my first graders wore name tags (red apples on a soft yellow yarn lanyard) during the day so the lunch staff, music, gym, media, and computer teachers would begin to recognize them and could begin learning their names. One day, upon my students' return to the classroom from lunch, I noticed that a student's name tag was on her desk. As I picked it up and handed it to her so she could put it on she vomited on me. Out of love and concern for her, I reassured her that this was NOT a big deal, quickly and quietly wrote a note to the school nurse, and had two students usher her down to the office.

Since it was read aloud time the other students waited on the rug for me, looking at the author Mo Willems' books that I had already read to them, so I used the classroom phone to contact a custodian to clean up the aftermath. As smoothly as I could, I cleaned myself off and sat down to read to the children, never raising my voice or making a fuss over the vomit. As I read, the custodian cleaned up and sanitized the affected area.

Next, the children moved back to their seats to draw a picture of their favorite Mo Willems' character in a setting they had seen in one of the books we had been reading. After they had drawn their picture they were to add labels or sentences—whatever they felt comfortable producing for this project. The little one who had shared her lunch with me came back to the room and I helped her get ready to go home for the remainder of the day. I wished her well and told her we would miss her.

As I was wondering around the room looking at what the children were creating and answering questions, one little girl called me over to her desk to look at her work. When I got to her desk, she stood up so she could get close to me and share her project with me. As she was speaking, I felt my feet and legs getting wet. It took me a second to realize that as she was explaining her beautiful work she was urinating on me. Again, out of love and concern for the child, I reassured her that this was NOT a big deal, quickly and quietly wrote a note to the school nurse and had the child ushered down to the office by two of her peers. Once again, I called upon the custodians to come and sanitize the affected area, cleaned myself off and never talked about it with the students. When the young lady came back to the room with dry, clean clothes she took her seat and began, once again, to consider her part in the classroom community.

The next day, both girls returned to class and were greeted with comforting smiles. Both were unsure as to how they would be treated by the class and by me. Neither accident was ever brought up in public. The little girl who urinated on me, however, discussed in private with me how awful she felt about the experience. I advised her that it was a normal bodily function, that everyone had accidents at some time in their life, and that she was not to worry about it anymore. These accidents brought the girls and me closer and although we never talked of them again they learned that the classroom was a safe place where they could learn and be loved and that their classmates accepted them.

After school that day, I had a meeting to attend. Of course, the first thing I did was apologize for how this first grade teacher smelled and laughed with my colleagues about the wonder of teaching.

~Linda A. Smerge
2009 Illinois State Teacher of the Year
Elementary teacher, grade 1

52

The Naughty Kid

Children are a great comfort in your old age—
and they help you reach it faster, too.
~Lionel Kauffman

After the first few days in a new classroom, especially if it is in a new school, your child is likely to come home and claim that he or she doesn't know the names of any other students.

"You can't remember even one friend's name," you'll say, desperate for all the details. But your child's lips are sealed. Only after relentless prodding will your child finally confess: "Well, there is this one kid...."

That "one kid," the only student whose name your son or daughter knows, is guaranteed to be the naughty kid.

Every class has a naughty kid. Other children quickly learn the naughty kid's name because they hear it called out by the teacher—with various undertones of anger and frustration—over and over again. Beware any child whose name is the first one that your son or daughter learns.

But what if your child is the naughty kid? How will you know? Your first clue might be if your son or daughter says there isn't a naughty student in the class. Remember, there is always a naughty kid.

ME (speaking to my five-year-old son, who just started kindergarten): "Owen, did you learn any friends' names today?"

OWEN: "No, Mom."

ME: "Not even the naughty kid's name? Your older brother always learned the naughty kid's name on the first day."

OWEN: "We don't have a naughty kid in our class."

ME: "No naughty kid? That's impossible. Every class has a naughty kid."

OWEN: "Not my class."

ME: "Well that's good. But you don't know anyone's name? You didn't hear the teacher saying someone's name over and over again?"

OWEN: "Nope."

The second clue that your child is the naughty one in his class: Other parents know your child's name.

ME (speaking to the mother of someone in Owen's class): "I'm sorry, what is your daughter's name? I'm still trying to match parents to children."

ANOTHER PARENT: "You're Owen's mom, right?"

ME: "Yes."

ANOTHER PARENT: "We hear a lot about Owen."

The third and final clue that your child is the naughty one in class: He or she seems to always have a new seat.

ME: "Owen, what was your favorite part of the week?"

OWEN: "That I'm sitting at my friend's table again."

ME: "You've switched tables already? It's only the second week of school."

OWEN: "I switch tables every day, Mom. Each time I get in trouble, the teacher finds me a new seat."

I was shocked when I finally put it all together. I didn't want my child—my Owen—to be "that kid." I didn't want him to be the naughty one. When I talked to my husband, Dustin, about it, he chuckled and said, "Owen has come a long way. Do you remember when he wouldn't talk at all? Do you remember how you worried that he would always be shy?"

Dustin is right. Just two years ago, our Owen, who has always been in the third-percentile for weight, was a scrawny four-year-old boy who couldn't keep even size 2T pants on his hips. He seldom talked and he cried every time I left him at preschool. He had trouble making friends.

Now our pint-size little boy—the one we used to call "Tiny Tim"—has blossomed into someone who apparently can't stop making friends. Even during Circle Time and Rest Time. And while it's nice to see him growing, that doesn't mean he should misbehave.

"I guess I need to call Owen's teacher and arrange a meeting," I said aloud to myself that night, and my oldest son, Ford, overheard.

"I bet the teacher will answer and say, 'Well, hello there you naughty parent,'" Ford said, bringing a whole new element into my dilemma. If every class has a naughty child, I guess it makes sense that there is a "naughty parent" as well.

Owen came into the room and heard us talking. "Oh come on now, stop," he said. "Let's not go calling my teacher, or anything. I've got it all under control."

Which, of course, is Clue #1 that you need a Parent-Teacher conference pronto.

~Sarah Smiley

Reprinted by permission of
Steven A. Barr ©2009

53

Classroom Fun

I am thankful for laughter, except when milk comes out of my nose.
~Woody Allen

Teaching second grade never ceases to amuse me.

One year, I had a young man in my class who occasionally seemed to have difficulty following the rules, especially during unstructured times such as recess. Whenever he was guilty of any infraction, I immediately knew because he would break into tears as soon as he saw my face, and he had a million excuses as to why the behavior occurred. My students were entering the room after lunch recess one day and one by one they rushed to inform me of Tommy's latest transgression.

I braced myself for the tears and excuses I knew were inevitably coming my way. As Tommy entered the room however, he marched with determination right up to me and said, "Mrs. N., I know you've heard about me making bad choices but you *really* need to hear my side of the story."

I was intrigued, as he had never come in so calmly, and I let him proceed. Tommy continued, "All I said was, 'Would you rather go to Heaven or go to Hell?' If you really want to be mad at someone, you should be mad at Billy because he said, 'Tommy, what the hell did you say that for?'"

Of course, sometimes I am the source of the amusement....

One day, I was standing at the whiteboard in front of my class, recording students' ideas for a writing assignment. After documenting one student's idea, I turned my head to call on another. Suddenly, I felt a sharp pain in my chin. I quickly discounted it and continued writing down ideas.

As I turned my head a second time, again I felt something sharp hit my face. This went on for quite some time. Then, one of my students raised her hand and said, "Look everybody... Mrs. N. has a new magic wand for us to use in the classroom and she's trying to hide it." I looked down and discovered I had popped the underwire in my bra!

~Lori Neurohr
2009 Wisconsin State Teacher of the Year
Elementary teacher, grade 2

Crayon Crisis

Life is about using the whole box of crayons.
~RuPaul

The telephone rang. It was my sister. She said, "Just thought I'd let you know I used your crayon story again." My sister is the media specialist in an elementary school. Every now and then, she will tell my story to the students who visit her library.

Forty-odd years ago, I sat in my first-grade classroom. The classroom's PA crackled to life, summoning me to the principal's office. The PRINCIPAL'S office! As I walked to the office, my six-year-old little life flashed before my eyes. What did I do?

I was a shy kid. I did my best to blend into the background. I hated to be noticed or singled out. For me, being called to the principal's office was my worst nightmare come to life. My black and white saddle shoes scuffed the floor as I walked ever so slowly to the office.

"Diane, the principal is not ready for you yet. Please have a seat," said the school secretary.

I climbed up onto the leather sofa and sunk as low as I could into the cushion. I was praying that the cushion would swallow me whole.

The intercom buzzed on the secretary's desk. "You can go in now," she smiled.

I pushed open the heavy oak door. It was worse than I thought.

Seated in front of the principal's desk were my parents. The real reason why they were there, I wouldn't learn until years later.

My father walked straight over to me. He held a stack of my drawings. "Why do you only use a black crayon when you draw?" he asked.

I couldn't speak. All I could do was shrug my boney shoulders.

"Show me your desk," said my father.

We returned to my classroom. It was recess time so all my classmates were out on the playground. I nervously pointed to my wooden desk.

My father pulled out my crayon box. He dumped the contents into his hand. A single nub of a crayon rested in his palm—it was black.

Puzzled, my father asked, "Where are the rest of your crayons?"

I quietly explained that I'd given all the other crayons to friends. I'd been sharing like my parents had taught me.

My father let out a deep controlled breath, "You were sharing."

I nodded my head. I looked at my father, then at the principal—both their faces were red. The principal mumbled that I could join the rest of my classmates for recess. I waved goodbye to my parents. My mother waved back, but I couldn't get my father's attention; he was too busy glaring at the principal.

I learned years later that my father's face was red due to anger and the principal's was red due to embarrassment. The principal, on seeing all my artwork done in black crayon, assumed that I had deep emotional issues. To him my crayon choice reflected my "dark and depressed nature." He had called my parents in to discuss "my problem" and to suggest some type of psychological counseling.

I was too afraid to admit that I only had one crayon. I was too timid to ask for my "shared" crayons back. Because I didn't stand up for myself, others assumed the worst.

That night, my father talked to me about "sharing and giving," and how the two are different. He also gave me a brand new box of crayons. He tapped the box and said, "These crayons are for you and you alone. I don't want you sharing or giving these crayons to anyone else, understand?"

I clutched the new box and said, "Yes, Daddy."

Today my sister tells her students, "Don't be afraid to ask a question. Don't be afraid to speak up. If you don't—I just might make the wrong assumption. And that's not a good thing. Let me tell a story about my sister, when she was around your age. It revolves around an assumption and a black crayon...."

~Diane M Miller

Full of Surprises

Every survival kit should include a sense of humor.
~Author Unknown

After receiving a staff e-mail containing pictures of outlandish things that kids do, I felt compelled to share with my fellow second grade teachers my own story of a student who could have easily been in many of those pictures. My first year teaching I thought my school administration was out to get me. As an inexperienced teacher, every child of a staff member who was in second grade was placed in my class. No pressure there, right? To add to that, I also taught five Spanish speaking students and I had not yet received my bilingual certification. At this point, my confidence level as a new teacher had declined tremendously. As unnerved as I was throughout my initial teaching experience, the year went by with minimal complications. Little did I know my second year of teaching would be filled with prolific challenges.

Let's call her Meredith…. Meredith was a beautiful child who could light up a room with her laughter and smile. She had a fantastic sense of humor and brought a great deal of joy to our classroom. However, Meredith had a tendency to find herself in unusual situations. Take the head stuck in the chair incident. How this happened, I have no idea. As I was at the chalkboard displaying new vocabulary words, Meredith somehow managed to wedge her head in an opening in the back of the chair. Lesson number one—do not turn your back on them for one second.

We abruptly discontinued our vocabulary lesson so that I could attempt to remove Meredith's head from its unexpected position. Meredith twisted and turned, stretched and pulled to no avail. As she began to cry, I thought her tears might provide some lubrication to help slide her head back through the opening. When that theory proved to be ineffective, I proceeded to call our head custodian. He came over right away armed with his tools and his sense of humor. He then attempted to have Meredith twist and turn, and stretch and pull. Once again… nothing. As a last resort, the custodian removed the back of the chair from its supporting pieces and Meredith was freed from her confinement. It did not take long for Meredith's tears to turn to impish laughter and we were able to continue with our day. Please note I did not schedule for a removal of head from chair in my lesson plans.

This was the incident that first came to mind after receiving the entertaining images of curious child behavior. But this is not my only story involving Meredith and her mischievous manner. Another vivid memory I have of that year involved measuring tape, students jumping and me flat on the floor. As part of a measurement activity, students jumped as far as they could and we measured the distance. We did this activity one student at a time with me on one end of the tape measure and one student on the other end. I asked students who were waiting for their turn or who had already finished to sit in a separate area and observe. As I moved forward and backward, and up and down, I trusted that I could do so safely. Lesson number two — do not have false confidence in your own physical wellbeing in the classroom.

As I blindly backed away from a student to measure a jump, I encountered an obstacle and fell to the floor. Through my legs in the air, there sat Meredith, scrunched in a ball on the floor in front of me. I couldn't decide if I wanted to laugh or shout. After briefly sharing a laugh with my students, I instructed them one more time regarding what should occur during this activity and stressed the importance of listening and following directions in order to maintain a safe classroom environment.

As I shared these stories with my colleagues who had just received the exuberant e-mail that triggered my memory, an innocent, inexperienced student teacher gasped in horror and said, "That's the kind of thing I'm afraid of!" I smiled at her and said, "Don't be afraid of these types of things. They're the kind of things that keep it interesting." As I thought about my response to her, I realized that my biggest disasters are some of my best memories. I learned that even the best plans can and will be interrupted by heads stuck in chairs and teachers crashing to the floor. And my memories of Meredith... she will forever brighten my day and bring me back to reality.

~Blythe Turner
2009 New Mexico State Teacher of the Year
Bilingual teacher, grade 2

Social Secretary

Wisdom doesn't necessarily come with age.
Sometimes age just shows up all by itself.
~Tom Wilson

I n my classroom, I have students as Class Council President, Vice President, and Ambassador. While I complete the morning tasks that frustrate so many teachers, the Class Council members set up the computers, run books to the library, and turn in any notes to the office and the nurse. This leaves me free to quickly handle any paperwork.

Last January, as I was completing my attendance count verification sheet, one of my fourth grade students approached the desk. Only half listening, I heard him ask, "Mrs. Breen? May I change the calendar?"

I glanced at the small daily calendar and noted it showed the third day of the month. I replied rather impatiently, "No, the calendar is correct."

"But Mrs. Breen, today is the fourth," Jason insisted. Jason is a very reserved student. He was finally beginning to trust me with his thoughts.

"Honey, the fourth is my husband's birthday and I'd remember that. It's tomorrow. Now, have a seat please." And I returned to my work.

He insisted and I finally looked at the large classroom calendar. I jumped up from my seat and went over to the calendar as if hoping it would change as I watched it. "Oh no! Oh my stars!" burst from me as I realized he was correct.

A horrified "You-forgot-your husband's-birthday?" statement floated past me from a horrified Jason. He stood looking at me with shock screaming from every pore of his body. With a disgusted and more than a little indignant expression, Jason returned to his desk and began to work on a writing project.

As he was leaving for the afternoon, Jason placed a piece of paper on my desk, gave me a reproachful look, and said not to read it, but to give it to my husband as soon as I got home. The letter read:

Dear Mr. Breen,

I hope you have a delightful dinner tonight. Mrs. Breen COMPLETELY forgot your birthday today until I reminded her of the correct day! She promised she'd take you out for a steak dinner. Happy Birthday.

Sincerely,
Jason

Properly humbled, I shared the letter with my husband and we went out for dinner. Upon returning, my husband wrote a note back to Jason thanking him for reminding me of his special day.

I thought that was the last of this issue until one day, as I was attempting to get the classroom Valentine's Day party underway, with twenty excited fourth-graders making suggestions, the phone began to ring. Our school secretary was asking about the student who had written the "birthday note" to my husband. Confused and thrown off balance, I told her it was Jason. She requested he be sent to the office ASAP.

Upon his arrival in the office, Jason was introduced to my husband Bill, who had brought roses for me. They shook hands and Bill thanked Jason for helping me to remember his birthday, and asked him to deliver the flowers to me.

Jason walked into the classroom with that "You're-going-to-be-so-sorry" look and I knew I had been had by Bill. Jason handed me the flowers and said, "Happy Valentine's Day. Mr. Breen remembered Valentine's Day and I didn't have to tell him." After laughing and thanking him for the delivery, I mentioned that we were going out for dinner again. "That's it?!" Jason said very indignantly. "You did that for his birthday."

I surrendered and am still laughing.

~Ilah Breen

Teacher Tales

Touched by a Student

*Some people come into our lives and quickly go. Some stay for awhile
and leave footprints on our hearts. And we are never, ever the same.*

~Anonymous

Letters from Home

To send a letter is a good way to go somewhere without moving anything but your heart.
~Phyllis Theroux

As teachers we are privileged to become a part of our students' lives. They share their joys, frustrations, worries, and fears with us on a daily basis. Sometimes the emotions appear on the pages of a journal, where the writer can pretend the admissions are merely the story line for a work of fiction. Other times they are shared openly and enthusiastically during a morning meeting. Over the years, I have been privy to stories of new babies in the family and soccer goals in the final moments of the game. I've helped students deal with nightmares, divorces, and the death of a loved one.

The stories Abby shared were laced with both fear and pride. You see, Abby's father was on active duty with the Army. As a result, she entered my second-grade classroom with an understanding far above her tender years, of the conflicts in both Iraq and Afghanistan. More importantly, she was aware of the impact these far-away places could have on her family. It wasn't long after school started that a somber-eyed Abby walked through the door. Her greatest fears had been realized; her father was preparing to leave the family to complete a six-month tour of duty. I remember listening to this brave eight-year-old tell her classmates the reason why she would miss the next day of school. She described the dreaded drive to the Army base and the moment she would tell her father goodbye in a voice laden with emotion. As Abby finished her announcement and turned to me for comfort, I said a silent prayer for her entire family.

That year was difficult for Abby. On a particularly upsetting day early in the separation, I suggested Abby write her father a letter. I quickly scrapped my lesson plans for teaching the students about the importance of adding details to their personal narratives and decided to introduce letter writing instead. While most of the students wrote letters to their friends about recess plans, Abby wrote to her father. She never mentioned her fears, preferring to create snapshots of family and school events he had missed with her words. We placed the letter in an envelope and I sent it home for her mother to mail. When Abby left the room that afternoon I sat at my desk and cried for the child who knew instinctively what her father would need to hear the most.

Abby's letter writing became her therapy that year. For her benefit, I started including stationery as a staple in my writing center. Soon her cheery letters started arriving on brightly colored paper. She lovingly decorated each letter she wrote with drawings and stickers. As we prepared for Christmas, all of the second graders at my school collected items to ship to the soldiers overseas. Looking at the pile of toiletry items, phone cards, CDs, and snacks one day right before Christmas break, Abby explained that we had forgotten something important. I frantically looked through my list of requested items, trying to find the one small object that we could have possibly left out. Abby informed me it was letters—the soldiers needed letters. Again, I threw out the planned lessons on fractions and traditions so that my class could write all afternoon. Later, I packaged up the donated supplies and carefully placed the handwritten letters and homemade Christmas cards on top.

Abby continued to write letters to her father most of that year. It seemed he was just as diligent about returning notes to his only daughter… until late spring. Abby hadn't received a letter in several weeks and the old fears started to return. I tried my best to comfort her, but it seemed hopeless. After a particularly difficult day, I made the decision to attempt to talk with Abby's mother when she came through the car line at dismissal. Abby was pressed to my side as we approached the car with the tinted windows at cone number four. I prepared to lean in and voice my concerns as I opened the door. I never got a word out because Abby started to scream. Her backpack dropped on the sidewalk as she flew through the open door, across the passenger seat, and into her father's lap! The tears ran silently down his face as he clutched his somewhat hysterical daughter to his chest. I took a seat beside Abby's book bag on the sidewalk and attempted to control the tears that poured from my eyes. The other cars were rerouted around cone four as the three of us struggled to regain control. As I watched Abby and her father drive away I again realized how privileged teachers are to be a part of their students' lives.

~Jenna Hallman
2009 South Carolina State Teacher of the Year
Science teacher, grades K-5

Teaching the Teacher

It's not that I'm so smart, it's just that I stay with problems longer.
~Albert Einstein

The end of the year had finally arrived. The first year of my teaching career would be over in a matter of days, but I dreaded Awards Day. Although I had a class of exceptional students, I feared one student wouldn't have an award. Brent just didn't have the high averages of some of his classmates.

As I sat down and began looking over my grade book, I filled in the blanks on the award sheet for highest grade in each subject. Then, I proceeded to "A Honor Roll" and on through the list. When I began checking averages for "AB Honor Roll," I knew Brent hadn't made it yet. But while the nine-week honor roll was determined by the average of all grades for a quarter, the yearly honor roll was the average of the final grade in each class for the year. Maybe there was a chance.

Brent's grades may have been considered average, but he was far from it. He was no quitter. If he failed a spelling test mid-week, by Friday, he would pass. If his math grade slipped a bit, he'd work to get it higher. Unlike the other students who would often attempt to "one up" one another, Brent's only competition was himself, and his goal for the entire year was the AB Honor Roll.

With each report card, his face had fallen when he'd missed that elusive B average, and although he'd never made honor roll, he'd never stopped trying to reach that goal. Now, he had one last shot. I entered his final grades into the computer and averaged. It was a B! I checked again. Yes, it was a B.

His grades had gone up and down. When he focused harder on one subject, another slipped a bit. Overall, he had a B average.

Now, I couldn't wait for Awards Day!

That May morning as I called out the highest averages in each subject, the students were excited, but there were really no surprises. They knew who would receive each award. Then came AB Honor Roll. I called Brent's name. His eyes lit, a big grin split his face, and he jumped up and whooped. While everyone who got an award made me proud, when Brent came to get his certificate, I blinked back tears.

Until that moment, I was the teacher and he was the student, but the tables had turned. Little Brent had taught me a valuable lesson—while the individual things we do may not be exceptional, together they just might add up to something amazing. Many school years have come and gone since then. I don't remember who had the highest math average that first year I taught, nor which student was my best speller, but to this day I still remember Brent and his amazing lesson in persistence.

~Lisa McCaskill

Ashley

When someone you love becomes a memory, the memory becomes a treasure.
~Author Unknown

The 2005 school year began after what seemed like a perfect summer break. Back-to-school business took attention away from a great storm brewing in the Atlantic. But my World Geography students had been plotting Hurricane Katrina's coordinates on tracking maps for days. When Central Office closed our school to comply with a mandatory evacuation of our area, my students were thrilled. For my freshmen, the hurricane was a great excuse to be out of school. They weren't afraid of what was happening.

Six weeks after the storm hit, I was back in my classroom, getting my room ready for the return of my students. Since our school was fairly intact, we had an influx of students from more heavily damaged areas. Our pre-Katrina student populations were typically from high socio-economic backgrounds and from second generation college graduates. But that would change. Our once homogenous suburban school now included teenagers from rural fishing communities, impoverished inner cities and tight-knit, indigenous ethnic populations.

It was important for the students to tell their stories of survival, so for the first few days, we listened to each one. The questions were endless. "Where did you evacuate to?" "What happened to your home?" "Were any friends or relatives still missing?" "What did you lose that meant the most to you?" It was heartbreaking, but it helped to be able to share those common experiences. There was one girl who stood out. When Ashley had first come into my classroom, she took one look around, beamed a bright smile and took a seat in front of the white marker board. She wore the telltale signs of a hurricane victim—a pair of flip flops on her feet and a T-shirt and shorts that clearly were not her size.

When it was Ashley's turn to tell her story, I could tell from her accent that she was from the especially hard hit parish of St. Bernard. She had lost everything in the storm—her home, her clothing, and all of her teenage treasures. There was only a slab where her house once stood. She said she missed just one possession—her pink jewelry. Pink was Ashley's favorite color.

That's when I realized why she loved my classroom so much. I sponsor an all-girl service club called Tri Theta, and our signature color is bright pink. Our T-shirts are pink and a fourth of my classroom and its wall space are dedicated to my girls in pink. In the corner closest to where Ashley sat were pink jeweled picture frames, a pink lamp, a pink shag rug and a huge mirror decorated with big pink roses. My classroom, with its burgundy painted walls, gold love seat and table lamps seemed more like a home than a traditional classroom. She told me on several occasions that she felt like she was back in her own pink bedroom when she walked into my classroom. I was happy that my penchant for creating a cozy learning environment was making one displaced student feel warm and welcomed.

Our urban and rural students soon became acclimated to their new suburban school. When new student IDs were issued, Ashley asked if she could buy one of the pink sequined ID lanyards that I wore on Tri Theta meeting days. I gladly gave it to her and she wore it all of the time. She confessed to me that it felt like a beautiful pink necklace. She couldn't wait for Tri Theta's meeting day so that she could see what kind of pink get-up I would wear to school. In addition to my pink club T-shirt, I often wore a hot pink boa, jeweled pink tiara and neon pink glasses. She loved it! But she especially commented on my jewelry—a pink crystal necklace and matching bracelet. It was apparent that she was missing her own pink baubles every time she admired mine.

I found myself asking Ashley if she had anything from her past. She said that luckily, she had loaned her aunt a "Mary Kate and Ashley in London" videotape before the storm. Since we were studying Europe, she asked if she could bring the tape in for the class to watch. I heartily accepted her offer. She was so proud to have something to give! When Christmas time came around, my Tri Theta girls collected toys for those children still living in shelters. When Ashley saw the toys piled up in my room, she brought in a brand new baby doll for the shelter kids and a pink gift bag for me. In it was the most delicious smelling hand lotion—Victoria's Secret's "Pink" of course! Here she was, giving to others after losing so much herself. I was in awe of her generosity.

Having Ashley in class was a joy. She was pure sunshine! After each class, I would notice a small flower drawn on the marker board behind her desk and the message "I (heart) Mrs. Tonguis." I never caught her writing it, but it was always there… until one day when she didn't show up for school. When I buzzed Student Services to ask if Ashley had relocated, I was summoned to my Vice Principal's office. Ashley had been in a fatal car accident early that morning. I sat in stunned silence. What Hurricane Katrina hadn't crushed in my spirit, this news did. Being a high school teacher, I had attended far too many teenage funerals. This one just might be the worst by far.

Her funeral was just what she would have wanted—a blanket of the prettiest pink roses on her white casket and hundreds of friends. Three friends who Ashley had volunteered to drive home from a slumber party survived the crash and were there with blackened eyes and broken bones, numb with grief. Her mother, after having lost everything in the storm, now lost her only child. As I stood looking down at Ashley, in my head to toe pink, a nod to her favorite color, I slipped the pink crystal bracelet she had admired so often from my "Pink" scented wrist, and placed it on hers. When I tried to return Ashley's videotape to her mother, she refused it, saying that Ashley loved my class so much that it belonged there for my students to enjoy.

The next day, when I returned to my classroom, I dreaded third hour when I would see Ashley's empty desk. I hadn't erased the last message she left on my board, but somehow the flower was rubbed off. It didn't matter. From that day forward, one of Ashley's many newfound friends from class would place a freshly picked wildflower on her desk. That was Ashley's desk… and it still is. The Art Club painted bright pink flowers all over it in her honor. No one has sat in that seat for four years. Perhaps someday I will be able to look at that desk and not see her there.

Katrina blew through southern Louisiana and took many things away, but it also brought people like Ashley into our lives, someone we never would have known if it hadn't been for that hurricane.

~Deborah Hohn Tonguis
2009 Louisiana State Teacher of the Year
Social Studies teacher, grades 9-12

Step by Step

The job of an educator is to teach students to see the vitality in themselves.
~Joseph Campbell

I'll never forget Chelsea. She was a wounded soul. Over the years she had always struggled—both academically and with self-confidence. In addition, her mother had died after a heroic battle with a terminal illness when Chelsea was a fifth grader. As she began sixth grade, Chelsea was still hurting. I worried about her with good reason.

Each fall my teaching partner and I take our sixth graders for a five-day adventure at Wolf Ridge, an environmental learning center nestled in the woods of Northern Minnesota overlooking Lake Superior. Our week is filled with learning, team building, and overcoming seemingly insurmountable challenges. We go in October, and the turning leaves—transitioning from summer green to fiery orange, brilliant yellow, and blazing red—come to symbolize the changes we see in our students over the week. The steps and growth students make at Wolf Ridge become a metaphor we use throughout the year as they face challenges in the classroom.

The culminating activity is the High Adventure Ropes Course, which stretches from tower to tower high amongst the treetops forty feet above the ground. I knew this experience would be particularly difficult for Chelsea.

When it came time for her to strap on the harness, Chelsea was already trembling. The harness hooks into a safety wire overhead and offers physical protection, but not much mental comfort when nothing but a slippery board or a wobbly wire is between your feet and the ground far below. Chelsea stepped hesitantly onto the Swinging Wood Bridge, and only after the instructor's encouragement, slowly made her way across its rickety boards up to the first tower. With the support of a chaperone stationed there, she began her way across the Burma Bridge, made of merely three wires and straps. Her trembling body added to its shaking. From down below, her ground partner shouted up supportively, "Come on Chelsea, you're doing great!"

She finally reached the second tower and told the chaperone, "I can't do it." But eventually Chelsea stepped out onto the next challenge—a single log—and slowly inched her way across. She now faced what for many is the most difficult activity: the Single Wire. She wouldn't even step onto it until I worked my way over from my perch on the last tower to the middle of the wire. I could see the terror in her eyes. I implored her to take just one step. With tears streaming down her face, she eventually did. And then another. Her classmates and our chaperones, sensing Chelsea's internal struggle, had gathered below and were offering constant words of affirmation while moving forward in a huddled group as she crept ahead, step by step. Ultimately, she reached the last tower—exhausted. She collapsed in my arms and sobbed.

"Just one more big step, Chelsea," I told her. The final challenge is a zip-line, which requires leaping off that last tower and trusting that the guide wire above will carry you safely down to the chaperones waiting 100 yards down the path. Chelsea just stood there for what seemed like hours. "I can't do it," she told me over and over again against the background cheers of the entire team now gathered below. Finally, when I was just about to say that she could turn around and go back (something I have never done), she looked up at me and in an almost imperceptible whisper said, "Tell them down there that I'm doing this for my mom. I know she's watching, and I want her to be proud of me." As I yelled, "This is for her mom!" Chelsea leaped.

Seconds later she was enfolded in the waiting arms of chaperones and students whose cheers could be heard echoing through the trees for miles. None of us there were ever quite the same. Especially Chelsea. And I was reminded why I teach.

~Derek Olson
2009 Minnesota State Teacher of the Year
Elementary teacher, grade 6

61

I Wish Every Teacher a Kevonna

When you are sorrowful look again in your heart, and you shall see that
in truth you are weeping for that which has been your delight.
~Kahlil Gibran

"Why do you want to be a teacher?" I never could explain it without the usual obvious reasons, such as my love of children or wanting to make a difference. It was not until I met Kevonna that I truly knew the reason I wanted to be a teacher.

I was running an after-school/summer program. A young girl just finishing seventh grade walked through the doors and I thought to myself, "This is going to be a long summer." She was a student at my school and I was well aware of who she was even though I was an eighth grade teacher. Her reserved place in the principal's office was well known by the eighth grade teachers as we prepared ourselves for those students who were going to need extra attention.

I racked my brain trying to figure out what I was going to do with her all summer. I had a new class of students with special needs. I usually had my older students act as classroom helpers for the younger grades, so I decided that this would be a good spot for her. Little did I know how that one little decision would change my life, not only as a teacher, but as a person.

Kevonna transformed before my very eyes. She showed

compassion and patience with the children in that classroom. She was responsible and caring and she began referring to those students as "her kids." I witnessed a natural teacher blooming. I had an unforgettable summer with Kevonna.

Soon the school year began and Kevonna and I were together again. This time our relationship was different. I was her teacher, not just the person in charge of her summer camp. Kevonna continued to make strides and prove that she had a different outlook on life. We had an eighth grade service learning club at the time. Our assistant principal was in charge of the club along with another eighth grade teacher. The other teacher and I approached the assistant principal about allowing Kevonna to join. He denied us at first based on her previous year's academics and behavior. We kept pushing, telling him that she deserved a chance. He finally agreed. Kevonna not only became a member of the service club, but was voted president by her peers.

Kevonna continued to volunteer with "her kids" at my afterschool program. She continued to make strides in school and impress people with her dedication and charm. Her smile was infectious and her sense of humor, astounding. In June, we always had a culminating activity with the service club and students shared what they enjoyed about their experience. I do not believe that anyone was prepared for what Kevonna had to say. She thanked every person there for believing in her and giving her a chance. She was genuinely grateful. There was not a dry eye in the room, students and teachers included. She had a wonderful year and walked across the stage at her eighth grade graduation to receive the Most Improved Student award. After the ceremony, we received gracious words of gratitude and praise along with tight hugs from her mother. What a proud day that was for me. Kevonna was extraordinary and her future was shining bright.

We continued to keep in touch when she went to high school. She still volunteered with "her kids" and still kept us informed of her academics and activities. Kevonna sent a letter to me, my colleague, and our assistant principal. In that letter, she thanked us again for giving her a chance and believing in her. She also stated that she had made her final decision and she was going to be a teacher! I don't think I could have felt more pride than I did at that moment. Her letter was taped to my refrigerator for months.

Over the years, I met other wonderful students, but no one quite like Kevonna. Every time I saw Kevonna, she put me in a great mood. She always had a gigantic smile on her face and gave me a great big hug. She truly loved life and I felt so special to be a part of hers.

We shared a quick dinner of her favorite, Italian food, one fall. She caught me up on everything that was happening with her. She was a member of Future Teachers of America, doing well in school, applying to colleges, all the fun things that a young girl does. She insisted on knowing every little detail of my life and what had changed at our school. It was a wonderful evening. I ran into her, her mom, and sister again at the grocery store right before Thanksgiving. When she saw me in the store, she squealed with delight as she always did and gave me a huge smile and bear hug. We shared a quick conversation and went our separate ways.

A couple of months later, on a Saturday morning in January, my telephone rang. I answered the phone and heard "Did you hear about Kevonna? She died last night in a car accident!" I closed my eyes and all I could see was her beautiful smile. My husband looked at me and when I told him, he stared at me in disbelief. I hung up the phone and began sobbing. She was my special student and my shining star. She had a wonderful future ahead of her.

I sent her mother a card, attached a contest entry that I wrote about Kevonna, and included the last picture of us. My husband and I attended her funeral; it was standing room only. Everyone there was touched by Kevonna. When it came time to pay our respects to her family, I did not know how I was going to face her mother. When she saw me, she hugged me and said, "She loved you so much." Through my tears, I responded, "I loved her too!" That day was filled with sorrow, but it was also a celebration, a celebration of Kevonna.

Now when I think about why I became a teacher, I think of Kevonna. She was truly an angel on earth. I miss her immensely. I have the last picture we took together hanging in my classroom as a daily reminder of why I am there. On those days when there are students who are testing my patience, I think of Kevonna and remember what a difference she made in my life. I wish every teacher a Kevonna; I am truly honored and blessed to have had her in my life.

~Patricia L. Marini

62

Special Treatment

We are all special cases.
~Albert Camus

Kayla sat in the back of my classroom. She usually had a rather dazed look about her, as though she'd just narrowly missed being hit by a bus. When I tried to engage her, she was always polite and respectful. She never broke any rules. However, I had a hard time determining her academic potential. She wasn't failing, but I had a sense that she was capable of more than the "C's" and "B's" she earned.

"How was your weekend?" I asked her one Monday morning.

Her rote response, "Fine," greeted my ears uncertainly.

"Is everything okay?" I asked. She seemed more dazed than usual.

Kayla shook her head and then nodded. "My brother was home for the weekend."

There was nothing in my file about her family situation. I mentioned her to a colleague who had taught her the previous year.

"Poor kid," she said. "Has two siblings with autism. One of them had to be institutionalized. Guess he comes home sometimes."

That explained a great deal about Kayla's behavior. She tiptoed past students, always on alert that one might do something unexpected.

"The kid was so shell shocked that at one point the parents thought she might have some sort of disability as well."

"I wish someone had told me this at the beginning of the year."

"Sorry," my colleague replied. "I went through the same thing last year. Should have given you a heads up."

Returning to my classroom with a new understanding, as well as a plan to look up more about autism, I saw Kayla at the lunch tables with a woman who looked vaguely familiar. She wasn't on staff at the school. Perhaps I'd met her at back-to-school night.

"How was lunch?" I asked her. "Was that your mother?" Most middle school children would have died of embarrassment at the thought of a parent showing up to have lunch with them.

Kayla smiled. "Yeah. She has lunch with me sometimes, when she can get away."

"What a nice treat," I responded.

"It is nice, and calm and quiet. The only time Mom and I can talk."

Suddenly I understood. "Must be hard at home with your brothers."

"Well, my parents work really hard and they try to find ways to give me attention, too. But I understand."

At that moment, Kayla seemed to me so mature for her age. She didn't care what any students thought about having lunch with her mother at school. She stole moments wherever she could find them.

I would never completely understand what life was like for her at home. Some days were better than others; I could always tell by looking in Kayla's eyes.

In fact, she shuffled in the day of an important test looking like she could use a good night's sleep.

"Kayla?" I began, but she interrupted, nearly in tears.

"I couldn't… I didn't… the test…."

"Bad night?" I asked without need for elaboration.

Kayla simply nodded.

I wrote a note on the health slip. "Here. Why don't you go lie down in the nurse's office until next period. You can take the test tomorrow."

The girl looked confused, grateful, and hesitant all at once. "I... I don't want any special treatment."

"Kayla, we are all special. And everyone needs a little special treatment from time to time."

~D. B. Zane

Clinton

Personal relationships are the fertile soil from which all advancement,
all success, all achievement in real life grows.
~Ben Stein

I have spent the past nineteen years teaching a wide range of mathematical concepts and skills. In that time, I figure I have taught the quadratic equation approximately 100 times, the Pythagorean Theorem at least as many times and I have certainly lost count of how often I have worked out the slope of a line on a chalkboard. I would like to think I did a fantastic job each and every time I presented those concepts to my students. Ironically, I don't have a strong recall of any of those instances. What I do have are powerful memories of specific students who touched me in a very real and personal way.

Faces and names beyond count have come and gone in my classroom. I truly believe in the new three R's of education — Relationships, Relevance and Rigor. Building quality relationships with my students is the key to my success as a classroom teacher. Sometimes, those relationships forged in the classroom are the difference makers for a student. I have been fortunate to watch many of my past students go on and become successful and happy. Each one has enriched me in some way. However, the most significant lesson I have learned came from one very special student.

Clinton was a great example of the student every teacher loves to have in class. He was the only student at school who was awarded scholarships from three different school-based groups including the administration, the certified teaching staff and the classified support staff. Looking back into Clinton's past, one would see that he had traveled far. An immigrant from the Philippines at the age of twelve, Clinton and his family worked hard to become legal citizens. I had Clinton for two years in high school. His future looked bright and he had his whole life in front of him. Knowing his family had limited English skills, I helped Clinton with his scholarships and applications. All of us were very proud when he announced he wanted to study to be a teacher because we knew he would impact students' lives in the future.

Unfortunately, Clinton never made it to college. Just two days after he graduated from high school, Clinton was diagnosed with stage four colon cancer. It was a terminal diagnosis and the doctors held little hope that cancer treatments would do more than prolong the eventual outcome. We were heartbroken. Clinton would never attend college. He would never teach. He would never marry. He would never have children.

Clinton's teachers and friends responded in the only way we knew how. We extended a hand of help and comfort to Clinton and his family. Fundraising activities were organized at the school and many of us helped the family navigate the complex avenues of the health care system. "Pack the Track" became a huge celebration of Clinton's life and what he represented to his friends at school, teachers and other community members. In the end, over $8,000 was raised at this event. Bills were paid, paperwork filed and many an hour was spent by Clinton's side in the hospital as his body deteriorated.

Clinton passed on October 16th. Those of us who had worked with Clinton at school of course were deeply saddened by his death. But, Clinton's experience also awakened a realization for us that the true mission of our school is beyond the factual knowledge and skills we teach to students. We are helping youngsters learn to grow and mature into caring people — people who value relationships as the key to a good life. And the three R's??? If teachers don't constantly work to build positive relationships with students, then we are failing those very same students. Clinton proved to me that relationships are the key. A T-shirt was sold to help raise funds for Clinton's medical care. On the front of that shirt was the following: "Love is a verb." For all of us who knew and loved Clinton, we have come to act on that statement and we believe that it will make all the difference in the world.

~Cindy Couchman
2009 Kansas State Teacher of the Year
Math teacher, grades 9-12

Not in My Class

In all affairs it's a healthy thing now and then to hang a question mark on the things you have long taken for granted.
~Bertrand Russell

"Please don't put that child in my class!" It was partly a prayer to God and partly a silent request to the third-grade teachers. I knew that they would be deciding how to distribute next year's fourth graders among the three teachers, and I was sure I wouldn't be able to love Danny.

"How can a teacher be any good if she doesn't love her students?" I had wondered. I know that children have an uncanny sense about when they are really liked, and I didn't want to try to teach a student who could tell I didn't like him.

Every school-day afternoon for three years I had observed Danny. He turned up his nose at classmates, made faces at teachers when their heads were turned, and pouted when corrected. "I will not be able to put up with that," I fumed. "I cannot have him in my classroom."

During the following summer, as always, I asked God to put the students in my room who I would be able to teach effectively. As I pulled weeds or washed windows or relaxed on the porch with a glass of tea, I wondered who they would be. Would there be new students? Would I get the cute little girl with the big eyes? The funny little boy with the adorable smile? The good readers? The natural actors? Surely I wouldn't get Danny; God knew I could not take Danny.

When August rolled around and faculty reported for in-service, each team of teachers met to compile class lists for the next grade. Since we knew the children, we knew who would work well together, which parents would be good for parties and field trips, which students would require extra attention, and who could be counted on to be teachers' helpers. We strove to put together good, balanced classes, ever aware that someone else was doing the same for us.

When all the lists were complete, our principal went over them for final approval, and that was that. The fact that we didn't have any part in choosing our students was really a protection for us as well as the children; we could not be pressured into including a certain child on our roster, and no student was used in any kind of deal. We trusted one another and our principal, but awaited these lists with high anticipation, eager not only to see who we would spend the school year with, but also to get started making name tags for desks and preparing displays to welcome our new students.

When Mrs. Harmon brought my list, I held my breath as I scanned the names. Some were unfamiliar to me. That was always fun; I enjoyed introducing new students to the class and helping them feel at home in a new school. There were also some names that made me smile — children I had watched over the years and already loved. Then… I could hardly believe my eyes! The one child I knew I couldn't teach was right there on my list. Instantly his round face — complete with that smirky, self-satisfied smile — flashed on the screen of my mind. "I cannot love this child!" I thought. "Surely there is a mistake." All those prayers for the class that was right for me, and now this.

But I was a professional. I took a few moments to feel sorry for myself, and got back to work. I would make the name tags, finish my bulletin boards, plan interesting lessons, and hope for the best. I had a brand new room that year in a new building. I wasn't about to let this little setback ruin my excitement.

Then came the first week of school. In the midst of discussing summer reading, diagnosing math needs, and making final decisions for field trips, my Danny dilemma was temporarily forgotten. We were all learning to work together. On an outing to a pond for some hands-on study, students shared magnifying glasses, nets, and pencils. Walking along a path through the woods and sitting around picnic tables with our lunch gave me a chance to get to know each child better—including Danny. I was not surprised to find that he was intelligent, but didn't expect him to have such a good sense of humor. Maybe he grew up a lot over the summer, I mused.

When Danny got into a fight with Joe, one of our newcomers, I discovered something else. Like a good teacher, I heard both sides of the story before taking the boys to the principal. Although I could not condone fighting, it did seem to me that Danny made some convincing points. When I saw scratch marks on his neck from the tussle, I felt very protective toward him. Could it be that I was learning to actually like the boy?

And that's how it happened. Again and again I found myself drawn to Danny and noticing more and more of his good points. By the end of the year, I could honestly say, "I love that boy!" It was one of those little ironies that make teaching so interesting. Danny eventually, of course, moved on to fifth grade, and in a few years I moved over to high school English.

To my delight, one August day I looked at my new class rosters for senior English and recognized many of the names, one of them Danny's. It would be interesting, I thought, to see how he had turned out. I found that Danny still had a clever sense of humor and an impressive vocabulary that made his essays a delight to read. We had a good year together, built on the foundation from years earlier. During class one day, I realized that Danny, who appeared to be studiously following along in the text, was instead reading a paperback concealed in his English book. I took the book from him and dropped it into my desk drawer. Many weeks later, near the end of the year, Danny stayed after class.

"Can I have my book back?"

"Yes. I hope you understand why I took it."

"Yes, ma'am. I shouldn't have been reading it. I'm sorry for the way I acted."

"I appreciate your good attitude. You know I like you, Danny."

"Yes, ma'am. I know"

As he walked out the door, I remembered my frantic hopes that this boy would not be in my class, and I had to smile. He had grown into a dignified young man who would certainly make us proud — one of those unexpected delights that come over and over to those who teach.

~Sherry Poff

The Heart of Emily

Optimism is the foundation of courage.
~Nicholas Murray Butler

E mily did not look like other infants when she was born. She had a distinct appearance facially, standing out among the other babies in the hospital. She was born with Apert Syndrome, which affects physical appearance in several ways. I was first introduced to many of the facts of this rare syndrome when Emily's mother came in to speak to me a few days before first grade. I began to feel a bond with Emily before meeting her because of the window her mother had opened, allowing me to get a sense of this remarkable child. I was also absorbing the very essence of Emily's mother's strength and wisdom as we spoke.

Emily had experienced sixteen operations by the age of six. Typically, children with Apert Syndrome are born with webbed fingers and toes. One of the surgeries Emily endured was to separate her fingers so that she could hold pencils, utensils, and other objects, despite not having knuckles with which to bend her appendages. Her face did not grow proportionally because she was born without an opening in her skull. This young child was all too familiar with hospitals, their procedures, and personnel.

Now Emily found herself in a new school, a different classroom, with unfamiliar classmates and adults. This amazing child required an aide to assist her with physical and academic tasks, though our goal was to help her achieve as much independence as possible. She located her name on a desk just as the other children did. The students had to follow my directions to empty their school bags and place supplies where directed. I noticed a little girl's startled expression as she focused on Emily. Emily smiled at the child and the little girl smiled back. Such incidents recurred during the day with Emily repeatedly rewarding a different classmate with a smile, a little wave, or both. Never did a student in my class question me about this kind, sweet, happy child or treat her unkindly. In fact, my classroom was a place in which we were all enriched by Emily's presence.

The first time my teaching aide had to leave the room, a child jumped up and asked if she could help Emily. This girl stood over Emily, dotting words and sentences for her to trace, exactly as her aide did each morning. My classroom was set up in tables, four to five desks making a table. Emily and this classmate did not sit at the same table yet she knew exactly how to help. She even whispered words of encouragement and praise. When the assistant returned, the precious little helper quietly returned to her seat.

Another time, two of the more lively boys in our class jumped up shouting out that they would like to be Emily's helpers. I allowed it and witnessed incredible changes come over the two. Each calmed down, gently helping Emily until the return of the aide. One morning a little girl who often had trouble concentrating on her work because she was very interested in what everyone else was doing was the first to ask to help Emily. As always, I responded, "Of course!" This child assisted Emily by helping her to count and add. Their collaboration met with success. And the other child managed to get all her work done, without looking to see what others had written on their papers. A cute redheaded girl often stared into space rarely completing required tasks. Despite this fact, this smart-as-a-whip, freckle-faced child was usually right on the mark when answering questions. Then one day she volunteered to help Emily. The girls hugged each other at the completion of the task, having remained focused the entire time.

During parent conferences I learned what some of the children shared with their parents. A very advanced first-grader who sat next to Emily spoke of her at home. His dad told me that his son explained that it was difficult for others to understand her but that he could understand everything she said. The parents did not know that Emily was special until they met her at a school function. Another parent told me that her son expressed that Emily was the prettiest girl in the class. A single dad told me his son repeatedly asked to have a play date with her. And he did! Indeed, many of the children had play dates with Emily.

Then came that day in March when Emily's mom told me she was to have facial surgery. Our blond sunshine would be out of school from the end of April through the remainder of the school year. In addition to being extremely apprehensive for Emily, I was deeply concerned about the other students. I had to explain her absence and clarified that Emily needed an operation on her face to help her feel more comfortable when speaking and sleeping. I was asked many logical questions. "Did it hurt?" "Can she speak?" "Will she come back?"

Emily's hospital conduct further illustrated her exceptional bravery. Her parents related how she walked into the hospital wheeling her pink carry-on filled with special photographs, letters, stuffed animals, and toys. She told her father, "I do not want you to carry me into the operating room." She explained to the attending nurse that she did not want any medicine and didn't want to wear the blue operating room cap or change into hospital clothes. She was not made to do any of those things while awake. Emily walked into the operating room for the seventeenth time on her own two feet! Her dad told me how he felt humbled when he saw the severe problems of other children in that hospital.

It was inevitable that some of the children would see Emily after her operation, before she came to school for a visit. I had to explain that she was wearing something that looked like a catcher's mask on her face. We discussed the casts one of the boys had on his legs following surgery during this same school year. They remembered that his legs needed to be protected and realized Emily's face needed protection as well. The mask was purple and Emily's doctors and family referred to it as Purple. Some of the children viewed Emily in her mom's car picking up her brother from school. Some visited her at home. Each child who saw her came to school elated and greeted the class by shouting, "I saw Emily!" My concerns for her classmates were allayed as not one child who had seen her mentioned Purple. And yes, my first-graders had the ability to perceive the heart of Emily and I feel certain that she will continue to use her remarkable strength of character to surmount the struggles she has yet to face.

~Stephanie Scharaga Winnick

Chapter 8

Teacher Tales

The Teacher Who Changed My Life

A teacher's purpose is not to create students in his own image, but to develop students who can create their own image.

~Author Unknown

Divine Intervention

One looks back with appreciation to the brilliant teachers,
but with gratitude to those who touched our human feelings.
The curriculum is so much necessary material, but warmth
is the vital element for the growing plant and for the soul of the child.
~Carl Jung

So many times I've been asked the notorious educator question, "Why do you teach?" Sometimes the answer is just purely simple and easy to answer, but when I scrutinize the multitude of reasons why I teach, the answer is much more complicated than meets the eye. One thing that usually comes immediately to my mind is that I need to teach! In all honesty, teaching is in many ways one of the largest defining facets of who I am as a person. I'm complete, genuinely happy and irrevocably addicted to watching my students grow as citizens, meet challenges and achieve success on a daily basis.

My journey of becoming a teacher began when I was in fourth grade....

In the fall of 1980, I was moving for the eighth time and I was only nine years old. Far worse than that, my father had recently passed away from lung cancer in late spring and my maternal grandparents had passed away as well that summer. To make things a bit more challenging, my mother was divorcing her second husband during all of this, and we were moving in with her new boyfriend who ended up being my second stepfather. My emotional state was quite fragile; I was extremely sad and had some anxiety about going to yet another new school.

By what I like to now call divine intervention, I was placed in Mrs. Dutton's classroom. This incredible woman recognized that at this crucial point in my life, my soul needed nurturing as much as my intellect, if not more, and she embraced this challenge. Daily, she provided me with encouraging words and praise, which ultimately made me want to believe in myself. Her enthusiasm for teaching, her compassion towards her students, and her ability to find what it was that made us individually shine was what made me want to teach. More than anything, I wanted to be just like my favorite teacher. By high school, my flame for teaching still burned brightly, as I continued on the path towards becoming an elementary teacher.

Throughout my teaching journey, Mrs. Dutton remained a guiding presence in my life. She attended my high school and college graduation parties as well as my wedding. Our relationship continued to grow even deeper when I was hired as a fifth grade teacher in the same school where she was working, the school where she first came into my life in fourth grade, Congin Elementary School. (The same school I still teach at, by the way.) As a beginning teacher she quickly put me under her wing and continued to nurture me as my mentor. Mrs. Roberta Dutton-Morrill has in fact, never left my side.

Our connection runs so deep, that when I was named a nominee for Maine's Teacher of the Year, my hometown newspaper, the *American Journal*, ran a story about me. Mrs. Dutton did not know this was happening at the time, as she was living at her summer home and had to go pick up her mail from the post office on the particular day the story was released. Like a true-blue Westbrook citizen, she still had the *AJ* forwarded to her home in Belgrade Lakes. That very day, as Mrs. Dutton went in to get her mail, a postal clerk asked her what she did as a profession before retiring. Mrs. Dutton told the clerk about her career as a teacher, and the clerk said something to the effect that she, Mrs. Dutton, must have touched many of her students' lives. My former teacher then went on to tell the clerk about this one little girl she had back in the early 1980s, a girl who had just lost her dad and was going through a tough situation, and ended her story with how that little girl grew up to become a teacher who stayed in touch with her on a regular basis. During that whole conversation with the clerk, Mrs. Dutton held in her hands that day's mail.

Upon returning home she started to browse her mail and there on the front page was the article about that little girl, the former student she so loved, me. When she started to read the article she was flabbergasted to see a large portion was dedicated to her; it went on to say how her influence had made a world of difference to me and how I value the whole child due to her guidance. Later that night my phone rang. You can imagine how thrilled I was to hear Mrs. Dutton's voice, the voice of an angel. As she told me the story about what had happened at the post office earlier that day, my body was encased in goose bumps from head to toe. That is when she also told me about how she always felt that I had come into her life not by chance, but rather by divine intervention; this statement brought me to tears.

Just this past fall, I was presented the extraordinary privilege of being named Maine's 2009 Teacher of the Year. Can you guess who was in the audience at the surprise assembly? When it came time to give my speech, all I could think to say was how so many times during my fifteen years as a teacher, I would mention to my students that I only wished I could be half of the teacher that Mrs. Dutton was to me. Every year I would talk about her, and my students all knew who my favorite teacher was without a doubt, by name. At that surprise assembly, I was given an opportunity to share with my students, colleagues, parents, family and community what this amazing woman meant to me and how she had made a profound difference in my life.

More importantly, as Maine's Teacher of the Year, I got to honor the many unsung heroes, our teachers! Mrs. Dutton never got an award such as this one; however, she did get something better than that—she will forever live in her students' hearts as someone who had compassion, respect, and an abundance of love for her students.

In her presence we all shined, and if you ask me, that is what teaching is all about.

Why do I teach? I teach, because it is my passion and it feeds my soul.

~Gloria L. Noyes
2009 Maine State Teacher of the Year
Elementary teacher, grade 5

It's a Great Day to Be Alive!

May you live life every day of your life.
~Jonathan Swift

I stink at math. I really stink at it. Early in life, this lack of skill laid the groundwork for a strong dislike toward the subject and an ongoing effort to avoid it at all costs. So how is it that the most influential person in all of my educational career was my high school math teacher?

As a freshman in high school I was far from a math teacher's dream student. My mind was full of things that high school girls tend to focus on: boys, boys, and well… boys. I immersed myself in my social life, and my classes often took a back seat to other priorities.

I walked into Mr. A's classroom a chatty and bubbly fourteen-year-old girl. My primary focus was on picking a good seat, surrounded by my friends and with easy access to the door. From day one, I was very vocal about having a distain for math and I was even more vocal about my constant confusion. It was not uncommon for me to give up midway through an assignment, or zone out during a lesson because I didn't understand it. It wasn't that I didn't want to do well, but simply that I didn't think I was capable of doing well. "I can't," became my permanent state of mind in all things math related.

However, I was soon to learn that "I can't" was not an option in Mr. A's class.

On the first day of class, Mr. A greeted us with his arms extended as he proclaimed, "Welcome! Smile! It's a great day to be alive!" That phrase, which I would hear frequently over the course of the next four years, became an ever-present source of comfort and familiarity. From that moment forward, it was clear that Mr. A had a true passion not only for math, but for teaching. His positive and uplifting attitude never faltered. If Mr. A ever experienced the bad days of normal life, he never showed it. While some teachers forcefully told us not to cross them, they were "just having a bad day," Mr. A greeted us with that same enthusiasm each and every day.

This welcoming and uplifting personality mirrored Mr. A's teaching methods. Not only were his methods engaging, but his positive attitude was contagious. He encouraged each student, from the valedictorian to the self-proclaimed "I can't" student.

I found myself looking forward to math class, despite the fact that I still despised the subject itself. There was just something about being in Mr. A's presence that made me feel good, as if I had the potential to succeed. However, my story is not one of overnight success. I did not become a straight-A math student, and I continued to struggle with several concepts. In fact, it was in Mr. A's class that I received my first failing test grade, and I can still remember my eyes filling with tears as I stared at the 63 in bold red letters. I had failed. And more importantly, I had failed Mr. A.

This 63 became a defining moment in my math career. I could have given up and used the score as proof to Mr. A and to myself that I was not meant to do well in math. Similarly, Mr. A could have given up on me. But instead, he did the opposite. He became even more determined to help me with my math, and even more importantly, to help me see my potential.

As the year progressed, my determination to succeed grew. I spent an increasing amount of time on my homework, and I met with Mr. A weekly. My classmates began to do the same, and it became "cool" to have lunch with Mr. A. We didn't know it at the time, but he was transforming our attitudes. My hard work began to pay off and my grades slowly began to climb. There were road bumps, of course. Low grades and difficult concepts threatened to deter me, and sometimes succeeded in bringing me down. But a frown on my face almost always resulted in a bellowing, "Kate, smile! It's a great day to be alive!"

The year came to an end, and my classmates and I were surprised to find ourselves sad to move on from ninth grade math. We had found a home for ourselves in Mr. A's class, a comfortable learning environment which we feared would be impossible to replicate in a different teacher's classroom. And it was. Tenth grade proved to be a struggle: a new math teacher, new topics, and a sense of solitude. Mr. A's engaging lessons were replaced with hours of busy work, and my grades reflected this lack of personal attention. I longed to be back in Mr. A's class, and I was overjoyed to find myself there again the following year.

My junior and senior years were marked with many milestones: prom, the SATs, graduation. But perhaps the most important milestones were the accomplishments that took place back in Mr A's class. A's on the math section of my report card, a nearly perfect score on my math SAT, and a feeling of inner pride that I had never before experienced.

High school is undoubtedly a time of growth, both physically and emotionally, as well as academically and socially. I can honestly say that I experienced much of this growth sitting in my second row seat, just behind the door, in Mr. A's classroom. Today, when the work is piled up on my desk and I feel my mind beginning to think "I can't," I hear a deep voice in the back of my mind reminding me to take a deep breath and remember: it's a great day to be alive.

~Kate Lynn Mishara

The Gift of Self-Esteem

To free us from the expectations of others, to give us back to ourselves — there lies the great, singular power of self-respect.
~Joan Didion

I remember the day. I was in Senior English, two weeks away from high school graduation. I lived two lives: one as an underachiever in the classroom and the other as the esteemed at-home tutor who helped my younger brother overcome the obstacles of learning with Attention Deficit Disorder. I wrote really bad raps to help him memorize those mundane history facts he would be required to regurgitate on a test. I used a picture of a hamburger to teach him the layers of writing an essay. I filmed plays in which I also took a role, hoping he would feel a sense of personal achievement. In short, I was more challenged and motivated by tutoring my brother than I was by my own studies or any teacher in school. My parents knew me as creative and talented but my teachers only knew me as a classic underachiever.

The epiphany came that day in Senior English. We had finished our work early, and bursting with my news, I walked up to my teacher's desk and stood watching her enter grades in her grade book. I waited for an acknowledgement. Getting none, I started, "I know what I want to do."

She didn't look up, but kept entering final grades. "Yes, Leanne, what is it you want to do?

"I want to teach!" I exclaimed, full of pride and purpose. Her pen came to a dead halt as she slowly removed her eyeglasses and looked up at me standing eagerly over her desk. She saw a 2.3 GPA standing in front of her with dreams that seemed to contradict that reality. She saw a shy, aimless young lady who seemed more interested in social aspirations than anything academic. She saw failure and indifference to success.

"Really," she retorted. It was not a question, but a comment. I nodded, waiting anxiously for her confirmation and encouragement. It didn't come. Instead, she advised, "You might want to rethink that decision because I'm just not sure you are college material." I digested that for a moment, waiting for anything else she might add, but nothing came. She stared at me as if I was supposed to digest those words of wisdom thoughtfully, so I sat back down, allowing her perception of me to define my potential and future.

That day I told my parents I would not be going to college. Luckily, my parents told me differently. Four years later, I graduated from one of the top three schools in education within the United States, at the time, and received a double major in Secondary English Education and Communications and Theater Arts.

I still remember that high school teacher and the effect she had on my self-esteem. With that personal experience, my mission statement is squarely mounted on my classroom door that, among other goals, highlights my purpose of "raising my students' self-esteem through personal achievement." Research and education journals agree with this ambitious goal, but ultimately the proof came for me on the day I was called to the principal's office. "Shut the door," she commanded. In my career, that sentence has never proved to have a positive outcome. Having taught at-risk students for several years, I wasn't sure if I was going to hear about some tragedy involving a student, or some personal reprimand; either way, I knew it was not going to be good news.

She began with an unexpected question. "Do you remember when you had some things stolen from your classroom a few years ago?" I did remember reporting several items missing from my closet. Important things like Little Debbie Swiss Cake Rolls, oatmeal cookies, moon pies, and Fruit Roll-Ups. Oh yes, and those caramels with the white crème in them that tastes like Christmas. These "important" things in my closet served as sanity snacks for my own children when the bus from the elementary and primary school dropped them off at the high school where I worked. My girls would go straight to the closet, get a snack, and start their homework. We had a routine that allowed me to get some work done before heading home for the day.

I remembered one day leaving my room for a few minutes during my planning period to run errands around campus, and when I came back all of the freshly stocked goodies were gone, boxes and all. I had reported the theft to the resource officer, but I had never heard any more about it. "Yes," I said, confused and curious. "I remember. Why?"

"Well, I am only telling you this now because the student has graduated, and I thought you should know the impact you are having on the lives of your students." She told me who had stolen those items—a boy in my English class who had little to no support at home, but had the heart of a champion and potential that I wanted him to see through my eyes. "Well," she continued, "we rolled back the tapes to see who had entered your room around the timeframe in question, and we saw him. We called him to the office, and he admitted it right away. When the school officer asked him if he had anything else he wanted to say, he said, 'I have one request. Please don't tell Ms. Maule because she's the only one who believes in me.'"

I sat there in her office welling up with tears at this story of a young man who was one of my biggest fans, showed such great potential, and was the "Rock" for me when I was absent, helping to keep others on task. He had me for the first time in three rounds of freshman English. I remember the day I saw him graduate and took my picture with him under the lights on the football field.

"I wanted you to know the truth, and I hope you understand why I waited to tell you for so long," she continued.

"Thank you, Mrs. Kellogg. Thank you," I said, leaving her office with the validation I so desperately wished I had from my Senior English teacher years before.

Yes, I teach to enhance student learning. Ultimately, however, I want my students to experience empowerment and self-esteem from personal achievement. When my seniors graduate, I share a quote from Henry David Thoreau: "Most men lead lives of quiet desperation and go to the grave with the song still in them." I challenge them to NOT be "most" men. I toast them as they continue their journey to find their heart's song as I have found mine. I tell them, "No money in the world can buy the feeling of waking up every day and doing a job you love that uses your talents in a challenging way. Find it and sing it." I could not wish a more precious gift for them than this.

~Leanne Maule-Sims
2009 Georgia State Teacher of the Year
English, British Literature teacher, grade 12

Reprinted by permission of
Patrick Hardin ©1988

Words of Wisdom

Put your future in good hands — your own.
~Author Unknown

As I walked into the elementary school, looking down at my new black Mary Jane shoes, my stomach turned from the biscuit I had just eaten an hour earlier. My mother held my hand (which was comforting but embarrassing seeing I was in fifth grade) as we made our way to Mrs. Blackstone's class. I was the new kid in town, enrolling in January which made it even worse. Desks had been assigned, rules established, friendships made and seats in the cafeteria taken. I wanted to be anywhere in the world but Fountain Inn Elementary School. I stood at Mrs. Blackstone's door. It was made of solid wood with a tiny glass window at the very top. I couldn't see in, but my mother could.

"Oh, Amanda, they look so nice! It's a big classroom. Ready to go in?"

The decorated door was full of pictures of the kids just on the other side.

"Wait," I pleaded. "Let's look at these first," pointing at the snapshots staring back at me.

My mom, always the optimist, "She's cute, I bet she'd make a good friend!"

Her encouraging words fell on deaf ears. I knew I only had seconds to spare if I was going to make a run for it. Before I attempted the great escape, the wooden door abruptly opened to the singsong voice of Mrs. Blackstone, my new fifth grade teacher.

"We've been waiting on you!" she said in an unusually high voice. With a wink and a smile my mom tiptoed away and I was left standing center stage in front of an unimpressed group of students.

Over the next few days, Mrs. Blackstone made it her mission to find me a new best friend, enroll me in choir and give me the all-important dream job of hall monitor. During history lessons, when I slumped into my desk because I didn't want to speak in front of the class (even when I knew the answer) she'd not only call on me but have me stand up to address my peers. She laughed at my awkwardness, like when I wouldn't get in line to sharpen my pencil, even when my lead was broken, for fear of being embarrassed. Her silliness made me smile and eventually feel much more at ease in my new surroundings.

One spring afternoon, when the bell rang at 2:30 for children to meet their parents in the courtyard, Mrs. Blackstone asked me to stay after class.

"I'd like to speak with you, Amanda."

My mind raced. Had I made a bad grade? Had I unintentionally hurt someone's feelings?

"Are you enjoying your new school?"

She sat comfortably behind her desk, surrounded by pictures of her former students.

"I want to tell you something, between you and me, not to be shared with anyone else."

"Okay." My throat all of a sudden felt very dry.

With her eyebrows raised she said, "I see something special in you. The way you interact with others, the kindness that you show — I think you have great potential to be something very important."

I listened intently, hanging on every word.

"I've been a teacher for over twenty-five years, I can see it. But you must believe it yourself. Confidence — Compassion — Common Sense. That's what is important. Remember that and you'll go far."

She then hugged me and said, "See you tomorrow."

Her singsong voice was music to my ears that day. I walked out of her class, not staring at my Mary Jane shoes, but looking straight ahead with my head held high. My teacher saw something special in me!

As an adult now, I recall those words often when I need them most. I later learned Mrs. Blackstone had that afternoon conversation with many of her students. I was blessed to have been one of them.

Mrs. Blackstone has gone on to impact and educate many lawyers, doctors, police officers, accountants, mothers, and like myself, teachers.

Not long ago, in the busyness of a spring afternoon, I sat down with a quiet, timid, ten-year-old. I looked into her eyes and repeated those words I'll never forget, "I think you have great potential. You must believe in yourself. Confidence — Compassion — Common Sense. Remember that and you'll go far."

~Amanda Dodson

A Teacher's Influence

The mediocre teacher tells. The good teacher explains.
The superior teacher demonstrates. The great teacher inspires.
~William Arthur Ward

My experiences this past year as Nebraska State Teacher of the Year have prompted me to give much thought to why I became a teacher. My parents were my greatest supporters when I decided I wanted to become a teacher as a senior in high school. There were also a few teachers who encouraged me without even knowing it. I decided to locate Mr. Eloe, my junior high Industrial Arts teacher, to let him know what his teaching and his class meant to me.

I located Mr. Eloe in another state and left him a message. One Sunday evening a few weeks later, I answered the phone and immediately recognized a voice that I had not heard in over forty years. Mr. Eloe began with, "Hello Dan, how should I know you?" I explained to him who I was and told him he had taught me.

Mr. Eloe had instructed us in forming a company, guided us in coming up with a product (The Doll Fly), helped us to learn how to advertise, assisted us in purchasing our shares of stock, constructed an assembly line, and guided us in selling our products. Mr. Eloe told me that he had attended a summer workshop entitled "Innovative Approaches to Teaching Industrial Arts" and tried it out on us that school year. I still had three of my doll flies; however, they were too valuable to use fishing. I told Mr. Eloe that the doll fly unit was instrumental in leading me to a thirty-five year teaching career.

In reflecting, I can easily remember those students who I know I had an impact on throughout my teaching career, but now I think of all those students that I maybe had an impact on without realizing it. I only hope that I have been able to instill a passion for industrial technology education and for learning as was done for me by Mr. Eloe, even though he didn't remember me.

One student who I know I helped, and whose name I still remember, was Bob. In the summer of 1976, I took a teaching job in a high school system with an enrollment of close to 1,000 students. I had taught just one year prior to this in a high school of approximately 150 students. So being a little anxious, I talked to some of the veteran teachers in my department about my class rosters. They looked at my student lists and when they arrived at Bob's name there was a huge pause. Bob had gotten into serious trouble at the junior high school.

Throughout the first quarter in our class, I covered the various machines used in a woodworking shop by giving lectures, machine demonstrations, and safety tests to determine who would be allowed to use the machines. Because of the modular schedule our school was using, seven days would pass between my lecture and the machine safety test. Bob received scores in the teens on the first couple of tests. As I went over the tests in the class, I could see anger and disappointment building in Bob because of another failing grade. He wanted to use the machines and knew these tests were keeping him away from what he had enrolled in the class to do.

I called Bob in after class one day to talk to him about his low scores and to see what we could do together to improve his testing. I learned he had some definite chips on his shoulder because of earlier failures in his education. I tried reviewing with Bob individually before the next test, but he received the same results. So, Bob and I had another talk about giving me his best effort. I asked Bob what I could do to help. Bob replied, "Nothing." For a freshman, Bob was tall and physically developed beyond his age, but that day I learned Bob had trouble even reading a comic book.

I was finally able to talk Bob into going down to the reading teacher with me so the three of us could develop a plan to help him with his work. For the next machine test, Bob agreed to go to the reading teacher's room so she could read the test questions and record his responses. Bob scored an 85% on most tests after this and he was able to do this by just listening, because he would rarely take notes.

Bob and I developed a good working relationship and I seldom saw his angry side. Bob completed the required project and found a passion for using the woodworking lathe. On the lathe, he was able to turn his wood into bowls and took pride in making them for his mom, sisters, and aunts.

I stopped worrying about keeping my eye on Bob during lab. My only problem was to get him out of the woodworking shop and on to his next class. He preferred to keep working in the woods lab. One day Bob came into class to find me upset because someone had lost one of my lathe parts, which made it inoperable. Bob looked at me and without hesitation said, "Mr. McCarthy I know where your part went. I am not a stool pigeon and I won't tell you who threw your part out the window, but your part is out there in the snow bank."

I asked, "Bob, would you mind going out to get it for me?" He went right out and found the part and returned it to me.

I know that Bob has not always had an easy life since he left high school. Recently, I ran into Bob at a convenience store. It has now been some thirty years since Bob was in my class. He looked at me and said, "You don't know who I am, do you?"

I said, "Sure I do. How are you doing, Bob? It has been a long time since I have seen you, so what have you been up to?" The biggest smile came across his face when he realized that I remembered him. We continued catching up with what each of us had been doing. I learned many of the bowls he had turned were still being cherished and used by his relatives today. Bob went on to express how amazed he was that I was still teaching. It was so good to learn he had his life on track and had a good position with a local concrete contractor.

Thanks to Bob, I learned very early in my teaching career that not all teachers relate the same to all students and not all students relate the same to all teachers. Without knowing it, Bob taught me that it is important to allow students the opportunity to show whether they can or cannot be trusted. With Bob's help, I learned to form my opinions about my students based on their behavior and performance within my classroom rather than by listening to opinions of others based on their experiences and perceptions.

~Dan McCarthy
2009 Nebraska State Teacher of the Year
Industrial Technology teacher, grades 9-12

71

A Lifelong Friendship

A master can tell you what he expects of you. A teacher...
awakens your own expectations.
~Patricia Neal

I met Mrs. Sase my senior year in high school. I was struggling greatly in her math class. On top of having always struggled with math, I was dealing with the fears and anxieties that come with being a foster youth and worrying deeply about the future that lay in store for me. I had been living with foster parents, and our agreement was that after graduation I was to move out and begin my life as an adult, at seventeen.

The burden of this anxiety resulted in a lack of motivation in school. Most teachers assumed I had senioritis or just didn't care. Mrs. Sase, however, took a closer look. I will never forget the first time she walked over to my desk and handed me a little folded note. It read, "Are you okay?"

I was shocked by her genuine care and interest in my wellbeing. Not only was she intuitive and sensitive enough to notice my reserve, she took the time to personally make a difference. She listened as I shared my most hidden fears about my past and the uncertain future that was closing in on me. She listened when others seemed to be too busy to show concern or too fearful to try. She agreed to write my letter of recommendation when I decided to apply for the Guardian Scholars program; a comprehensive program committed to supporting ambitious, college-bound students exiting the foster care system.

Her letter was meticulously thought-out and meaningful, even with the high demand of students who wanted her to be the one teacher to write their letters of recommendation. It is something I will always treasure.

I found new ambition through Mrs. Sase's support and devotion to my academic and personal success. If I was sick and had to miss school, I would still go to school for the one hour of Mrs. Sase's math class. Not only did my grades dramatically improve, so did my confidence.

There is something very powerful in feeling that you have someone who truly cares for you and deeply believes in you. Mrs. Sase gave me the support I needed to overcome the obstacles in my life. Because of her personal influence and encouragement, I found faith in myself and came to believe that I could achieve academic and personal success. I believe that the most healing and important thing in a mentoring/helping relationship is consistency. She has not missed one hard day, one tear, one birthday or one celebration. She is truly a beautiful teacher, friend and mentor.

I owe a great deal of my success to Mrs. Sase, not only for the profound and lasting impact she had on my life in high school, but also for her continued support after graduation. The most amazing thing about Mrs. Sase is that I am just one of an army of students who would confess that Mrs. Sase changed their lives as well. Her entire classroom is filled with memorabilia and letters of utmost gratitude for her and the life-changing impact she has had on so many students.

While getting to know Mrs. Sase my senior year in high school, I learned that she had recently lost both her parents to cancer. She had moved home to Irvine to care for them and teach at Woodbridge High School. When I look back on the generosity and love she gave so freely to me, it's overwhelming to know that my first day meeting her was also her first day back to school after the loss of two of the greatest and most important people in her life.

I received an e-mail my senior year in college from a friend informing me of the Carlston Family Foundation, a foundation that recognizes teachers nominated by former students who credit their success in high school, college and beyond to one special educator who made a difference. The teacher that is chosen is given the title "Outstanding Teacher of the Year" and receives a $15,000 check from the Carlston Family Foundation. The school where this teacher teaches also receives a $5,000 prize.

I immediately felt compelled to write. In fact, it was hard to limit myself in all that I wanted to share. I wanted every reader to truly understand how important Mrs. Sase is. I guess it wasn't hard to see. She was chosen and received the award with awe and humility. The award ceremony is one of the greatest memories I have. I am so thankful that I was able to give back to someone who has shown me that there are people in this world who are genuinely good, who care for others and believe that each and every person is smart, strong, and fully capable of being successful and are worthwhile.

By some miracle, I was in Mrs. Sase's math class. The identifying term "math teacher" robs her of all the incredible titles this woman possesses. Mrs. Sase is an angel who spreads her wings so far and wide that all who find themselves in her path feel forever protected, believed in, and cared for. She's so much more than a teacher. She's a friend and a big sister. The Orange County Register quoted Mrs. Sase in an interview after she received the Carlston Family Foundation award saying, "the kids are my heartbeat." She is mine.

~Jayde Rossi

72

Not So Accidental

Out of this nettle, danger, we pluck this flower, safety.
~William Shakespeare

I was sixteen and life could not have been more difficult. My cousin had admitted to the entire family one year ago, on Thanksgiving, of course, that she was a lesbian. My strict Irish Catholic family had a few issues with that, and had decided to disown her. Rather than jumping on the bandwagon, I decided that what she did with her life was her choice, and that I would not let that affect the way I felt about her. After all, she was my cousin.

Now, one whole year later, it was Thanksgiving again, and after a year of not speaking to me because of my choice to love my cousin unconditionally, my family had invited me to Thanksgiving dinner!

I had mixed feelings about whether or not I should attend the bash. After all, it had been a whole year since they had spoken to me. It seemed almost too good to be true. I remember sitting in science class, when Ms. F, as I will call her, waved a beaker in my face and asked me what planet I had been on for the last few minutes. I jumped quickly back into reality and attempted to take notes again, with little success. Thanksgiving break started the next day.

After class, as I drifted towards the door, a figure entered my path. It was Ms. F. I feared she would chastise me for my inattentive state in her class, but she did just the opposite. She hugged me.

As a junior in high school, the last thing you want from a teacher is a hug. Of course, I resisted. Then, she said the most important thing of all: "I understand. I've been there."

I was wondering what on earth she was talking about. Somehow, though, she knew about all of my family's soap-opera-like drama. She sat me down and we talked for the entirety of her planning period about the angst that I was feeling about going to dinner. I remember telling her how afraid I was of what would happen. Then, she said the oddest thing.

"No matter what happens, don't drive."

Of all the strange things to say after I had poured my heart out, that was all she managed to come up with? I was confused, to say the least. She looked at the puzzled expression on my face and told me that I'd understand when it came to be time.

So, with this puzzling thought in mind, I embarked on one of the longest journeys of my childhood, the trip to Thanksgiving dinner. I drove to my grandparents' house, not even thinking twice.

Dinner, I must say, went horribly. After bowing our heads to say grace, my family declared that I was a lesbian. After I got over the initial shock of having my sexual orientation declared for me (incorrectly at that), I bolted out, car keys in hand. Somehow, though, through the bitter cold and the streaming tears, I remembered something. The raspy voice of my wacky science teacher rang loud and clear inside my mind: "Don't drive."

For some reason, which I still do not know to this day, I chose to listen. I ran a long way, but I did not drive. My cold, tired body didn't appreciate it that day, but later I understood.

A few months after Thanksgiving, I called my cousin. Though the phone rang and rang, I got no answer. After a few days of no answers, I called my brother and asked what had gotten into my cousin.

"You don't know?" he gasped.

"Know what?"

"Madeline's…" He couldn't finish.

"She's what?" was all I could manage. I thought she had run away again.

"She's gone."

My cousin had gotten into an argument after she called her mother to try to work things out and had gotten into a car accident. She and her friend had been crushed below a tractor trailer. She had chosen to drive.

All of a sudden, Ms. F's advice made sense. I began to wonder if I would have met the same fate had I chosen to drive.

I never got a chance to thank Ms. F for her advice. By the time school had begun again the next year, she was gone. However, as I enter my first year of teaching in a classroom full of tough, urban kids with bigger problems than I could ever begin to understand, I remember Ms. F's caring advice. I try to incorporate her wisdom and caring nature into all that I do. I hope that someday I can pay her back by passing the torch on to another confused student.

~Brooke M. Businsky

The Dunce Row

Good teachers are costly, but bad teachers cost more.
~Bob Talbert

"Take out your math homework," Sister Mary commanded from the front of the room.

There was a rustle of papers and a fumbling of books as the class of second graders rushed to comply. This was Catholic school in the early 1960s, and when you received an order, you obeyed. Sister Mary ran a tight ship. Fifty students in a class could be a recipe for disaster. Not in her class. Students followed the rules or else.

To a seven-year-old, Sister Mary was an imposing figure. In those days, nuns still wore the traditional habit: a long black polyester dress belted at the waist; jet black stockings; black leather shoes that reminded me of the ones the Pilgrims wore except without the buckles; and a rosary that hung from her belt and nearly touched the floor. The beads of the rosary were the size of dark brown marbles. The cross was made from wood, painted black and was roughly as large as a man's fist. Sister liked to twirl the rosary. The cross made large circles in the air as she patrolled up and down the seven rows of neatly arranged desks.

I was nervously flipping through my math book searching for my homework when this sinking feeling of despair began to spread over me like floodwaters spilling over the banks of a river. My panic started growing. Flip and search... page after page... no matter how many times I looked, my homework wasn't there. I was in shock. I couldn't believe it. No one, I mean no one, neglected homework. It just wasn't tolerated. As the seconds ticked by, my brain was racing through all kinds of horrible scenarios. My hands were shaking as I glanced around. Every desk had a math paper on it except mine.

From the front of the room, Sister Mary surveyed her domain with the eyes of an eagle. Her piercing gaze settled on my paper-less desk, and she immediately approached. My eyes traveled up the length of her long black habit until I met her cold stare. Her chunky face, encased in the white cardboard of her headpiece, revealed an expression of pure annoyance.

"Where is your homework?" she asked sternly.

"I forgot it at home," I whispered softly.

She fingered her rosary, examining me up and down as she pondered my fate.

"Class, it seems Miss Porzio has forgotten her homework. Who can tell me what the punishment is for not having your homework?"

I knew then how prisoners felt while they were waiting for the judge to sentence them. No one raised his or her hand. They didn't have to. We all knew perfectly well what the punishment was. I was to be banished to the dunce row.

The dunce row was a line of five empty desks snuggled against the right wall of the classroom. The first desk in the row bore the sign that labeled it the dunce row. During the first week of school, we had a lesson on the uses for this row. We had been instructed that dunce meant stupid. That row was reserved for stupid people. Stupid people who couldn't follow the school rules, and stupid people who forgot to bring in their homework.

Sister Mary then spoke the words we all knew were coming, "Pick up your books and go sit in the dunce row."

Slowly, I rose from my seat. I gathered up my belongings, hung my head, and with lead feet, trudged over to take the first desk in the row. I was sentenced to remain there for the entire week. As I sat down, shame and humiliation swirled around inside me. My eyes watered, and a tear threatened to trickle down my cheek. Somehow,

I managed to keep from crying. The last thing I needed was to be labeled a crybaby. Being branded a dunce was bad enough.

That event happened nearly fifty years ago, yet the memory is still painfully vivid. It serves as a constant reminder of how powerful the words and actions of a teacher can be. Words can hurt; actions can cause humiliation. When my students move on, I want them to remember a teacher who established a classroom as a community of learners where interactions were based on mutual respect, cooperation and dignity. Sister Mary taught me that, because in second grade I was banished to the dunce row.

~Deb Fogg
2009 New Hampshire State Teacher of the Year
Language Arts teacher, grade 7

Chapter
9

Teacher Tales

Tough Kids

*We expect teachers to handle teenage pregnancy, substance abuse,
and the failings of the family.
Then we expect them to educate our children.*

~John Sculley

Unforgettable

If a doctor, lawyer, or dentist had 40 people in his office at one time, all of whom had different needs, and some of whom didn't want to be there and were causing trouble, and the doctor, lawyer, or dentist, without assistance, had to treat them all with professional excellence for nine months, then he might have some conception of the classroom teacher's job.
~Donald D. Quinn

In my second year of teaching eighth grade I had a student named Gabrielle whom I will never forget. Although she was placed in a lower level class (students were tracked at this time) she had the potential to excel—if only she would behave for me! Gabrielle was rude, obnoxious, and disruptive. She didn't do any homework and rarely completed her classroom work. She was failing the eighth grade. Most of the other teachers on my team had already given up on her and routinely sent her to the dean's office rather than deal with her disruptive behavior. But I was determined to find a way to win her over.

I tried every strategy I had in my bag of tricks. Everything either failed or backfired! Eventually I resorted to keeping her after school. In my detention, I sit and talk with my students, hoping to build a relationship rather than tearing one down. Gabrielle and I talked for over an hour and she told me a little bit about her life. She cared for her three younger siblings and her cousins and lived with an aunt. Her mother had been murdered when she was only seven years old. (I would later learn from a guidance counselor that her father had stabbed her mother to death in front of her and a younger sister.) She told me she was late to school every day because she had to drop off her siblings and cousins at the elementary school every morning. She told me she made them breakfast every morning and dinner every evening while her aunt worked. She told me she made sure they had all showered before they went to bed.

Gabrielle was the caregiver in her home; she was "the mom" to her younger siblings and cousins! What I came to understand was the only place she could act her age was at school—and that was where she acted out because it was the only place in her life where anyone would pay attention to her! She didn't care what kind of attention she got—good or bad—she just wanted someone to pay attention to her.

After our conversation I thought I had finally made some progress with her—that we could move beyond the rude behavior in class and that she would finally begin to work to her potential. But the very next day she was so out of control in class that I had to send her to the dean. I was devastated! I didn't know what to do... but I wouldn't give up on her.

Our relationship continued this way for a couple more weeks. I kept trying everything I could think of, but still nothing seemed to change her behavior. Then suddenly one day everything changed. She became one of my best students—not in any of her other classes, just mine. She started to help other students in the class with their work. She became the classroom leader I knew she was capable of being. She even reprimanded other students who were misbehaving in my class! Slowly her grades started to climb. What had happened? Did I finally get through to her?

Well, in a way, I had—she found out I was pregnant with my first child. One thing she knew how to do was to take care of children. She had been raising her siblings and cousins since she was seven years old! When I asked her what had caused the change in her attitude, she told me that the stress she was causing wasn't good for my unborn child.

This was to be our connection—my pregnancy! This became

the basis for our relationship. Gabrielle finished the eighth grade and went on to graduate from high school. She came to see me after graduation and proudly presented me one of her high school photos. She started at a local community college, but never did finish. She was pregnant with her first child at twenty. I learned that in teaching not all relationships are what you think they will be—in education you take what you can, you build on it, you nurture it and you try to be the most effective teacher you can because the future of that child depends upon it.

~Barbara Walton-Faria
2009 Rhode Island State Teacher of the Year
Science teacher, grade 8

75

A Tale of Two Students

Teachers are expected to reach unattainable goals with inadequate tools.
The miracle is that at times they accomplish this impossible task.
~Haim G. Ginott

It was pouring down rain and forty degrees at the DuPont Country Club in Wilmington, Delaware, where I was completing work on a major sports contract. I was forty-two, and I had spent my life building my own successful production company, directing, designing, and writing for theatre, commercials, sporting and musical events in the professional world.

But I was more interested in convincing one of my temps to get his GED and put his prison life behind him than I was in completing the viewing area on the ninth hole for LPGA Open. Something was missing in my life. I was often asked to conduct workshops in theatre for young people and for teachers at schools around the area. I began to seek out these opportunities on a regular basis because I found them to be more satisfying and rewarding than my normal career.

So, in the middle of a driving rain storm, when the current theatre supervisor for Jefferson County called and asked me if I wanted to teach at Shades Valley High School, I embraced the opportunity. With the support of my wife, I took the job and accepted the challenge of developing a theatre program where there was none.

On my first day of teaching at Shades Valley, I had a student arrested in one of my classes on a drug charge. In my second week, a student was arrested in another one of my classes and charged with raping a girl at school. I was seriously considering reopening my production company. At the end of my second week, a senior student (Cody) came into class with a joint behind one of his ears. I called the office and an administrator came down. In the hallway, the principal asked Cody what was behind his ear. He reached up and realized what he had done and threw the joint onto the floor replying, "Nothing." The principal asked him what that was on the floor, to which Cody answered, "Why, Mr. Galloway, I think that's a joint. I wonder where it came from." Mr. Galloway asked, "Just how dumb do you think I am, Cody?"

Cody responded by saying, "Right now, Mr. Galloway, I hope you're really, really dumb." Unfortunately, Cody got in and out of trouble the rest of the year. I tried to get him involved in my developing program to no avail. Eventually, he just stopped coming to school, and I never heard from him again.

During the second day of auditions for our school play, I asked Kitty, one of the students sitting in the classroom, to read for a part. She said she wasn't interested. She said she was just there with the person who was giving her a ride home from school. In fact, she was going to drop out of school the moment she was old enough. I looked around and didn't see enough people to cast my show, so I asked her to read again. "What could it hurt?" I said. "I might not be here that long myself."

She read. She was good, and I cast her in the lead. Two years and many roles later, she graduated from high school. She went to college on a full scholarship. She is now married with a family and just completed her PhD in anthropology from a school in New Mexico. There's no way to accurately determine what role casting Kitty in the play had in keeping her in school. It's hard to say, but I know that she is a major reason that I stayed in the classroom that first year, and she says she would have quit school if I had not put her in the show and gotten her involved with my department.

My program is now one of the largest in the country. We have traveled all over the world and won countless awards, but I still remember those two students and their stories. One became involved and became a success. One vanished and has never been heard from since. I often wonder what became of Cody. Did he get his act together? Did his life fall further apart? Is he even still alive? I have buried too many of my students.

I also wonder what would have happened had I taken the job even two years before I did. Would I have made a change in Cody's life? I know there is no answer to that question, but I try to remember him when I see a troubled student. I know what a kind word can do when I get the postcard or e-mail from a student who I can barely remember that says, "You may not remember me, but I became a teacher because of your class," or "You may not remember me, but the things I learned in your program have made me the person I am today." What an incredible and terrifying responsibility.

Even though my program is established and at times overwhelming, I try to look at it as a collection of individual young people with hopes and dreams, fears and weaknesses. By doing that I hope that I am able to touch them on an individual level in such a way that they develop the confidence and the courage they need to survive in the word in which we live. By doing that I hope to give them the skills and the strength they need to dare to succeed. By doing that I hope that they will not become a statistic like Cody but they will become a success like Kitty.

~Roy Hudson
2009 Alabama State Teacher of the Year
Theatre teacher, grades 9-12

76

Chicken Soup for the Soul

Chad's Award

He who opens a school door, closes a prison.
~Victor Hugo

Although for a number of years I had considered trying full-time teaching, my first job actually came out of desperation. With my savings account dwindling to an uncomfortably low level following several months of unemployment, I reluctantly accepted a job teaching Spanish at a charter school for at-risk high school students in downtown Houston. The salary was about half what I'd earned in my previous position at a law firm. The school was under the direction of a woman whose only credential was certification in teaching home economics. On the plus side, teaching certification was not required for my job, and there was no contract. I wouldn't have to invest time and money in certification programs yet. And if I hated the job, I could just give some notice and take off.

Characteristics of the charter school included open enrollment, a self-paced curriculum (hardly appropriate for a large population of special education and below-grade level students), a director who changed the curriculum daily and hired and fired personnel at the drop of a hat (even members of her own family and lifelong friends), and students in and out of jail and/or rehabilitation programs. When the year concluded at the end of May, only a handful of students sitting in my classes had been there since the doors opened in August.

Chad was one of them. He started out in my first semester Spanish I class. He had taken the course twice already without earning a credit, which was not an uncommon phenomenon at the school. He was hyper at times (at our school, the teachers joked, ADD was contagious), but fairly bright, and he never missed a day of school during the first semester. With some prodding and encouragement, Chad earned credit for first semester Spanish and moved on to the second.

I noticed a huge change in him when he returned from Christmas vacation. He was quieter and more focused. He began class each day by retrieving his folder and working diligently through his assignments. He asked questions and participated. I was impressed by his dramatic improvement, which one teacher attributed to new medication.

Towards the end of the spring semester, Chad missed several weeks of school. When he returned, he wrote in a warm-up that he was soon being shipped off to "year-round school in another state" and he didn't know if he would finish out the year.

The day I submitted Chad's name for an award, I discovered that the "year-round school" was prison. I was shocked to learn that he had broken into someone's house and threatened the occupant with a "deadly weapon" (a BB gun). Some of the teachers called Chad a punk. "You should give the award to someone else," one suggested, and I considered it. But in the end I decided to judge Chad only on what he had done in my class. "If we take their extracurricular activities into account, we might as well call this whole awards thing off," another teacher pointed out.

It was the first awards ceremony ever at our "school for the criminal professions." Some teachers said that we should be handing out awards like "Most Likely to End Up on Death Row" or "Most Likely to Test Positive for HIV." But even the most cynical among us were moved by the kids' enthusiasm. Some of these street-tough kids covered with gold chains and tattoos had never received any kind of award in their entire lives. They swaggered up to the awards table, flashed victory signs when teachers presented them with handwritten certificates in front of their peers, and asked how they could make copies of the awards for relatives and friends or convert the awards into posters.

Chad's sentencing had been delayed, and he made it to school that day. He hardly reacted when I presented him with an award for Most Improved. But after the ceremony, my quiet, cooperative student ambushed me with a hug. "Thank you," he said in a voice thick with emotion. "Now I have something to show my mom."

Chad didn't finish second semester Spanish, and he never got credit for the course. But I'd like to think that award made a difference. That having something tangible for his efforts would remind him that he could accomplish things, and that he would turn his life around. Or was it already too late—his last achievement in the civilized world before embarking on a career in crime?

Even if the award didn't make a difference in his life, it certainly did in mine. I realized that while I couldn't remain at that particular school, interacting with those kids—trying as it was at times—was much more meaningful than anything I had ever done. I knew I would never return to the corporate world. I earned my standard teaching certificate a year later and have taught full-time ever since.

~Cheryl Y. Brundage

77

Going the Distance

Teaching is the greatest act of optimism.
~Colleen Wilcox

B
eing treated unfairly is never easy. I once called a parent to inform her that her child had used inappropriate language in my ninth-grade math class. She yelled at me, questioned my integrity and accused me of picking on her child. I began to shake and tears streamed down my face. I spoke calmly in a professional voice and ended the call as soon as possible. I never spoke to that parent again. For me, the call was only a ridiculous example of the extreme lack of parental support that teachers must sometimes face. As the years went by, my focus changed: How could I build trust with these parents? How could I reach out to my next challenging parent?

Seeing beneath the surface of a problem is difficult, though often rewarding. Cassidy had long black hair and a face that usually stared blankly or was frozen with a frown that said: "I would rather be any place but here." Cassidy refused to participate in the class, do her homework, or even pretend that she was trying. She was failing Introduction to Algebra and my strategies to engage and motivate her were not working. Hands-on activities with mathematical manipulatives did not even dent her apathy. My words of encouragement fell on deaf ears. Including her in the lesson as we discussed how to solve a problem gained nothing but an icy stare. At the end of class one day, she handed me a letter filled with anger, rude words, and a strong challenge that no matter how hard I tried, she was never going to do any work in my class.

I phoned Cassidy's mother and shared the contents of the letter. I was concerned about her response in case she was too angry with Cassidy; we were going to work together to help Cassidy be successful. I was correct in that Cassidy's mother was going to be very angry, but incorrect as to where the anger was going to be directed. "Why are you picking on my daughter in class?" she accused. I explained that I often call on numerous students during a lesson to ensure that everyone understands. If I only call on a couple of students who raise their hands, perhaps only two students understand the lesson while the rest of the class flounders. Randomly calling on students is one of several ways in which I monitor student engagement and how well the class is learning. "Teachers can say whatever they want but I think they are just trying to humiliate students," she retorted.

My strenuous efforts to convince her that I would never try to humiliate a student only met disbelief. As the phone call continued, her complaints progressed and delved into strong criticisms of public schools in general. I felt like I was under attack and had a dozen arrows in my chest and my back, metaphorically speaking of course. I was being characterized unfairly. My efforts to teach and help Cassidy were being perceived in ways that I found horrifying. Cassidy was never going to pass Introduction to Algebra. Somehow, I needed to pull all the arrows out of my chest and set them aside so we could help Cassidy—the focus of any good instructor.

I listened to the phone conversation and tried to peel back the layers below the strong words. It started to make sense. Cassidy's mother did not have a positive experience in high school. She felt strongly that she had been treated unfairly and that teachers exclusively liked certain rich, smart kids and ignored the rest. She feared the same thing was happening to her daughter.

The feelings were so strong; I searched for words to convince Cassidy's mother that I truly cared about her child. If this were a baseball game, I was in the first inning and down by fifteen runs. A baseball game, however, is played over nine innings. The game was not going to be won with just one swing of the bat. I did not need to repair all the negative feelings Cassidy's mom had toward teachers and public schools in one phone call. I had the entire school year to win her over.

I waited for a lull in the conversation and took in a deep breath before finally speaking: "It seems to me that you do not have a lot of trust and confidence in public schools in general or in me as Cassidy's math teacher in particular. I am sorry you feel that way. I want you to know that I want to regain your trust. If we can schedule extra tutoring in class or tutoring before or after school, I will do it. If it means not calling on Cassidy in class until you are convinced that I am not picking on her, we can still keep track of how hard she is working and if she is doing her homework. I want to regain your trust and see Cassidy be successful."

Cassidy's mother paused. "Well, it wouldn't take much." I did not win the game, but by the end of the phone call I was down by only ten runs. Over time, and with further phone conversations with Cassidy's mother and continued encouragement to Cassidy, we cleared away the wreckage of previous negative school experiences and built a new foundation for a trusting relationship. Cassidy started doing her homework. She passed a test. Finally, we reached an agreement where I could call on her in class once a week. As time went on, the agreement changed to being able to call on her twice a week and then three times a week. Gradually, little by little, the trust was rebuilt.

By the end of the school year, I could call on Cassidy in class just like any other student. Cassidy passed Introduction to Algebra both semesters. At the end of the school year, I knew that Cassidy, her mother, and I had worked as a team. We won the game in not one inning, but slowly and surely over nine innings.

Baseball games often have certain pivotal moments that determine the outcome of the game: a missed double-play ball that would have ended the inning but resulted in three more runs, or a pivotal strike out with the bases loaded.

The pivotal moment for Cassidy, her mother, and me was that first phone call. It was difficult to set aside the strong words and accusations and not take them personally. Had I demanded the courtesy and respect that I deserved as Cassidy's teacher and ended the phone call early, I would have missed my pivotal moment to turn the game around.

Cassidy and her mother taught me an important lesson. Teachers do not have the luxury of only working with parents who have a high level of trust with teachers. As teachers, we need to accept that some parents have had previous negative experiences with public schools, meet those parents wherever they are at, and patiently work to rebuild that trust over time.

~Bob Williams
2009 Alaska State Teacher of the Year
Math teacher, grades 9-12

78

When Grace Steps In

Forgiveness does not change the past, but it does enlarge the future.
~Paul Boese

It was probably her giggling that drew my attention. Sentence diagramming really wasn't all that funny as far as I knew.

It was early May and I was facing a class of sixteen inner-city kids in South Central Los Angeles. Though I had almost three years of teaching under my belt, this particular sixth grade class had pushed me to the limits of my patience far too many times, and I was more than ready to wave goodbye to them for the summer.

I had come a long way from the idealism of my first year of teaching and living in the inner city. That first year I'd covered up the bullet hole in the window with an inspirational poster. I'd plastered the walls with pictures of places worlds removed from the industrial buildings across the street. I told the kids daily that they had something worth saying and that I could help them say it. Together we would work hard and make something of their lives.

The problem, of course, was that my ideals kept crashing up against reality. Not just the spirit-deadening reality of the inner city—gang pressures, poverty, drug-destroyed families. I was also up against the basic, universal reality of the twelve- and thirteen-year-old mind. A mind with the switch tuned in almost permanently to the channel called "You can't make me!"

And now I was faced with a giggle when I should have had only rapt attention.

Walking over to the young offender, I asked for the note she had in her hands. Frozen, she refused to give it to me. I waited, all attention in the room on the quiet battle between teacher and student. When she finally handed it over she mumbled, "Okay, but I didn't draw it," the first clue that this wasn't just an ordinary note being passed.

After getting the class going on a sentence diagramming competition, I finally had a chance to sneak a peek. It was a hand-drawn picture of me, dress details down to perfection, teeth blackened, nostrils flaring, and the words "I'm stupid" coming out of my mouth. The artist had done an amazing job and there was no doubt about who it was supposed to be.

I managed to fold up the picture calmly and return to directing the competition. My mind, however, was working furiously as I wavered between wanting to cry and wanting to ream a certain few students up one side and down the next. I figured I knew the two most likely candidates for drawing the picture. It would do them some good to get taken down a notch or two, and maybe it was high time that I did it!

Thankfully, that's when Grace intervened.

Somehow, in those moments of very real hurt and fury, God was able to save me (and my students) from myself, by asking me very softly, "You want to do it your way, or My Way?"

I'd had almost three years of mostly trying to do it my way, and my head and my heart were really beginning to hurt from pounding against so many little twelve- and thirteen-year-old walls of resistance.

"Okay, Lord," I silently prayed, "what should I do? How can you ever bring good out of this?"

With loving faithfulness, God showed me.

When there were about six minutes of class remaining I had the kids stop what they were doing and get out a piece of paper. Then, suppressing my pride, I showed them the picture. The whole class was silent as I told them how hurtful this was for me. Struggling not to cry, I told them there must be a reason behind why someone would draw such a picture and that now was their chance to tell me anything they needed to tell me. Then I let them write silently while I sniffled in the back of the classroom.

As I looked over the notes later, many of them said something like, "I've got nothing against you," or "I'm sorry your feelings were hurt." A number of them said, "You give us too much homework." One student said, "We're afraid of you." And two notes, from the girls I figured were behind the picture, had a list of issues. I was too mean, too strict, and I picked on certain people too much.

Reading those notes, I realized that over the course of this year of slipshod work and incomplete assignments I had moved from being disappointed to being downright angry. Instead of encouraging my students, I had begun commanding them to achieve. I'd set high expectations without allowing for grace. Where I thought I was driving them to success I was actually driving them away.

I had some apologizing to do.

When the kids walked into my classroom the next day one boy and one girl each handed me a card. The one signed by all the boys expressed sincere regret for the ugly joke. The one from the girls asked for forgiveness.

I was dumbfounded. And more than a little humbled. I had my little speech all ready to give to the kids, but they'd beaten me to the punch. God had not only been busy softening my heart but also the hearts of my students.

If only I had let Him lead more often before this. If only this was the only time I would need to be taught this lesson.

It wasn't. And with the help of this recalcitrant class, who I would also have as seventh and eighth graders, God gave me many more chances to learn just Who was better at teaching (and loving) inner-city kids.

~Amy Morrison

79

Angry Blue Eyes

Anger is short-lived madness.
~Horace

At the start of my ninth year of high school teaching, I walked into my fifth-hour class and faced angry blue eyes. The student slouched at his desk, arms folded, and glared at me.

Even a novice teacher wouldn't have misunderstood this silent challenge. I caught the implications and wondered what confrontations were ahead.

Sending up a silent prayer, I introduced myself to the class, explained what the course would cover and then called roll. Many of the students preferred a shortened version of their formal names, such as "Chris" instead of "Christopher." But when I read the name of the student with the angry blue eyes, he insisted I call him by his full name: Kenneth. He quickly added that only his friends called him Ken. Obviously, teachers didn't fit that category.

In the weeks that followed, the tension grew. Kenneth would meet even the simplest request with a penetrating stare and plain stubbornness. He would wait until the other students did as I asked before complying. And his compliance was always accompanied by a smirk.

Occasionally, he would nudge his textbook onto the floor when I was trying to make an important point. The noise would disrupt the class, and his sarcastic "oops" always would draw a chuckle from the rest of the students.

I tried all the normally successful teaching techniques in the hope of having Kenneth take an interest in some part of the course. But I couldn't penetrate the wall around him. Talking privately with him did no good; he merely shrugged, and the same critical eyes would greet me at the next class.

Finally, I decided I had to stop worrying about him. But, still, I continued to mentally replay each day's encounter and wonder what would take down the emotional wall.

One Monday evening, while thinking about Kenneth's sullen ways, I poured boiling water over tea bags in a pitcher I'd used hundreds of times. But this time, the tempered glass shattered, throwing the scalding kettleful onto my thighs. Even though I received immediate medical attention, the burned flesh formed painful blisters.

The doctor suggested I take the rest of the week off from work, but I didn't want to subject a substitute teacher to Kenneth. I assured the doctor I would arrange my lessons plans so I could remain at my desk. I appreciated his "suit yourself" shrug, but wondered if Kenneth would choose this time to cause more problems since I wouldn't be able to physically assert any authority.

The walk to my classroom the next morning was torturously slow, and I didn't arrive until all my students were seated. Upon limping in, I was greeted with cries of "What happened?"

I briefly explained the accident to the class. As I did, I thought I saw a flutter of compassion in Kenneth's eyes. I dismissed the thought and began the day's lesson.

The hour passed quickly, and I drew a deep breath, relieved the class had gone well. I dismissed the students and began to gather my books and papers for the walk across the courtyard to my next class. Then I realized Kenneth was standing by my desk.

"I thought you might like me to carry your stuff," he said. "I have study hall, and Mr. Kelly won't care if I'm late."

Surely Kenneth was teasing me. But he remained by my desk, quietly waiting.

I gratefully handed him my briefcase.

Kenneth carried my briefcase for the rest of the week. Slowly we began to talk about the weather, his job and his other classes.

On Friday, we arrived at my next class early since I was walking better. No one else was in the room. Kenneth placed my briefcase on the desk and stood, head lowered, with his hand still on the strap. Finally, he looked up.

"What degree are your burns?" he asked quietly.

"Only second degree, Kenneth," I answered.

"Oh," he said. "Mine were third."

So my burns were the reason for his change of attitude. "How awful," I said. "What happened?"

His words tumbled out about the model airplanes he'd loved working on when he was seven, the almost empty tube of glue he'd held over the candle in an attempt the soften the last drop for the delicate wing, the flash of flames, the long weeks in the hospital and the numerous cosmetic operations.

To emphasize his final point, Kenneth lifted his chin slightly and said, "See? They can't get this spot to heal right, even with the skin grafts. I still have this ugly scar. Everybody is always looking at it!"

"Kenneth, that is a bad scar," I said. "But I never noticed it until now."

He stared at me intently, wanting to believe me. "Really?"

"Yes, really. Your eyes are what people notice first."

"Really?" His unexpected smile erased the bad moments he'd given me in the previous weeks.

"Yes. And, Kenneth, you have a wonderful smile. You should show it more often."

His smile widened as he turned to go.

"Kenneth," I called. "Thank you for telling me this."

"That's okay." He paused. "You know, Mrs. A., you can call me 'Ken' if you want."

I smiled. "I'd like that very much, Ken."

The following Monday, he greeted me with a smile. And his eyes were no longer angry.

~Sandra Picklesimer Aldrich

80

Getting Away from School

I feel like a fugitive from the law of averages.
~William H. Mauldin

My California town is a tiny burg of a place. It's mostly a Latino, worker-breeder-feeder for the wealthier communities nearby. And the elementary school I teach in is well... as we say in the lexicon, "challenged." Challenged is a polite, politically correct way of saying hosed, and we can't talk about specifics. That "challenged" appellation is why my fellow teacher, Mr. Frost, and I skedaddle ASAP during lunches.

When the clock's hands hit lunch time we shoot out like a sniper's 50-caliber shot straight to target. There isn't much that can slow us down. We have learned over the years that if we stay at school things will find us. Things like problematic parents, crazy kids, saddened secretaries, testy teachers, prickly principals, and saturated superintendents, or a combination of any of them with any variety of the descriptor before the noun. Translation: we boogie. Not that we go far, just across the street, behind the Super Max store.

On one of our getaway days, Mr. Frost drove, as he usually did. He parked in front of Subway while I ran in and ordered one of my three favorite choices, a foot-long, five-dollar: tuna, meatball, or Italian sandwich. I B.S.'ed with the former students working there and Mr. Frost stayed in the car and gnawed halfway through his own homemade sandwich before I rushed back. He drove us the few remaining feet to our lunch spot. This we have done for many years, like clockwork, and we park under a stand of sky-grabbing, peeling eucalyptus trees.

That day, we dug into our sandwiches and bitched about the kids, their parents or, more likely, current guardians, and all the inputs of poverty which make our school "challenged." We always sit beneath our trees parallel to the highway and try to have a brief respite to detox, to breathe kid-free fresh air, to indulge in a few minutes of relative quiet without the pressing immediate needs of students.

No respite exists even in our shady refuge. Many days we have company, other parked vehicles, containing Latinos on their lunch break. They eye us, assume we are undercover cops, or with Immigration, and most leave with their worried eyes focused in their rearview mirrors. We are rarely alone. A homeless encampment supports the even more desperate. We usually eat and keep our eyes on them, and they on us, as they walk near the car. Rarely do we acknowledge each other. A mutual unspoken treaty of indifference reigns.

Mr. Frost and I started complaining that day. "Man… oh man!" I said. "Never thought I could say I'd have a worse class than last year. But these guys. Jesus H."

Mr. Frost laughed, "Hey, I warned you. I suffered with those kids all last year. Now they're yours." Mr. Frost stopped chewing. "There's a first." He pointed at the homeless encampment. "Anglo female down there. She's coming our way, too."

"Holy, Holy Cow!" I said as I rolled down my window.

"What are you doing?" Mr. Frost looked worried.

The young woman smiled and stopped two feet from me.

"Mr. Karrer?"

"Chelsey? Chelsey Morgan?"

She smiled, then looked down at the encampment, waved and yelled, "John! Come here!"

"Who's John?" I asked.

"My hubby." She yelled again, "John! Come here. Bring the cat. It's my fifth-grade teacher."

"Chelsey, this is Mr. Frost." I pointed at him. "He teaches fourth grade at your old school." She bent at the knees to look in and waved at him.

Mr. Frost's eyes got bigger right in front of me. We were getting way out of his comfort zone.

Her hubby John showed up, cradling a gorgeous black cat in his arms. Chelsey explained, "Our friend Roberto got thrown in jail. Nobody's watching his cat so we're here on a rescue mission. John came up to the window. Chelsey chuckled. "So what do you think of my husband? Not too many teeth, but he's still pretty good looking. Lot older than me, but I'll keep him."

John protested, "Hey, forty-one isn't so old."

They both laughed.

"Chelsey, how old are you now?"

"Twenty-four."

" Wow. That means I had you fourteen years ago. Hey, do you still have nine brothers and sisters?"

"Nope." She flashed the inner side of her right forearm. A blue tattoo with the name "Sarah" covered most of it. "You remember Sarah. Her husband killed her about four years ago. Only nine of us now."

I didn't dare look at Mr. Frost. We had just oozed way out of my comfort zone too. "Oh... Mr. Karrer. Remember Sun Kim in our class?"

"Sure do. What's he up to?"

"We were in the hospital last year. Somebody shot Roberto and Sun was there trying to get drugs. He changed since you had him. Well, we have to go feed the cats. Great to see you, Mr. Karrer."

"Thanks Chelsey," I said. "Nice to meet you, John."

The two of them turned and walked down the embankment. I hit the switch to roll up my window.

Mr. Frost and I just looked at each other. "You want the rest of it?" I asked.

"More? There's more? I can't process what I just heard. How can there be more?" Mr. Frost shook his head in disbelief.

"The kid she talked about, Sun Kim. His family came from Korea that year. The school put him in my class because of the basic Korean my wife taught me. His mom and my wife became friends. One Thanksgiving Day his family went to Big Sur and Sun saw his mom and dad get swept out to sea by a rogue wave. His mom died. His dad lost everything including his mind. Sun's been on his own ever since. Poor kid."

We drove back to school in silence. Sometimes it is hard to get away from school even under our eucalyptus trees.

~Paul Karrer

Becoming an Educator

Too often we underestimate the power of a touch, a smile, a kind word,
a listening ear, an honest compliment, or the smallest act of caring,
all of which have the potential to turn a life around.
~Leo Buscaglia

"Do you want to go to jail?" These words actually came out of my mouth my third year of teaching. These are not the worst words I said that year to my young first graders, and I am certainly not proud of saying them. I actually remember my breaking point that year. Surprisingly, it was not when one of my first grade boys greeted me one morning with a slap on the rear end and "Hey baby." It wasn't the day I got a phone call that nine of my boys were in the office because they decided that when I told them to make sure to go to the bathroom outside at recess, they actually "went outside." It wasn't when Jared colored green in everyone's nose on their self-portraits, when Matthew asked a little girl to "lick his chest" on the playground or the hundreds of angry and mean things my eighteen boys said that year. No, my breaking point came the very last day of the second quarter. I had made it to Winter Break and I was ready to quit. I wandered over to my desk to breathe a sigh of relief when I saw a crumpled piece of paper on my chair.

I remember this moment vividly as I prepared for what unbelievable thing I might read this time. I sat there feeling overwhelmed with shame when I read the words on the flowery stationery:

Dear Mir Baid,

You are cool.
I like you so mush.

Love, Jared.

I read the note over and over and thought about how ironic it was that Jared still wanted a relationship with me. Ironic because I was once a little girl who was desperate for relationships and wanted nothing more than a teacher to believe in me, and yet as a teacher I was not working to build positive relationships with my students. How could it be that after all of the lectures and yelling, this little boy still wanted a relationship with me? Then this moment came where I realized, if they all seem so naughty, could it be… it was my fault? I was the problem?

My identity as a teacher changed in that moment and I have never been the same teacher since. I confronted my teaching and I tried my best to use the rest of the year to build community and find routines and procedures that made my kids feel successful. I'd like to say it was easy and the year ended perfectly. On the contrary, it was the hardest year of my career and every day was a challenge. Though we made some progress as a class, I honestly cannot say that the little boy who left me that simple little note believes that I cared for him that year.

I had an opportunity to practice my newfound passion for relationships the very next year with Payson. Payson was a loving little boy who just didn't quite fit. He would say, "Ms. Baird, I'm so in loving with you." However, he did not complete a single assignment that year. He took apart anything and everything that he could in my classroom and he constantly made noises. But, what Payson wanted more than anything in the world were relationships. He had this terribly sad look whenever it was time to go out for recess. "No one will play with me," he'd say with his head hanging. So every day, I walked Payson outside and we looked for someone to play with and we practiced asking, "Can I play with you?" He tested my patience every day, and every day I reminded myself that I would never make another child wonder if I cared for him as a human being.

Payson struggled all year to make friends. He did get invited to his first birthday party, but he never really found a best friend. After that year ended, I moved to teach at a new school. I heard over the years that Payson still struggled, both in the classroom and with peers. I always worried about him and hoped that his teachers would see the loving little boy over anything else.

The year I was named Arizona Teacher of the Year, I had this amazing opportunity to ride on top of the Wells Fargo wagon in Arizona's Fiesta Bowl Parade. It was an indescribable experience, hearing complete strangers cheering and clapping and yelling, "Sarah, we are so proud of you!" and "We love teachers!" It is a feeling of appreciation every teacher should get to experience. Amidst the cheers, I heard a little voice yelling, "Ms. Baird! Ms. Baird!"

And there was Payson. Bigger, older, but still Payson. Standing in front of the crowd waving and screaming. I was so excited to see him! I quickly raised my camera and took his picture from my parade position. As I rolled by, I heard him scream, "I knew you loved me!" then he turned to the crowd and proudly yelled, "She took my picture, people!"

I don't know if I will ever get that same chance with Jared, but he is a child I will forever hold in my heart and I will be forever grateful to the little boy who helped me find my identity as an educator.

~Sarah Baird
2009 Arizona State Teacher of the Year
Math teacher, grades K-5

Teacher Tales

Reconnecting

We only part to meet again.

~John Gay

The White Car

To conquer fear is the beginning of wisdom.
~Bertrand Russell

The worst thing that can happen to any driver is to run over a child. That thought crossed my mind when I braked at a stop sign and saw two boys on bikes weaving circles on a side road. My house was fifth from the corner. I turned and accelerated slowly to twenty miles an hour. Suddenly, the younger of the two riders angled in my direction. His bike moved alongside my window, the boy struggling to control it.

I slammed my foot on the brake. The tires screeched. Two thin wheels, a child and a pair of handlebars disappeared under my bumper. I looked into the rearview mirror, bracing myself to see a crumpled body and a mangled bike. Nothing was in the road. "Dear God," I thought, "he's still under the car." And my second thought hit me like a death sentence: "I've killed a child."

Opening the door, I stumbled into the street in front of the house where the boy was headed. A woman flew out the door and started screaming. Her husband stopped his work in the open garage and headed toward my car. I ran to the mother, crying "I'm sorry, I'm sorry." I couldn't even look in the direction of my small white car. It had become a murder weapon.

Suddenly, a neighbor approached, holding the hand of a dazed but calm child. She had looked under the car and discovered him clinging to the underside of the bumper. His only damage: slight road burns on his back. His dad followed behind, carrying a twisted bike. The mother bent down to examine her son, anguish melting from her face as she hugged his thin body.

The boy, a dark-haired child with large brown eyes and freckles on his cheeks and nose, squirmed out of his mother's arms and scurried over to his dad. "I'm okay," he insisted with a macho attitude.

Two months later, the family moved away from our neighborhood. I had meant to replace the boy's bicycle, but my busy work routine made me forget the promise. No one knew where they had gone. Since their presence had been a reminder of how close I had come to taking the life of another person, I felt relief, but regretted that I had never made good on the bike. Seven years went by. Then something so unexpected happened that I can only explain it as a second chance to make restitution.

I taught English at the local high school and often assigned my eleventh-graders to write an autobiographical incident that taught them something about life. For a question that always triggered ideas, I would ask, "How many of you have ever been in a car accident?" This particular year, a lanky young man with curly black hair and pale skin cheerfully volunteered, "I had one, Mrs. La May. Remember? You hit me."

I searched my mind for a time when I had hit any car, let alone one driven by a student. Giving up, I frowned at Orlando. "I never had a car accident."

"Yes, you did," he insisted. "I was nine years old. You ran over me with your white car."

The class went silent. Blood rushed to my face. I did remember! It came back to me that the boy I hit that day had an unusual name—Orlando. He had black hair and the same smattering of freckles on his cheeks and nose as this handsome sixteen-year-old who now innocently brought back my past.

Recovering quickly, I joked dramatically, "My past has come back to haunt me."

"I'm still afraid of white cars," Orlando ventured with a wry grin.

Of course my class wanted to know the details. Together, my student and I reconstructed the crime scene, including the fact that an investigating policeman absolved me of blame. As the year progressed, the story forged a connection between the two of us and became a light form of banter. Still, Orlando did remind me with a laugh that I never bought him a new bike. I could only apologize for my oversight and hope that I could make it up by helping him with his studies.

Orlando was a struggling ESOL student usually earning a borderline "B." But second term meant research papers. He tried, but it was too big a project for him to grasp. His average veered to a dangerously low "D." Toward the end of the term, he came up to me while the rest of the class was engaged in group work. "Am I going to fail?" he asked, with a note of dread in his voice.

Without a second's hesitation, I answered, "Orlando, there is no way on earth that you will fail my class."

With a sheepish grin, he headed back to his seat. I looked gratefully at his healthy head of hair, his bright eyes, his dancing freckles. He was back at work, confidently adding to his group's discussion, panic and worry gone from his eyes. I couldn't give him a bike and I couldn't take away his fear of white cars, but I could give him a little boost to get through the years ahead.

~Sharilynn Townsend La May

A Lesson in Friendship

A teacher is one who makes himself progressively unnecessary.
~Thomas Carruthers

I t is difficult to believe that I won't be getting a card from Mrs. Hanson at Christmas this year — or any more birthday cards filled with glitter hearts or multicolored, balloon-shaped confetti. For almost twenty years I looked forward to receiving a greeting or a handwritten letter from my fourth grade teacher, and I really thought she might come to my wedding even though we hadn't seen each other in sixteen years, since my family moved from Horsham, Pennsylvania to a rural town almost five hours away.

• • •

When homeroom assignments came out in the summer of 1989, I was petrified and immediately wanted my room changed. As a third grader passing Mrs. Hanson's classroom at Round Meadow Elementary School, I'd occasionally heard her voice coming from her classroom doorway when she raised it above the noise of her students instructing them to "pay attention." I knew she probably yelled, and I was sure that fourth grade was destined to be a year I would never forget. I was right.

I dreaded the start of school. I had new glasses that I hated. Big and round and pink and blue, they took up most of my face and magnified my cheekbones. Nearly all of my friends had gotten braces over the summer. My teeth were still crooked. While some of the other more popular girls in my class were starting to experiment with purple eye shadow and mascara, I went without any. Just plain Julie Mellott. No pierced ears. Mousy brown, unstyled hair. And giant glasses.

Mrs. Hanson was a sixty-year-old, slender woman with her hair dyed a light reddish brown and styled on the top of her head. Eventually, I learned that Mrs. Hanson didn't yell, but she kept order in her classroom and encouraged respect. While some of my classmates called her "hard," I really liked the challenge that having her for a teacher presented. And she was always nice to me. She showed compassion toward me when others teased me on the playground and when I learned my grandmother was very sick. She even nominated me to speak in front of the senior class about the dangers of drinking and driving. I loved Mrs. Hanson and I loved fourth grade.

I still stopped in to visit Mrs. Hanson after moving on through school, and she became my pen pal at her suggestion. Since I was moving away and she was retiring, Mrs. Hanson thought it would be nice if we kept in touch with each other. Over the years I continued to send her letters and pictures—sharing my success stories and my firsts. She would tell me about her travels and visits with family. I always looked forward to a lengthy letter each summer. She always called me her "special girl."

After graduating from college and living on my own for a few years, I took a job in Boston and lost touch with Mrs. Hanson for a few months. Settling in to a new job, a new apartment and a new lifestyle took up most of my time. The first opportunity I had to reach out to Mrs. Hanson was over the holidays.

Days later, I received a card in return:

...Wishing you peace,
and wishing you love.
Merry Christmas!

With much love,

Mrs. Hanson

We never lost touch again.

Recently, I received a voicemail from Greg Hanson. Although we had never spoken before, I sensed that he knew me already. "I'm Janice Hanson's son. Mom is in a hospice," he explained. "She's asked me to contact you—she would like you to call. We've been hearing all about you for years." Tears filled my eyes because I knew a hospice could only mean one thing, and I had to prepare myself mentally and emotionally to contact my teacher for what might be the last time. "She's having a good day, and you are on her top-ten list, if you want to call it that. We're keeping her comfortable and you are one of the people she wants to know that she is here."

I hadn't talked to Mrs. Hanson in nearly a year. The last time we had spoken, I called to tell her about my engagement. I couldn't wait to share my excitement with my oldest friend. The news of her suffering from chronic obstructive pulmonary disease (COPD) was rather surprising, because in all of our conversations, all of our letters, Mrs. Hanson had never let on that she wasn't feeling well. After several hours of trying to collect my emotions and to talk without crying, I picked up the phone and dialed her hospice.

I will never forget the seven minutes that I spent on the phone with Mrs. Hanson. It was so easy not to cry because it seemed like nothing had ever changed. Although she was a little more difficult to understand and I could hear the sound of her oxygen in the background, her voice was the same, her laugh was the same, and her memory was so clear. "So how was your second winter in Boston? I bet you got a lot of snow. Do you like your job? What are you doing now? I've always been so proud of you. Thank you for sending the ivy plant. It's a nice gift to remind me of a special girl."

I could tell that it was getting more difficult for her to talk, and she wrapped up the call, "Well, I'll let you go. But if someone would ever get me some paper around here, I would write you a letter. Maybe I'll call you sometime."

My mind was spinning because I knew our conversation was ending. How could I say goodbye to an important part of my life for twenty years—for more than half my lifetime? "You are a very special part of my life," I started. "I'm so happy that we've kept in touch over the years. I love you."

"I love you, too," she said.

Mrs. Hanson passed away in her sleep two weeks later.

I wish I could say that I remember the first day of school or the first lesson that Mrs. Hanson taught to me, but I can't. What made Mrs. Hanson a special teacher to me was not what I learned in her classroom. It's not the books that she read to us or the facts that she taught. Mrs. Hanson inspired me in so many ways. I learned to be kinder and more compassionate. I aspired to make a difference in the lives of others. But more than anything she could have instructed from a text book, Mrs. Hanson taught me a lesson in friendship. I learned it can span generation gaps, twenty years and 300 miles. I learned friendship lives forever.

~Julie Mellott George

84

A Chance Encounter

A teacher is a compass that activates the magnets of curiosity,
knowledge, and wisdom in the pupils.
~Ever Garrison

After thirty years in the classroom, I have come to realize that the tiniest of gestures can make a world of difference for a child. This is one such story.

I received an invitation to attend the mayor's summit on education being held at the alternative high school. The students who were enrolled in the chef's preparation program had prepared the meal.

As I looked over at the buffet line, I noticed a young girl who looked familiar. I knew she had been a student of mine. I racked my brain trying to remember her name. My inability to do so frustrated me, as I have always been able to recall former students.

Her eyes met mine and she threw her arms around me and said, "Mrs. G. it's me, Sarah, and I'm still writing!" The memories came flooding back. You see, Sarah was never a student in my classroom. Sarah's mother had abandoned her, and her biological father was absent from her life. She was sent to live with foster parents the year I met her. Sarah was angry, often in trouble and often in the office.

It was during one of those office visits that I first encountered her. She was furiously writing in a notebook. I introduced myself to her and asked her what she was writing. Sarah shared her story with me. Her writing spoke to me. It filled my heart and I know it was healing for her to put her thoughts on paper. Every morning before school she would come into my classroom and we would work on her writing skills.

Upon meeting Sarah at the alternative high school, ten years later, I knew her journey had not been easy. Our conversation that evening was filled with hope and optimism. She was turning her life around and looking forward to going to the community college to major in journalism.

Driving home, I could not help but realize the tremendous impact for both good and bad that teachers have upon their students. Taking the time to connect with a child has the power to truly change that child's life. That's why I teach.

~Sharon Gallagher-Fishbaugh
2009 Utah State Teacher of the Year
Elementary teacher, grade 2

85

Garage Sale Revelation

Many things grow in the garden that were never sown there.
~Thomas Fuller

Garage sales are a peculiar pastime. I am not one of those people who enjoy rummaging through other people's unwanted items. My mother was, and she convinced me to accompany her one cool and dreary morning. I jumped at a chance to hand off my new baby to Grandpa and spend some adult time with my mother.

We went to several garage sales and finally stopped at a pleasant cottage in the woods. The elderly owner told me that he and his wife were moving into a retirement complex. His wife had been a teacher before she had a stroke and retired. She missed teaching with all her heart.

As we were perusing the sale items, I heard the gentleman's small, frail wife say her name to someone, and I immediately realized who she was. She looked at me and said, "You are Lisa Miller." I stared at her in awe, for it had been nearly thirty years since I had been in her class.

My mother immediately apologized to her for any trouble I might have caused. She did that routinely now after learning that my brothers and I were not the sweet little angels she thought. She assumed that if this woman remembered me after so many years, I must have really done something horrible. My teacher looked at my mother and softly said, "Oh no, she was very good," and my mother stared at her in disbelief.

My teacher explained that during the last week of school, I brought her a plant from my mother's garden. It was a Lamb's Ear, a small plant with leaves that look and feel like a lamb's ear. She said it came to her roots and all and was probably pulled out that morning as I ran out the door. (My mom knew that it was probably a peace token, and I had in fact done something that needed some sort of atonement.) She took us to a patch of plants and told us that she planted the Lamb's Ear in her garden, and over the years it spread. As I looked down her driveway, I was taken aback at the site of Lamb's Ears lining both sides of it. She looked at me and said, "Every day when I leave my house and drive up the driveway, I think of you. And when I come home these plants greet me, and I think of you." Tears welled up in my eyes. There at her home, among all her belongings, was a piece of my life that she had nurtured.

In that moment, she taught me more about life than I could imagine. We give pieces of ourselves every day without thought or expectation. We rarely envision the effects that we have on others' lives. That piece may grow and spread, becoming an integral part of a life. In the end it is not the big things that matter, but the small things that make all the difference in the world. This is the lesson that I take with me to my classroom every day, and the lesson that got me through lymphoma and chemotherapy. I never had a chance to thank her, but I hope she took a Lamb's Ear with her to her new home.

Garage sales are a peculiar pastime—you just never know what you will find. I found my calling.

~Lisa Miller Rychel

86

The Treasure Chest

Teacher appreciation makes the world of education go around.
~Helen Peters

Working one late afternoon on a lesson plan we were to teach the next day, my teaching partner and I were startled by the sudden appearance in the doorway of a tall, lanky young man in an intimidating dark trench coat. His red, spike Mohawk caught our attention as well as his heavy-metal T-shirt. Then, he flashed that remarkable grin that told us it could only be Jacob. He had grown a bit since we last saw him and his demeanor was certainly different, but under that "tough guy" exterior, we both recognized the lost, insecure first grader we had taught and loved many years ago. Some children do not have the privilege of a nurturing family where unconditional love helps them survive the bumps of everyday life. Jacob was one of these children.

In the first grade, Jacob required constant reassurance and redirection from his teachers. He often was unable or unwilling to participate or cooperate in our classroom. As a first grade team, we shared the responsibility for not only Jacob's education, but his social and emotional needs as well. He quickly became one of our favorites. The extra attention manifested itself in a more confident student who began to willingly engage in the process of learning.

Even after Jacob left first grade, he would return year after year, willing to give up his recess time to volunteer in our classrooms. He simply needed that unconditional acceptance. Family circumstances eventually took Jacob to another state, and with heavy hearts we thought we would never see him again. We were worried how life would treat Jacob. So, we felt great relief and joy to see him standing in the doorway.

Jacob's eyes darted around my classroom. What was he looking for? Suddenly, with a laugh, he asked, "Do you still have that treasure chest for your students?" I reached under my desk to pull out the old treasure chest. Jacob began digging for his favorite candy. We all sat down for conversation over peanut butter cups and Smarties. Jacob must have eaten ten before he was finished. On the way out he gave us both a squeeze and a look of gratitude. His stomach as well as his emotional "bucket" were filled.

A classroom is more than four walls filled with textbooks. It should be a safe haven filled with unconditional love. It needs to be a place where children like Jacob can return year after year for a refill of love and attention. Don't we all need a trip to the treasure chest once in a while?

~Robin Sly with teaching partner Sherry Dismuke
2009 Idaho State Teacher of the Year
Elementary teacher, grade 1

87

Simple Pleasures

Time you enjoy wasting, was not wasted.
~John Lennon

I taught high school for years in St. Louis County and had the joy of knowing many wonderful kids. Of all the students I taught, a few still stand out in my mind like gifts, each one changing and adding to my life.

One student, Scott Wood, was especially close to my heart and still is to this day. One of the subjects I taught was Creative Writing, a topic that lent itself to getting to know my students personally through their writings. Scott came as a junior, a new student in the area and at Lafayette High School. He wrote brilliantly. I mean, there it was, that ingredient one cannot "teach" into someone. He was able to express through his written word how much he was struggling and it enabled me to light his way a little.

Scott and other students were often in my home, at my kitchen table, sharing supper. It was amazing to me that what I said to them about life and love, and making time for the important things actually sunk in. I watched them put these lessons into practice as I followed their lives after graduation. Scott, especially, did this, and still does this today.

I know this because we stay very connected via e-mail, letters, even visits. The thing is, he has done just as much for me. I get discouraged sometimes because of ill health, pain, and family tragedy, and sometimes I tell him this. Recently I told him I felt particularly down. Here is what he e-mailed back to me:

I remember you coming into class one day late. You were rushing to get the class started but you had a great big grin on your face, like the cat who had eaten the canary. Anyway, you proceeded to tell all of us in the class that you were late because of a very special reason. It had snowed the night before but instead of scraping the ice off of your windows in the car, you let the car heater take care of it and you sat and watched in wonder as the water slowly started flowing down your window. I think about this a lot when the weather begins getting cold, how most of us miss the simple treasure—ice melting. Just like a sunrise, I suppose. Every day is a blessing, right? Is that not what you always told us? That is how you lived and that is how you told us to live.

Ice melting. I do not recall this incident but, thinking back, it rings very true. That is what I believed, that is what I taught. After reading his reply, I just sat back in my chair and, in my heart and mind, I returned to those days. When did I lose my ice-melting self? Had I lost it?

The more I sat and thought and traveled back, the more I realized I hadn't really lost my ice-melting self, just sort of pushed it aside too often. I remembered the day on the beach right at sunset when my husband Gene and I married. The sky was pink and the air salty and there was such love there that day that even two raccoons and three joggers stopped to feel it. Gene actually stopped the ceremony to ask everyone with us to be aware of the perfection of the moment. It, too, was an ice-melting moment.

You know, just to make it clear, an "ice-melting moment" to me is that moment you stop time for—you stop everything for—because it is too precious to miss. Scott, my student long ago, made me remember to never be too busy to stop the world, stop the clock for the magical moments in our daily lives.

~Jean Brody

88

Stoop to Conquer

*Education is the ability to listen to almost anything without
losing your temper or your self-confidence.*
~Robert Frost

Before I present the subject of this story, it is important that I set the tone and share the cultural milieu in which it is set. The Virgin Islands were colonized under seven different nations—(The Netherlands, Denmark, Britain, France, Spain, Malta and the U.S.) from a period beginning in the 1600s until they were purchased by the U.S. from the Danish in 1917. The natives are a mix of African stock brought to the Islands during the slave trade. The African Diasporas is prevalent here in the Virgin Islands and the languages were lost many years ago influenced greatly by the colonial powers occupying the islands at any given time. Today on the now four Virgin Islands (St Croix, St John, St Thomas and Water Island) we also have natives of French, Puerto Rican, Danish, and some German ancestry.

The Virgin Islands dialect is filled with colloquial sayings from Dutch, French, and English Creole origins with what some may call an accent, broken English or a West Indian twang. There are two great books written by Virgin Islanders: one titled *What a Pistarckle* by Lito Vals, sort of a Creole dictionary, and the other *Herbs and Proverbs* by Arona Petersen, both out of print. Arona's book has a lot of useful information on local herbs and their uses as well as it is filled with sayings/proverbs. For example: "Do for do is no Obeah"

(Just retribution is to be expected), "Tongue and teeth does fall out" (Good friends quarrel), "Monkey always know what tree to climb" (never a sandbox tree) plus many more, including, "Stoop to conquer but never too low."

My assignment to my students was to use these two volumes as source material to select a saying—a proverb that resonates with them and then graphically illustrate it as best they could. The intention was to give my students an art assignment that focused on their culture, while at the same time the challenge was that they had to think creatively and problem-solve all within a time frame as if the art work was to go to press.

Wellington did not display any particular impressive art skills and aptitudes while a student of mine in the mid-1980s. He was raised in a low-income district on the narrow backstreets with long row wooden houses and swept dirt yards, architectural elements left from the Danish Colonial days—an area not seen by the many tourists who visit the Island of St Thomas.

Despite a slight stutter speech impediment, Wellington was not a rude or deviant teenager angry at the world for the cards dealt to him. He would do his assignments with the normal hesitancy of most beginning or foundational art students fearful to make mistakes on that clean white sheet of drawing paper. He struggled to come up with an idea as the submission deadline was fast approaching.

Wellington managed to earn a passing grade—a low "B" for his semester final project work, which for that matter was a typical grade for a non-art major. The childlike image he drew was that of a slave worker kneeling at the foot of the slave master stepping on a book. The irony of the image will be revealed later.

Looking back at my grading criteria, I emphasized drawing ability and to a lesser degree the concept or idea. Content did and always will matter, yet we had an art major program and so my task was to discover talent and the ability to carry an idea to its full and best development and reward that with an excellent grade. The next year, Wellington graduated and then joined the army.

Years later, after honorably fulfilling his military obligation,

Wellington returned to St Thomas and visited me in my classroom. It was at that time he shared with me the most wonderful story. While in the army Wellington had difficulty following the strict regime of the military and was constantly challenged by his superior officers to the degree of being threatened with physical harassment and worse — incarceration. He said all throughout his military career and ordeals he carried with him in his head that image of the drawing representing his idea of "Stoop to conquer...." He further said that that saying and image saved him from going to the brig on many occasions.

I did not remember the illustration at the time; however he mentioned to me the book in the illustration was his secret weapon to success. Wellington realized from that art assignment exercise that despite all the trials and tribulations that may be heaped upon him he would seek knowledge even if it meant being beaten by a slave master. I was touched by that — to have a former student express to me an actual example in action of the true meaning of the axiom that says a "teacher never knows where his or her influence might begin or end." It was an "AHAA! I got it" moment for me. "Discretion is the better part of valor" is another way of looking at the proverb Wellington selected — yet to have him remember that classroom art assignment and many years later find it relevant, real and a reliable source of strength for him to persevere is something I will never forget. Who would have thought that a simple art assignment would carry a former student through his army soldiering years long after high school and beyond?

As time went by, Wellington became a public servant/Corrections Officer and from time to time we kept in touch. At those times we would reminisce about the past and how students of today's generation are so much different from his school days. The irony you see is that Wellington had become sort of a slave master himself, guarding the inmates under his watch. Now, he was in a position to see someone operate under difficult conditions, who may perhaps use the same saying "Stoop to conquer but never too low" as a lesson on how to manage to survive and yet even thrive under difficult circumstances.

As we saw each other over the years Wellington would always refer proudly to me to whomever we may meet as his art teacher.

Today my sympathies go out for Wellington, who is suffering from an eye disorder that he is struggling to combat. Although he has retired — "20 Years and Out" — and moved to the mainland to be near better medical treatment, Wellington will always remind me of the type of student we sometimes get at some point in our teaching experiences. As public school teachers we have no choice who comes into our classrooms. We must teach them all, teach the whole child and teach them the lessons of life.

~Edney L. Freeman
2009 Virgin Islands State Teacher of the Year
Comprehensive Academics, grades 9-12

89

More than Math

The hardest arithmetic to master
is that which enables us to count our blessings.
~Eric Hoffer, Reflections On The Human Condition

She was one of my second grade teachers. She taught me math, and at that time I thought she was teaching me everything that I would ever need to know about math, and for that matter about life itself. Well, not really, but Mrs. Pillar was a great teacher and I learned so much from her when I was eight years old. However, I will always remain indebted to her for what she did for me more than a decade later.

As a sophomore in college, I was involved in a near fatal "accident" when I walked into a robbery at a convenience store. One of the thieves shot me in the head. The thieves, as well as most people, thought that I was dead or would soon be dead. Obviously, they were wrong. However, it was a severe and difficult battle getting back into the mainstream of life. I had to drop out of college.

Even after I was discharged from the hospital I endured many hours of intensive therapy each day. I had to relearn practically everything, including walking, talking, and yes, even math.

To help me with that task, Mrs. Pillar volunteered to come to the hospital and later to my house once a week, to work with me. At first, the material that she presented appeared, to most people, to be very basic math skills. Then, as time progressed, and I made progress, my "homework" became progressively more difficult.

I remember vividly how she would come to my home on Sundays, sit with me at the kitchen table, and throw various coins on the table. She would ask me to show her 38 cents, 17 cents, 63 cents.... It was challenging—but she also made it fun.

After one-and-a-half years had passed, I had progressed sufficiently both physically and mentally to return to college. Once there, I continued therapy regularly, but I was enrolled in college. I was back at the University of Texas.

Four years after I returned to college, I graduated at the top of my class. Following that, I went on to graduate school.

As the years went by, I always kept in touch with Mrs. Pillar.

One day my parents informed me that Mrs. Pillar had suffered a stroke after open-heart surgery. Now it was my turn to help her. When I walked into the ICU, Mrs. Pillar was in a hospital bed and could not speak. I thought that the situation was extremely ironic. Nothing had changed except for who was in the bed and who was standing beside it.

I told Mrs. Pillar that I would be back and that I would work with her just as she had worked with me years earlier. As the days went by, I saw Mrs. Pillar progress each time I visited her.

One day, when I was visiting her, I pulled some coins out of my pocket, dropped them on her bed, and asked her to show me 12 cents. The nurse thought that my action was extremely strange until Mrs. Pillar smiled. I began working with her just as she had worked with me years before. I would point to the dimes and the pennies and she would put them together when I would ask her to give me the proper amount of money.

Mrs. Pillar was eventually transferred from the ICU to a private room and then to a rehab room. As she moved from room to room, there was no doubt in my mind that she was improving.

When I visited her, I would always ask her to tell me something good. She would then slowly and hesitantly answer my question. As the days would go by, her responses were quicker and more fluent. Mrs. Pillar made wonderful progress and was eventually discharged from the hospital with a prescription to continue with speech therapy as an outpatient.

One day I called her to wish her a happy New Year. She spoke into the phone quite fluently and said, "Happy New Year to you and your family, Michael. Thank you for everything you've done for me."

I quickly responded, "Thank you for everything you've done for me."

Mrs. Pillar was one of my second grade teachers, but she taught me so much more about life than mere mathematics.

~Michael Segal

Chapter
11

Teacher Tales

Reflections on
Being a Teacher

When people go to work,
they shouldn't have to leave their hearts at home.

~Betty Bender

90

Making a Difference

*Don't judge each day by the harvest you reap
but by the seeds that you plant.*
~Robert Louis Stevenson

Reflecting on more than two decades of teaching is not as easy as it may sound. My experiences have been many, the students diverse, the days long, my patience tested, but my endurance strong. You see, I always promised myself that I wouldn't just do something to "do it." I wouldn't just occupy a desk, office, or classroom for the goal of punching in and punching out. My goal was to wake up in the morning with a purpose, spend my days helping children understand, and fall asleep knowing that I made a difference. It was a good goal... noble, respectable, and simple.

I've never been confused about my purpose and I thoroughly enjoy being involved with a child's learning and understanding. However, have I achieved my goal? Do I fall asleep every night knowing that I made a difference that day? Humbly, the answer is no. As a matter of fact, the days spent hoping that I am making a difference far outnumber the days of knowing.

Living in a small agricultural community in Iowa, I am surrounded by cornfields, bean fields... and more cornfields! The farmers often talk about seed, time, and harvest. They always know what to sow, when to sow it, and where to sow the seed. I witness the farmers planting seed with a work ethic and fervor that instantly gains my admiration. They cannot afford to focus on anything other than sowing seed!

Once the seed is in the ground, with absolutely no evidence of a single plant in the field, the farmers begin watering and fertilizing that which was sown. They invest countless hours providing for and protecting their unseen crop. They realize that time is an essential ingredient in producing what they desire. The expectation is high, regardless of what they have seen up to that point. After a while, the crops are fully grown. The farmers get to harvest the fields, and see the result of their labor. They no longer wonder if the work was worth it… they know that it was!

There are days when I come to school with important decisions, deadlines, family issues, lack of sleep, etc. taking priority in my mind. I look at the lesson plans prepared for that day, knowing that I could easily hit the Auto-Pilot button, coast through the day, and pass the time until I could attend to more "important" matters. I glance up at my class and notice several elementary-aged children with similar concerns. They are also coming to school with important decisions, deadlines, family issues, lack of sleep, etc. They want to hit the auto-pilot button worse than I do!

I have had to pause and ask myself, "What could possibly be more important than watering and fertilizing these precious seeds?" I am happiest when I am reminded of this fact, and understand that a difference will be made regardless of the evidence that is shown that day.

I've sown seeds impacting the lives of hundreds of students over the years. I do my best to stay in touch with my former students, hoping to get a glimpse of the harvest that I've sown. I hope I have made a difference to all of my students, but I know I have made a difference to some. They've expressed that to me in a variety of ways. At times, former students come back to my classroom to show me their report cards, just come to talk, or bring me schedules of the extracurricular activities they are involved in. However, I will never forget the day I received a specific letter from a former student.

This letter came at the perfect time. I had just spent several days hoping that I was making a difference, seeing little to no results in my classroom. I still have the letter and look at it often. It reads:

Dear Ms. H:

> *You were my teacher in fourth and fifth grade. I still remember the lessons that I learned in your class to this day. I remember how I used to sit in my seat and complain about certain math problems and how I'd never learn how to do them. You insisted that with your help and lots of effort on my part I would understand. You were right. You taught me that it is important to work hard and try because nothing is impossible to learn or do.*
>
> *You have been there for me on countless occasions with both academic and personal issues. For example, you were willing to listen and help me when I was having a hard time dealing with my parents' divorce. You became someone I look up to, trust, and admire. You always said that we were your children because you didn't have any of your own. I know you truly care for all of us this way.*
>
> *So, for always being there for me in the good times and the bad, I want to thank you and let you know that you will always have a very special place in my heart.*

A teacher's commitment never begins and ends with the first and last bell of the day. A teacher's thoughts never remain in the school buildings overnight. A teacher's love for his or her students never fades at the end of the school year. A teacher's greatest reward is impacting lives, knowing that a difference has been made.

~Linda Heffner
2009 Iowa State Teacher of the Year
Elementary teacher, grade 4

Attitude of Gratitude

If you want to turn your life around,
try thankfulness. It will change your life mightily.
~Gerald Good

"**D**reading going back to school?" my husband inquired as he tossed some junk mail into the recycle bin.

"Why do you ask?" I replied.

"Because I see a heap of loser scratch tickets in the bin. The number of lottery tickets you purchase has a direct correlation to your feelings of desperation about your job."

It's true. After twenty-nine years in the classroom, I seem to have lost that giddy first-day-of-school feeling and it saddens me. I want to be excited about another year of possibility. Yet lately it seems I've been feeling like all another school year holds for me are more problem students and a principal concentrating too much on standardized test results. In my first years of teaching there was time for creativity and for getting to know the students. Now it's just coach, coach, and coach for the state exams. It's not much fun for any of us, student and teacher alike.

Good educators know that our attitudes are as important as the information we impart. Classroom climate can make or break a situation, and my goal has always been to treat my students with the respect and compassion that they deserve as human beings. So what can I do to adjust my attitude?

My sister gave me a wonderful idea. She said that I should strive to develop an attitude of gratitude towards my job and my difficult students. It works! I try to feel grateful that my principal put his faith in me to guide and help these students. I am grateful that some of my colleagues didn't get a particular pupil because their personalities would have clashed and it could have been a yearlong disaster for both. I am sincerely grateful for my own children, and profoundly thankful that they don't have to cope with the situations in which many of my students find themselves. And finally, I feel gratitude because next year some other teacher will have the pleasure of that difficult student's company.

I also decided to keep a journal of funny things that have happened during the school years. For example, one day while the students were supposed to be working on their science lab I observed two of my third graders arguing furiously. I stepped in demanding to know what was going on. The first girl said, "Carmen says that her ears are so good she can hear a dog whistle, and that isn't true, is it?" I replied that even if Carmen had really keen hearing, most likely she couldn't hear a dog's whistle. "Yeah, I knew that," the girl said. "Cause dogs can't whistle."

Another time the students had been given a spelling list and asked to write a sentence using each word. Mercury was on the list. One of the students wrote, "Lord have mercury on my soul." Many a time since then I have repeated those words," Lord, have mercury on my soul too!"

My assistant commented on a student's name. "Sturgis, that's a cool name. Did you know there's a town in South Dakota named that?" she inquired.

"Yep, I'm named after that town. My mama rode her motorcycle there for a rally and she went into heat and I was born."

Now folks, you just can't make up stuff like that. I only wish I had started keeping track of these stories earlier. I could have retired on the book deal. When I have just about reached the end of my rope, these stories reel me back in.

Teaching is a hard job. What a huge understatement! We all strive to do the very best for our students, trying to remember that as precious as our own children are to us, so they are to their parents. We may not agree with how they are being raised and we often feel distressed at the lack of guidance they seem to be given, but for this one school year they are ours.

What do you remember about your own school days? Chances are you have two vivid memories: the teachers that made you feel like you mattered and the teachers that in some way left you feeling humiliated or traumatized. We hold the power to create memories for students that they will carry with them for the rest of their lives. We do make a difference in the lives of children, and I am grateful for that opportunity.

~Tommie Ann Grinnell

"School starts tomorrow. Keep reminding me that teachers make a difference... before I make a run for it!"

Secrets Students Keep

Be kind, for everyone you meet is fighting a hard battle.
~Plato

Teenagers are unusually honest, telling us we have marker on our faces or our shoes are out of style. Yet, sometimes it's what they don't tell us that we really need to know. The secrets students keep might surprise you.

One of my students, Mandy, was a tall, beautiful blonde. She happened to ride the bus. Everyone in our high school knows that bus students come from the "free and reduced" lunch group. They cannot afford a car, not even the gas to get back and forth to school. They feel marked for social ostracism, unless they can conceal their economic disadvantage or somehow gain acceptance through exceptional academic or outstanding athletic abilities. Mandy had some academic specialties so she had a few friends in the upper echelons. Although social standing shouldn't be so important, it is very important to every teenager in the world!

Our student council was hosting the annual food drive for the less fortunate at Christmas. It was a contest between the classes to creatively design a food box or basket containing all the essentials for a holiday dinner, with the winning class receiving a pizza party. Our class made a list and passed it around for students to sign up for a beverage, vegetable, fruit, dessert, or decoration. We had cleverly decided to make our food box into a gingerbread house.

The entire class was eager to participate. Students began to bring items in, filling the gingerbread house. There were only two more days until the entries would be judged. Mandy and a few others had come in during lunch to help glue on the last of the candy decorations. It was a sight to behold! It looked just like a doll house with windows and doors arched with candy canes. Strings of colored gumballs lined the snow-laden roof. Kisses and chocolate bars adorned the house and lollipops formed windows.

We checked the list to make sure every item was in the box. A few students, including Mandy, still had not brought the items they had volunteered to bring. That day, Mandy lingered after class near my desk. She gave me a note, said "Don't read it now," and ran out the door. It was folded over as many times as possible, indicating top secret. It read, "I cannot bring the dessert I signed up for. My family cannot spare even one can of food and we may not even have Christmas this year."

I fought back tears as I met the next class. The note in my pocket poked at my heart all the way home and I cried as I considered how difficult it was for her to admit she had nothing. I opened my own cabinet and felt embarrassed at how much food I saw.

I brought two packages of cake mix and two cans of frosting to school the next morning and found Mandy before her first class. This was for her: one to take home and one to contribute to the class. She smiled. Her smile was even bigger when she brought up her contribution as her name was called in class that day. It was our secret and no one would know.

Our amazing gingerbread house won the competition and Mandy proudly ate her share of the pizza. When the student council sponsor was loading the baskets and boxes for delivery, I shared Mandy's story, choking on the lump in my throat. He immediately decided to deliver our entry to Mandy's house. It was a glorious day!

We never mentioned the gingerbread house again that year, and she and I would only say hello when passing in the halls, until two years later, when Mandy was graduating. She came by my room and hugged me goodbye. She said she would always remember me. She started to leave, then turned back and whispered, "No house ever tasted sweeter than our gingerbread house."

Another student was burdened with a much darker secret. Sam was in my last class of the day. He sat near the back in a roomful of mostly repeats, students who had not been successful at math, yet had to fulfill the graduation requirement. It was a 90-minute block algebra class that seemed much longer if I failed to actively engage the class from the beginning. The creative sketches the class made on their homework papers, and too often on their desks, had inspired me to design the conics lesson around art.

The class followed my every step for drawing cones intersected by planes to produce each of the four conics sections. They were focused. I watched Sam. He had his head propped up, cupped into one enormous palm, in his usual tired manner. He was a large fellow, so polite that you knew he would never cause trouble, yet he often chose not to participate. It would have been easy to overlook him that day, with the rest of the class so excited about combining their artistic interest with algebra.

As I made my way around the crowded room, offering assistance, words of encouragement and praise, I came to Sam. He was asleep with his head on his desk. When I roused this gentle giant, he rubbed his eyes and said, "I'm sorry, Mrs. Bryan, I'm just not getting enough sleep at night." I softly reminded him he needed to pass, and he could do today's work if he just tried. He said again, "You don't understand. I can't sleep at night." I suggested getting in bed earlier or not staying up playing video games. My tone was neither harsh, nor punitive, and Sam simply put his head back down and said he would do better, maybe tomorrow. The look in his weary eyes told me he really needed rest more than algebra.

When the final bell rang, Sam left the class and drove home, walked in his house and found his mother dead. She had taken her own life.

Later I learned that Sam had been staying up at night to protect his mother from his abusive stepfather. He had been taking care of his younger siblings, as well. It was more than any sixteen-year-old boy should have to bear.

I never saw Sam again, as he moved that weekend to live with his father in another school district. The students wrote individual notes of comfort and support to Sam on notepaper I provided the next day. We bundled them together to deliver as one package. It was all we had to give. There was no public funeral service, not even a way to receive friends and family—just a private burial. The sadness engulfed the entire class as we mourned his loss for the next few days.

I was glad I had not pushed Sam to work in class that last day or penalized him for nonparticipation. His quiet words still ring in my memory, "You don't understand. I can't sleep at night." My sensitivity toward any student who falls asleep in class will forever be heightened. As teachers, we see only what students will allow us to see. We move closer when we can, but the entire picture may be blurred by pain, or shame, or fear that cannot be formed into words. Students may be bodily present, yet far removed from what is going on around them. I will remember Sam and the tragedy he faced at the end of an ordinary school day. Sleeping in class that day might have been the last peaceful sleep he would have before his sleep would be filled with haunting nightmares of coming home that fateful day.

~Luajean N. Bryan
2009 Tennessee State Teacher of the Year
Math teacher, grades 10-12

Brand New Starts

Drop the last year into the silent limbo of the past.
Let it go, for it was imperfect, and thank God that it can go.
~Brooks Atkinson

"Hey, do you want me to tell you about your students?" one of the second grade teachers asked, reaching for the class roster I'd just received.

I was new to the building and anxious to make friends, so I smiled and said, "Sure."

The teacher scanned the names of the children who would comprise my third grade class that year. She made a few clucking noises and said, "Wow, you're going to have a rough school year."

She began pointing to my students' names. "This one," she said, pointing to a little girl's name, "is sweet, but not too bright. Oh, and her mother is a real pain in the neck. Oh, and this boy is nothing but trouble. He'll be in jail some day, mark my words."

She continued down my list, saying something negative about nearly every one of my students. Her words rang in my head. This one is a foster child. That one is a liar and a thief. Her father is in prison. His mother is on her fourth husband.

Finally, she stopped and handed me back the list. She smiled and said, "Now you'll know who you're dealing with."

And as each student came through my classroom door on the first day of school, her words were all I could think about.

"Hi, I'm Mrs. Stark," I said. "What's your name?"

"I'm Darren," a tall, skinny boy said. He's nothing but trouble, I couldn't help thinking.

I met child after child, subconsciously prejudging each one. Her dad is in jail. That boy is in foster care. This one can't read and that one can't sit still.

When all the students had arrived, I went over the class rules and began to hand out their supplies. All while the second grade teacher's warnings echoed in my head. "You're going to have a rough school year."

At lunch time, I went into the teacher's lounge and sat down to eat. Since I was new to the building, a few of the other teachers asked questions about what school I had come from and what grades I'd already taught.

I shared a bit about my life. I was married with two children. I'd taught kindergarten at my previous school. I had gotten my degree from Indiana University. I answered all of their questions honestly and I was pleased that they cared enough to want to get to know me. But in the back of my mind, I knew something wasn't quite right.

I had answered their questions, but I had only told them what I wanted them to know. I didn't mention the time I'd misspelled the word "Brian" so that my hallway bulletin board read "Happy Birthday, Mr. Brain!" I didn't tell them that I'd flunked high school chemistry or that I once received two speeding tickets in the same day. No deep, dark secrets revealed there. No, I only told them what I wanted them to know.

And there was no one there pointing to my name on a list, saying, "Oh, that Diane Stark, you'll have to watch out for her. She's not a very good teacher. She uses all the toner in the copy machine and never refills it. She waits till the last minute to do her lesson plans. Oh, and the worst part is that she bribes her students with candy to get them to behave." There was no one there, giving away all my secrets and telling the other teachers about my shortcomings.

I was given the benefit of the doubt. And I realized that my third graders deserved the same chance I was getting. They deserved a fresh start.

Back in my classroom, I discarded my plans for that afternoon's lesson. Instead, I asked each child to write me a letter. "Tell me three things you want me to know about you," I said. "They can be things about school, or about your family or your house. You can write about what you like or what you don't like. You can tell me anything you want me to know."

When I collected their letters, I was both surprised and touched by what the children had chosen to share with me. Many of them wrote about their siblings, their pets, and their favorite foods.

But a few of them got more personal. The little girl whose father was incarcerated wrote, "My dad is in jail because he sold drugs. He did a bad thing, but that doesn't make him bad. It doesn't mean I'm bad either, even though kids make fun of me."

Another child wrote, "My favorite foods are pizza, macaroni and cheese, and spaghetti. But sometimes when I'm at school, I can't think right because I'm so hungry. I miss breakfast a lot. And sometimes dinner too. But I get to eat lunch at school. I like school."

But Darren, the boy who I'd been warned was "nothing but trouble," wrote, "I hate school and I hate teachers. I'm bad but I ain't stupid so don't say I am." I didn't know how to handle this situation, but I knew I had to say something. When the rest of the students went to art class, I asked Darren to stay behind.

"I asked you to stay back because I had a question about your letter," I said with a smile. "Can you read it to me, please?"

He shrugged, but took the paper from my hands. "It says I'm a bad kid," he said and handed it back to me.

"Darren, that's not what it says. Besides, you're not a bad kid. You seem like a very nice boy."

"You don't know me yet," he said. "Once you do, you'll think I'm bad." His gaze lifted to mine as he added, "And stupid too."

"Darren, when you wrote this, what were you trying to tell me?"

He took a deep breath and said, "That I'm stupid. That I used to try in school but I couldn't get it. So I stopped trying and just started being bad. Now, nobody remembers that I'm stupid."

It was true. His teacher from last year had only mentioned his rebellious behavior, not any academic deficiencies. His little cover-up had worked.

"Hey, Darren," I whispered. "Can I tell you a secret? Someone once told me that I was going to have a bad school year. But I decided that I wasn't."

"You can just decide to make things better?" he asked. "How?"

I shrugged. "You have to try your best. And remember that every day—and every school year—is a brand new start."

Darren smiled. "Last year doesn't matter now?"

"Not with me it doesn't."

He thought for a minute. "I don't want to have a bad school year either."

The next morning, Darren gave me back the letter he'd written. He'd done some editing and it now read, "I used to hate school and I used to hate teachers. But that was last year."

I laughed and hugged that "nothing but trouble" boy.

And I thanked God for brand new starts.

~Diane Stark

Springtime Memory

And in today already walks tomorrow.
~Samuel Taylor Coleridge

Spring is an exciting time in a school. As the weather turns warmer, the mood turns brighter, and teachers and students alike are excited about new possibilities. But for me, the coming of spring takes me back... to the memory of some news I heard in April of 2003. Every spring I begin having the same thoughts... thoughts of Brian....

It all began in 2001 when I sent a little story in an e-mail to my stepdaughter, Heather, who had graduated from high school with Brian in 1996 and her husband, Chad, who was in the Marines at the time. It went like this:

> One of the joys of teaching is that everywhere you go for the rest of your life, you run into someone you taught, a relative of someone you taught, or someone who knows someone you taught. This morning I was having breakfast with a friend when I recognized the waitress as Letitia, the sister of my former student Brian.
>
> Brian was in my seventh grade language arts class in the 1990-1991 school year. I had him 4th period. How do I remember that? Because I had the entire junior varsity football team 4th period! I told Letitia that on game days, the players

would wear their jerseys to school, and the entire room would turn red.

Brian was a good-looking guy and a talented football player. Schoolwork was not his favorite activity, but he did it, knowing that I would talk to "coach" if he didn't. He did an average job on that work, but he played football like a hero... with a passion that most seventh graders haven't yet found. He was also polite and had a smile that never left his face. No matter how hard I was on him... for forgetting his homework, for talking about football instead of doing classwork, for begging me daily to take the class outside so the boys could throw a football around, he would sit and grin at me. On the days that he would wear me down, and we would go outside after lunch, he was a natural leader, breaking everyone into teams and calling plays.

Letitia broke into my thoughts, saying, "Brian is in the Marines now."

Do you know how that feels? Someone reaches into your memory, pulls out a seventh grader, and makes him a man. "They can't break him," she said. "But they're trying."

I thought, "Nope, they won't break him. They'll try, but he'll just grin..."

Then I thought back to my 4th period class of 1991. There, in the back, looking bored, and counting down the minutes to the football game, sits Brian Anderson, future Marine.

In April of 2003, I found a copy of that e-mail and added the following:

Today I heard some bad news. Brian, the Marine they wouldn't "break," was killed last Wednesday outside of the Iraqi city of Nasiriyah. I think of all the clichés—he loved what he was doing, everyone who knew him is proud, the world will be an emptier place without him, and so on.

But mostly, I think of that grin... and when I look back

across that 4th period class, the last desk... in the middle row...
is empty.

The world has just experienced our sixth spring without Brian Anderson. But I have learned something important. Now I look at my seventh graders not so much for the lanky-legged, giggling kids they are now... but for what they will be someday. They may become heroes like Brian. But for now, I'll just enjoy watching them grin at me... and think about that sweet smile that always sat on the face of Brian Anderson, the middle school football player and future Lance Corporal of the United States Marine Corps.

~Cindi Rigsbee
2009 North Carolina State Teacher of the Year
2009 National Teacher of the Year Finalist
Reading teacher, grades 6-8

Teacher's Summer List

Someday is not a day of the week.
~Author Unknown

Picture my wife, Rita, bald with a single earring in her right lobe, wearing a white T-shirt and white pants. That's her. That is what I have seen this week: Mrs. Clean. Just like in the ad on TV for her first husband, she shows up just when you need her. She has been into her list for the summer.

She, like all teachers, has a list for what she is going to do for the summer. This is a list that is made the day that school gets out. Allow me to give you a picture of what happens. On the last day of school, when the bell rings at 3:10, the students get on the buses and wave goodbye, join their mothers or fathers and head home for eleven weeks of fun. At 3:11, the teachers leave. In small groups they gather at some teacher's backyard patio and consume wine or beer (or soda pop for the still uptight ones), and rejoice in their newly-won freedom.

After the bottles are emptied, they head home to their own stashes. As they unwind over yet another beverage, they know it is time to make a lesson plan for their summer. "Whoops," they say, as they realize that they are still thinking school instead of real grown-up adult talk. They realize that what they have to do is make the "List."

Now this list basically comes in three parts. The first is what they are going to do to recover from the school year: sleep past 10

AM, ignore any human beings under five feet tall, eat non-school lunch food, and definitely do nothing that even remotely looks like they are complying with "No Child Left Behind." This is considered the god-given, necessary, "unwinding" phase. During this phase they accept no responsibility for any household chore, grocery shopping, or husband acknowledging activity. By Jove, they put up with those brainless twits for nine months, so they deserve some time to themselves.

The second part deals with having fun: coffee with the neighbor ladies, lunch with teacher friends, trips to see her side of the family, trips to see my side of family, shopping trips, betting at the race track, more lunches with friends, some contact with grown children but not a tiring amount, etc. This phase is the "recreating" phase. This is necessary to retain their sanity which has been robbed this past year by those snot-nosed, whiney, despicable know-nothings. This also is a god-given right and no husband better interfere for any reason.

The third part of the list is the chores that they have been putting off for nine months. What normal working adults do on weekends, teachers put off until the summer when they will have that whole nine weeks to do things. In their minds each year, they really think that they can keep a house well maintained by doing things to it only in the summer. As this includes things like replenishing the toilet paper supply, I hope that they all buy a lot in July. As will happen, this part of the list gets tackled during the last nine days of their freedom. This is what the wife is involved with at the moment. She is a whirling dervish, cleaning anything in sight. She goes back to the classroom next Thursday.

Now this list has small items, such as paint the house, clean all of the cupboards, re-landscape the backyard, take down the Christmas decorations, remodel the bathrooms, and learn Microsoft Excel.

Frankly, I don't know why they write a new list every year, as they never finish the one from the previous year.

Once your spouse, the teacher, passes age fifty, she doesn't even try to convince you that cleaning and repair will be on her summer list. She just tells you it will have to wait till she takes early retirement.

~Kenan Bresnan

Reprinted by permission of Off the Mark
and Mark Parisi ©2002

96

A Simple Place

Act as if what you do makes a difference. It does.
~William James

I have never been able to explain how I know. Does the pattern of lights in the classroom windows look different? The sound from the playground—is it quieter or perhaps more noisy than usual? My husband thinks it is the posture of my colleagues that even from a distance looks different, wrong.

Every time tragedy has struck in the tiny community of Strafford, I have known it here first, in the empty silence of the school parking lot. Today the feeling is so strong I fight the urge to climb back into my car. I would like to go home, pretend I do not know, pretend that the air is not thick with it. Instead I take a deep breath. My hand trembles. I grasp the knob of the heavy main door. This morning, I know, I will find it open.

Strangely, I feel no curiosity. Whatever has happened, has, in a very real way, happened to me. That is how I feel when they tell me, as if it had happened in my house, as if I had been there. I hear the siren of the ambulance, fight the cold, the confusion, the sharp finality of the diagnosis. For a moment, I am the neighbor called in the dark of morning by thirteen-year-old Sylvia, "Please come, my dad is dead."

All of this hurts. As I did in the parking lot, I long now to put a distance between myself and this grief. Instead, I let it wash over me. I know that this feeling is the foundation for what will come next;

the foundation for what I can see has already begun to happen at the Newton School this morning.

Around me is the quiet hum of activity. Someone has left to call the guidance counselor, the minister. Others are making a list of children most likely to be affected by John's death: the friends of his children, a handful of students who were tutored in John's home. The rest of us are discussing what to tell the students. John died only hours ago; few people have heard. Together, we make a plan. All the children will be told, quietly, and with care.

The remainder of the day moves slowly. The air is heavy and the building is strangely hushed, except for the incessant ringing of the phone. In front of the eighth-grade room, small knots of Sylvia's classmates gather to whisper and cry. A steady stream of students moves to and from the counselor's office. A few adults visit there too.

It is almost the end of the day when the school secretary comes to get me. She puts her hand on my arm. Her voice is unusually soft as she says, "I've just come from the second grade. Your daughter seems very sad." I thank her and head toward Meg's classroom.

The second graders are oddly peaceful. Some are working on cards for Anna, Sylvia and Brian; others play quietly. My daughter is huddled close to her teacher, the only child with tears still running down her face.

I reach out to hold her, puzzled by the intensity of her grief. Meg did not know Mr. Frisco well; she did not play with any of his children. We talk and cuddle, finally decide to make a card. I watch her shape her pain into big second grade letters, which seem to struggle free from the purple crayon:

I feal so sory for you Anna that your Daddy died.

I look at her tiny seven-year-old face, searching for something more complicated than the simple grief I see there. But what my daughter feels requires no elaborate explanation. A terrible thing has happened to Anna. Meg, with all her heart, wishes that it had not.

After school, the staff gathers in the library. No one has announced this meeting, but we are all there. I wait silently for what I know will soon begin, drawing strength from the group around me.

What happens next is so familiar it should not surprise me, yet it always does. A phone call is made to find out what is needed. Within a few hours, we are done. Meals have been arranged, flowers ordered, a bank account opened for donations. Drivers have volunteered to ferry the Frisco children to basketball and drama. Sylvia's teacher is chosen to keep in touch with Marie Frisco. She will call daily for a while, to make sure that we are doing all that can be done, to be sure Marie, Anna, Sylvia and Brian know that we care. I sit back, exhausted. Newton's teachers have just taught their most valuable lesson.

Anna, Sylvia and Brian will learn this lesson, as will the children of people bringing meals, and the students who glimpse the Frisco girls in the back seat of their teachers' cars. Year after year, they will see, as I have, bills paid, clothing found, houses cleaned, groceries appear on people's doorsteps. Gradually, they will come to understand that the inevitable sadness in our lives is also an occasion for caring, for sharing the experience of being human. Over time, it will become clear that this sharing is both a responsibility and a privilege.

In my town children understand this quite early. Even the littlest ones make cards, deliver cookies, pick flowers. When six-year-old Meg had pneumonia, my neighbors brought us chicken soup and homemade bread; their children sent a box filled with toys and games from their own closets.

It was hard, I'm sure, to give away those beloved toys. It is hard to find time to make chicken soup, to go miles out of your way to take someone else's child to basketball practice. It is hard to visit sick people in the hospital, to go to funerals, to explain death to young children, to lie awake at night worrying about other people's problems. None of this, however, is as hard as living in a world where people do not do these things.

I think of this as I sit at my dimly lit kitchen table, struggling to write a sympathy card to the Friscos. Nothing is coming out right. It seems there are no words for what I want to say.

I finally decide to begin in the simplest place, in the place where good schools begin, in the place where good people begin:

"I am so sorry, Anna, that your Daddy has died…"

~Diana Leddy
2009 Vermont State Teacher of the Year
Cluster teacher, grades 3-5

97

A Loss for Words

I can live for two months on a good compliment.
~Mark Twain

"Attention students...." As usual, it sounded important. Throughout the day, classes were interrupted by meaningless chatter. "...Nohemi Treviño was an honor student. We will all miss her greatly." A girl had died, and to my relief, I didn't recognize the name. I had a Nohemi, but not a Nohemi Treviño. "Excuse me, I'm sorry. Her name was Nohemi Torres." And that's how I learned of the loss of my student. Nohemi Torres was sixteen years old. She was shot in the head by her ex-boyfriend.

Two weeks before, she had asked me to write her a recommendation for National Honor Society. Knowing it was a formality, I quickly filled the small space provided: "Nohemi is a diligent worker and an excellent person. Her dedication to her work and to after-school PSAT preparation is unmatched." I left out her most special qualities. Attentive and interested, serious but happy, she justified my decision to teach.

But Nohemi was more than that. I believe she was a symbol for the future and potential of all students of all races and economic backgrounds. Her determination and pride in her work was a demonstration that all one needs to succeed is the will to try. Her death, to me, was a metaphor as well. It represented the unfairness and randomness that destroys the hopes and dreams of too many good people.

Nohemi's last words to me were "Thank you," after I gave her back the recommendation form. I don't remember my last words to her. I know they weren't "You're welcome" or "Congratulations, you earned it." And they were certainly spoken in my trademark monotone with my expressionless mouth.

Don't smile until Christmas.

That was my simple philosophy of classroom management. The previous year, my first year of teaching, I learned the unpleasant consequences of being nice. I so feared another year of screaming that I refused to express any emotion and instead became a robot.

Be their teacher, not their friend.

To the students, my stoic presence could have been interpreted as anything from apathy to seriousness to contempt. I wasn't concerned with their impressions. What mattered was that my classes were quiet and learning. The strategy was successful and, so it seemed, flawless. Two hours before I heard the announcement, I had casually marked Nohemi absent in my first period class. The students were not surprised at my lack of reaction, even though they assumed I already knew.

Once you establish control, it's easy to lighten up.

I'm not sure when, but I must have slipped — negligently allowing the pleasure of knowing a student like Nohemi to penetrate my façade. When I heard the announcement, I felt like crying, but I didn't. I couldn't.

The next day, I addressed her classmates and her empty desk: "I wish I knew how to teach you to deal with this. Actually, I need someone to teach me. Maybe you're thinking 'what good is going to school and learning Algebra if I could be dead tomorrow?' I don't think Nohemi would have said that. She's probably up in Heaven now, and as great as it is there, she's probably wishing she could be right here. She loved school. Nohemi is dead, but her dreams are still right here. You know what they were: To learn. To have a successful future. She knew that to fulfill those dreams would take courage and effort. Now it's you who need that courage and effort. Because now it's your responsibility to adopt those dreams, and keep them alive."

Since that day, I'm a changed teacher. I say "hello" when I pass by my students in the hall. When I give back tests, I say something encouraging. Generic teacher comments like "Nice Job," written on the top, are not sufficient. I never again want to be haunted by the question "Did she know I cared?" To Nohemi, I never said it. I wrote it, but that's not the same. It's speaking it that matters. It's looking at the person and genuinely saying, "I'm really proud of you." No one wants to read about how they're "diligent" and how their work is "unmatched." If Nohemi knew how fond of her I was, she knew in spite of my efforts to hide it. She was perceptive enough to do that. I'm almost positive.

~Gary Rubinstein

A Greater Purpose

In teaching you cannot see the fruit of a day's work.
It is invisible and remains so, maybe for twenty years.
~Jacques Barzun

A former student, who is now a teacher at my high school, walked by me in the hall this afternoon and said with a smile, "Ms. H, I know you love our word of the week. I heard it on the announcements this morning and I immediately thought of you." I replied, "Thank you Pharen; that pleases me." She went on to say, "I always remember you talking to me about integrity and character and how important they were." I thanked her again and she continued on down the hallway.

As I reflect on this interaction, it brings a smile to my face. Of the many words that she could associate with me, the fact that she associated the word "integrity" is an important testimony to my influence as an educator. I believe that she associated the idea of honesty and moral and ethical character with me because of the example I have set with my life. I am far from perfect but I have chosen to make a conscious effort to live a life of integrity in my classroom, in my home and in my community.

Pharen did not pursue a degree in science — the discipline area that I teach — but I am happy to think that I have served to improve her life by what I taught her. I *believe* that the subject matter I taught has improved her life but I *know* that the life lessons will pay into eternity.

This scenario served to remind me today of my greater purpose in teaching school. It calls to mind a favorite scripture from Galatians 6:9 — "Let us not grow weary in doing good for at the right time we will reap a harvest, if we do not give up."

I am thankful for a reminder today — when it seems that no one is "getting it" — that the important lessons are being *caught* and *taught* if I just keep "doing the right thing."

~Chantelle Herchenhahn
2009 Mississippi State Teacher of the Year
Science teacher, grades 9-12

First Day Jitters

Mighty things from small beginnings grow.
~John Dryden

I wake with no need for an alarm. I don't need one; it's the first day of school. I spring from my bed and head straight into the bathroom with such excitement, trying to decide whether to wear the pink blouse with my Old Navy fitted grey pants or the black cotton, three-quarter sleeve top with the white capris.

I turn on the shower and let the warm water run from the top of my head, down my shoulders and soak my toes before deciding on the white capris with the black cotton shirt. "Black is grown up," I tell myself. "It looks serious but subdued," and after all, how much longer will I be able to wear white capris with September lurking around the corner? I towel off, get dressed and spend just a few minutes more than normal blow-drying my hair.

My lunch, packed the night before in preparation for the "big day," even has my name on it… in bold permanent marker… the way my mother showed me! It consists of an apple, yogurt, turkey wrap, two bottles of water, three graham crackers and just in case… an orange and sourdough pretzels.

I stuff my lunch into the quilted Vera Bradley bag I bought with my sister over the summer. She bought the same style, but hers is more sedate compared to the bold red, black, blue and yellow swirly patterns on mine. She said it would look great if I wore it with my "funky chunkies," a pet name she gave to my multi-colored, cork-heeled sandals I also picked up with her on a previous shopping trip. "I guarantee all the cool kids will like them!" she promised me as we paid at the register.

Standing at my breakfast counter, I'm not so sure I should be wearing this crazy ensemble that shouts, "Look at me!" But the sensible side of my brain takes over and tells me "Too late now... it's 7:03...." Shoving the last bit of corn muffin into my mouth, I run out the door, only to return several more times as I check and recheck that I have everything.

The cool leather upholstery in the car sends a slight shiver down my spine as I desperately try to think of something witty to impress the people with whom I will spend the next 180 days.

It's 7:48 by the time I reach school, and already a sea of children are forming outside the familiar old brick building. Most of the kids look happy to be there... that's a good sign! Taking a deep breath and heading straight for the crowd, my smile is tight. I don't want the butterflies in my stomach to fly out my mouth the minute I say something. Working my way through parents, teachers and kids, I am encircled and soon everyone wants to know how I spent my summer and where I bought my capris.

Conversation is cut short, however, by the sound of the first bell. Everyone races to stand in their appropriate lines... something you can only learn by watching others over the years. Thank goodness I am not new! I race over to the third grade lines and wait for my name to be announced... suddenly all eyes are on me! As other teachers begin calling their students' names, my line begins "the walk"... down the corridor, past the library, toward the computer room until we stop outside a friendly classroom decorated with apples and bright posters. A sign on the door reads, "WELCOME to THIRD GRADE!"

I walk toward the front of the room and watch as others scramble for a seat which will get them closer to friends, allowing them secret whispers before the teacher starts her introduction.

"Good morning," a cheery voice says. With surprise, I recognize the voice as my own! "My name is Mrs. Benoit, and I will be your teacher this year. I look forward to our getting to know one another better."

Minutes turn into hours and soon, in an empty classroom, erasing the day's dusty memories from the newly painted chalkboard, I smile to myself. "They like me, they really like me!"

~Amy Benoit

An Indian Teaches American-Style in Polynesia

Travel and change of place impart new vigor to the mind.
~Seneca

This is a story of my transformation from a student to an office executive to a teacher with many wonderful experiences in a short span of time!

I was born and brought up in India. I have travelled with my parents and was educated in different cities and towns of India as my father was in the air force and moved from one station to another.

My first teaching assignment was when I was just seventeen years old, while taking my first year Bachelor's degree course in Science (Chemistry, Physics and Math). A tenth-grade boy approached me for tutoring, and initially I hesitated to commit, but my grandmother inspired me to take up the challenge.

Tutoring another high school chemistry student during my second year program was my second teaching assignment, which we successfully completed, as that student was very consistent and forced me to be consistent too! During my higher education courses, I continued tutoring high school students.

After my graduation, I joined the masters program for science in Chemistry but I had to discontinue that after almost two years to take a job in Dubai due to the attraction of a white-collar job with an immediate income to start my married life. After moving to Dubai in the Middle East, I worked with a group of companies continuously for ten years in administration and accounts. At the same time I continued tutoring high school students in Chemistry and Math, part-time.

When my wife Beena got the offer to teach in American Samoa I readily agreed because I liked to teach and wanted a change from the monotonous and high pressure office work.

I started working at Leone High School in the beginning of second semester in 2003-4 and it was hard to cope. There were a bunch of good students in each class but unfortunately I had many spoiled ones too who gave me a lot of headaches. Those days I even thought to return to my previous job. But as a last attempt I started experimenting with different approaches and teaching methods for managing the large classes. It was effective and I was tempted to continue.

Next I decided to do the certification courses and after that there was never an end. I attended all the workshops that were available.

For my current teaching practices, I heavily rely on my experiences from my high school education. While I teach I recall what happened in my high school classrooms. I remember the good teachers and the bad ones. I mostly do not remember the mediocre ones.

I remember the good ones because they were the ones who either had good relationships with us as students or who taught us with utmost sincerity and dedication even if they didn't have an outstanding relationship with us. I remember the bad ones too because either they were very brutal or totally mean and full of vengeance against adolescent behavior. The mediocre ones were not good or bad enough to remember. Now while I teach, whenever I take a step to do something in my class, I compare the situation with my own former classes. That way I am able to predict almost 80% of the psychology of the current students and plan my classes accordingly. I have experienced success in this.

David is an example of this. David came to my class when he was a freshman. He walked into my Physical Science class three years ago. I noticed first that he was very much a village-lifestyle oriented boy. His language was poor. But I found that he was an enthusiastic kid who was willing to participate and learn. I used to give extra science reading and pronunciation practice, as I had other students also who were poor in language, but not as bad as David was. When I encouraged him to read, he readily picked up that challenge. That made him understand the science concepts much better than before and he started getting improved scores in the subject. I even discussed his reading/language problem with his English teacher and she also gave extra care to him for his improvement in reading and speaking skills.

I found that David was not ready to give up, even when other kids teased him while he read. He tried harder and eventually improved his reading skills and he now as a senior speaks well and he gave a speech in English while he ran for the student body president post! He was chosen! He received better scores in science and had better grades than what he was getting in the beginning. And now he is taking Physics in my class as he can read and interpret Physics concepts very well.

As David has his hair trimmed like President Obama and is the student body president, students gave him the nickname "Obama." He used to get annoyed in the beginning but now he likes to be called that and even every employee in the school calls him "Obama!"

We may be located in the middle of the Pacific Ocean, but we are still an American territory with American traditions. Every Thanksgiving period we have an annual school and PTA-organized turkey run (a distance of around five miles) to have a community get-together and fun activities. Professional runners, various community members, teachers as advisors to different classes, power walking teachers, and joggers take part.

Even though I monitored and helped at various water stations I was not participating in the run. But three years ago some of my students challenged me in various ways to participate in the turkey run. I thought I would heed my students' request even though I was not that confident. (I used to take part regularly in long distance running events in the track and field programs back in my school and colleges.)

I decided to use my previous knowledge in running and trained for a couple of weeks and on the turkey day run in 2006, I could beat many of my students, to their surprise. It was fun and the association with them made us closer. I gave them tips for endurance and training and I saw many of them beat me in the next year. I am a regular participant now!

~Murali Gopal
2009 American Samoa State Teacher of the Year
Science teacher, grades 9-12

Editor's note: American Samoa is an unincorporated territory of the United States in the South Pacific Ocean, located about 2,700 miles from Hawaii. The population of about 65,000 lives in a land area a little larger than Washington, D.C.

Touching the Future

The direction in which education starts a man will determine his future life.
~Plato

I am honored and blessed to work in the greatest profession. Despite the long hours and hard work, I finish each day feeling as though I have made a difference. This is the drive that keeps teachers invigorated and passionate. As Christa McAuliffe said "I touch the future, I teach."

When I was named Maryland Teacher of the Year, I received a congratulatory e-mail from a former student, Morgan, who is currently attending Georgetown University and is an officer of the student-run Women in Politics group. I recently turned on the television to watch a college basketball game to find another former student, Austin, running up and down the court for Georgetown. Walking through a shopping mall recently, I encountered a former student, Olade, dressed in a suit. After a brief greeting, he handed me a business card for the company that he just started, at age twenty-two. Another student said he is in the process of applying for law school at Howard University. Believe it or not, I encounter former students with similar success stories nearly every week. One student, Ta-sha, is off to the University of Maryland, Eastern Shore next year to study, of all things, Social Studies/Education. Now that's a student after my own heart!

Seeing the success of former students and knowing that I was able to make a small contribution to their success during the time that they sat in my class, is the greatest reward. Sometimes, while I am watching my current students working and interacting in class, I try to picture what they will be doing ten years from now. I wonder if I am looking at a future senator or judge. Can you imagine being able to say, "I taught Senator Thomas government in tenth grade?" I would not trade my career for any other. We literally touch the future each and every day.

~William Thomas
2009 Maryland State Teacher of the Year
Social Studies teacher, grade 10

Meet Our Contributors

Angela N. Abbott is a fifth grade teacher who earned her Master's degree from Pittsburg State University; she speaks professionally for Abbott Learning (abbottlearning.org), and was named Wal-Mart Teacher of the Year. More than anything, she enjoys spending time with her family. Angela can be contacted at abbottlearning@yahoo.com.

Sandra Picklesimer Aldrich, president and CEO of Bold Words, Inc. in Colorado Springs, is a popular speaker who wraps insight, humor and encouragement around life's serious issues. She is the author or co-author of eighteen books and contributor to two dozen more. Contact her at BoldWords@aol.com.

Sarah Baird (Arizona STOY) received her BA in 1999 and her MA in 2002 from Northern Arizona University. She is a National Board Certified Teacher and was awarded an honorary doctorate in 2009 from Northern Arizona University. She taught 1st grade in Phoenix for six years and currently works as a K-5 Math Coach.

Steve Barr lives in the mountains of North Carolina. His cartoons appear in a wide variety of magazines and newspapers, and he is also the author and illustrator of the *1-2-3 Draw* series of art instruction books for children. In his spare time, he likes to draw and collect minerals.

Amy Benoit graduated from Worcester State College in 1988 with a Bachelor of Science in Elementary Education. She was chosen Worcester Telegram's 2001 Teacher of the Year. Amy enjoys teaching third grade, writing stories for children, vacationing on Cape Cod and spending time with her husband and family.

After graduating from Williams College in 1973, **"Bing" Bingham** worked in the music and television industries, eventually turning to writing full-time. His credits include TV specials for A&E and the screenplay for the Emmy-nominated film, *Faith of My Fathers*. He teaches at a private school in Kent, Connecticut.

Jan Bono taught public school for thirty years on the Long Beach peninsula in the southwest corner of Washington State. She now works as a life coach, writing coach, writing workshop instructor, Law of Attraction presenter and freelance writer. Check out her blog at: www.daybreak-solutions.com/blog.

Richards and Suzanne Boyce have been blessed to work with amazing students, faculty, and beginning teachers throughout Missouri. They enjoy traveling to visit family—especially their two adult children. Please contact them via e-mail at ricksboyce@sbcglobal.net.

Ilah Breen delights in teaching fourth grade in warm and sunny Florida. After spending many years in the cool, foggy lands of Humboldt County, California, she celebrates life by spending time with her family, playing with grandchildren, writing, gardening, and painting.

Kenan Bresnan is a professional salesman with four grown children who enjoys writing stories. Originally his stories were inspired by his children growing up, but then they did and moved away. Often Kenan's inspirations come from his wife, but daily life always seems to present new ideas and concepts.

Jean Brody has a BS in Journalism and Education plus she has done graduate work in Animal Behavior. She has fifteen published Chicken Soup for the Soul stories. Jean has written a weekly newspaper column for twenty years plus a magazine column monthly for eighteen years. She lives with her husband Gene and their animal friends.

Sally J. Broughton (Montana STOY) has a Bachelor of Science, with highest honors, from the University of Illinois and Masters of Education from Montana State University. She received the American Civic Education Teacher Award 2008. She teaches language arts and social studies in a rural middle school.

Cheryl Y. Brundage earned a BA (creative writing) from Oberlin College and a Master's (Spanish) from the University of Houston. She taught English in Spain from 1991-1998 and currently teaches Spanish in Houston, TX. She has published essays in the *Houston Chronicle* and fiction in Spanish in *The Barcelona Review*.

Luajean N. Bryan (Tennessee STOY) was also *USA Today's* All-USA Teacher 2006. She teaches Calculus and Pre Calculus, using project-based learning to make math real, from hot air balloon flights to overnight cavern expeditions. She co-authored the 2011 edition of *Glencoe Pre Calculus*. E-mail her at lbryan@bradleyschools.org.

Brooke M. Businsky received her Bachelor of Arts in English, with honors, and a Master of Education from Towson University. She taught high school English and Journalism for six years.

Cindy Couchman (Kansas STOY) is a National Board Certified instructor in her nineteenth year of teaching high school mathematics in Kansas. She received her BS in Education and Masters of Science in Administration from Kansas State University. Cindy loves to golf, is a Cub Scout leader, runs triathlons, and serves on the church Education Committee.

Bebi Davis (Hawaii STOY) received her Bachelor and Master of Education from the University of Hawaii and is pursuing a PhD. She is a physics and chemistry teacher, a math and biology college instructor, and 2005 Milken National Educator. Bebi loves to help students and hang out with her husband Harry.

Amanda Dodson is a wife and mother to three. She home schools and is a contributing writer to her local newspaper, *The Stokes News*, in Walnut Cove, NC. She has also contributed to other *Chicken Soup for the Soul* books. She can be reached via e-mail at amandadod@roadrunner.com.

Stephanie Doyle (Virginia STOY) received her BA, with honors, from Roanoke College in 1999. She teaches sixth grade U.S. history and reading in Roanoke, VA. She is the founder and director of Girls Rising Onto Womanhood, a non-profit mentoring organization for girls in grades 7-12. Stephanie enjoys traveling, spending time with her family, and mentoring. E-mail her at sdoyle@rcps.info.

Beth Ekre (North Dakota STOY) teaches 6th graders in Fargo, ND. Beth enjoys photography, family time at their Minnesota cabin, coaching track, and participating in service-learning projects with her students. She can be reached via e-mail at Beth_Ekre@fargo.k12.nd.us.

Susan Elliott (Colorado STOY) is an award-winning teacher of students who are deaf or hard of hearing. She also is a National Board Certified Teacher. As a scholar-practitioner, Susan is currently working toward her Ph.D. in Education with Walden University. E-mail her at sjsuz@aol.com.

Malinda Dunlap Fillingim loved teaching at Haliwa-Saponi Tribal School in NC and wishes she had never left. A Rome, GA resident, she works as a hospice chaplain but longs to return to the classroom. She and her husband sing and tell stories to whomever will listen. Contact her via e-mail at fillingim@comcast.net.

Deb Fogg (New Hampshire STOY) has spent the last ten years teaching seventh grade Language Arts in New Hampshire. She loves spending time with her family: Steve, Sara, John, Becca, Mike, and a Golden Retriever, Willy. She enjoys writing, cooking and listening to the loons on Maidstone Lake. Please e-mail her at dfogg@sau36.org.

Edney L. Freeman (Virgin Islands STOY) received his BA from City College of New York in 1977 and his MST from Rochester Institute of Technology-School for American Crafts in 1995. He teaches high school ceramics, sculpture, and calligraphy in St Thomas, VI. He enjoys traveling, languages (Spanish and Arabic), creating his unique sculptural ceramics works, swimming and martial arts.

Sharon Gallagher-Fishbaugh (Utah STOY) received her BA, with honors, and an MA from National University. She is also a National Board Certified Teacher. Sharon has taught for thirty-one years and currently teaches second grade. She enjoys traveling, reading, and spending time with her family and dogs!

Julie Mellott George graduated magna cum laude from Penn State Altoona with a Bachelor of Arts degree in English. She works as an assistant director of marketing for college admission in Boston. Julie enjoys reading, writing and traveling with her new husband.

Karen Gill (Kentucky STOY) teaches physics at Henry Clay High School in Lexington, Kentucky. Her husband, Scot Gill, also an award-winning teacher, teaches physics at Tates Creek High School in Lexington. They enjoy traveling and kayaking and are expecting their first child in January 2010.

Christine Gleason (Texas STOY) received her Bachelor of Arts and Master's degrees from the University of Texas at El Paso. She teaches English 4, Advanced Placement English 4 and Dual Credit at Fabens High School in Fabens, Texas. She has a wonderful husband and a four-year-old son who inspire her tremendously.

Murali Gopal (American Samoa STOY) was born and raised in India and now lives with his family in American Samoa, where he teaches at Leone High School. Murali likes working with students to engage in science research works inside and outside the classroom, reading, travelling, and spending time with family and friends. E-mail him at murligopal@yahoo.com.

Dorothy Goff Goulet (Dept of Defense Education Activity STOY), an Air Force spouse, lives in Germany where she teaches French and Social Studies at Ramstein High School at the U.S. Air Base. She is pursuing a doctoral degree in Educational Leadership. She enjoys travel, cooking, and art projects. She is a native of Ruston, Louisiana. Contact her via e-mail at Dorothy.Goulet@yahoo.com.

Tommie Ann Grinnell received her Bachelor's degree from Texas A&M University. She spent thirty years in education as an elementary teacher and librarian. Tommie is now retired and pursuing a career as a writer. She lives in Tyler, Texas.

Jennifer A. Haberling (Michigan STOY) has been blessed to teach high schoolers and middle schoolers in English classes for the last sixteen years. Jen lives with her husband Tim, her son Devin, and her daughter Ali. She enjoys camping, cooking, creating and reading.

Jenna Hallman (South Carolina STOY) received her Bachelor's degree from the University of SC and her Master's from Clemson University. She taught second grade at Calhoun Academy of the Arts. Jenna has a wonderful husband and two fantastic sons.

Patrick Hardin is a cartoonist with degrees in Philosophy and Psychology. He currently enjoys the halcyon settings of his home town—Flint, Michigan. He may be contacted via e-mail at phardin357@aol.com.

Tania Harman (Indiana STOY) received her BA from Bethel College, Mishawaka, IN, in 1985, an MS from Indiana University in 1996, and is currently pursuing an EdD in Educational Leadership from Walden University. She has been teaching for twenty-two years in South Bend Community School Corporation where she is employed as a New Language Teacher.

Linda Heffner (Iowa STOY) completed undergraduate studies at Briar Cliff University in Sioux City, IA. She received her Masters in Administration from Wayne State College. Linda began teaching in 1984 at Everett Elementary School in Sioux City, IA. She still teaches at Everett today. Linda enjoys hiking, athletics, and time with family.

Chantelle Herchenhahn (Mississippi STOY), NBCT in Adolescent Science, has taught Chemistry, Physics and Biology at Forest High School for twenty years. A native Mississippian, she holds a BS degree from Tarleton State University and an MS from University of Southern Mississippi. She has one adopted son, DeVardrick Carter.

Roy Hudson (Alabama STOY) is the Director of Theatre for the acclaimed Shades Valley Theatre Academy in Birmingham, Alabama. His plays have been produced all over the world including Off-Broadway and in Edinburgh, Scotland. He credits his wife, Alane, for giving him the courage to teach. His e-mail is rhudson@jefcoed.com.

MaryLu Hutchins (West Virginia STOY) carries on a family tradition of excellence in public education. Her grandfather, grandmother, and mother experienced distinguished teaching careers. As a family, they accrued 125 years of combined educational service. Hutchins, a first grade teacher and Phi Delta Kappa honoree, is a doctoral candidate at West Virginia University.

After teaching for nineteen years, **Robbie Iobst** put her chalk away to become a full-time writer/speaker. She lives in Centennial, Colorado with her husband John, son Noah and dog Scooby. E-mail Robbie at robbieiobst@hotmail.com or check out her blog at robbieiobst. blogspot.com.

Steve Johnson (Nevada STOY) was awarded a Bachelor of Science degree in 1986, and a Masters of Science in 1998. Steve teaches chemistry at Churchill County High School in Fallon, NV. He has received the Presidential Award of Excellence in Science Teaching and National Board Certification in 2003. Steve likes hiking, musical theater, art, and target shooting.

Susan Johnson (Washington STOY) teaches high school English Language Arts in the Cascade Mountains. She is also a Co-Director of the Central Washington Writing Project. Her love of language and literacy drives her teaching as well as her writing.

Ronald W. Kaiser, Jr. received his Master's degree in English Literature from the University of New Hampshire. He lives and teaches English in New Hampshire's Lakes Region. Writing stories is his second passion, next to his radiant wife. And then of course there are his two terriers.

Alex Kajitani (California STOY) is known around the country as "The Rappin' Mathematician." He also speaks nationally about "Making Math Cool!" Visit www.MathRaps.com to check out his music and videos!

Paul Karrer has been published in the *San Francisco Chronicle*, *Christian Science Monitor*, and reads his stories regularly on NPR affiliate radio station KUSP in Santa Cruz, California. He teaches in central California. To contact him look at his writer's website: www. paulhkarrer.com.

Alice L. King (Wyoming STOY) has a degree in Speech Communication and Secondary Education from Augustana College, and a Master's from Lesley University with a focus on Integrating the Arts. She teaches high school seniors, and coaches the speech and debate team. Alice spends time traveling with her family and reading a great book. Please e-mail her at aking@ccsd.k12.wy.us.

Paul Kuhlman (South Dakota STOY) received his BS degree in Biology Education from North Dakota State University in 1988. He also holds Master Degrees in Secondary Administration and Natural Science, both from the University of South Dakota. Please contact him via e-mail at paul.kuhlman@k12.sd.us.

Sharilynn La May received her BA in English at SUNY in Albany. Retired now, she lives in Florida and writes in several genres. One of her plays recently won second place in the *Writer's Digest* competition. She plans now to publish poems on teen angst, based on her observations while teaching.

NBCT **Jean (Brophy) Lamar (Florida STOY)** received her B.A.E. and M.Ed from the University of North Florida and is past-president of the Florida Council of Teachers of English. She is teaching high school English and reading while working on her doctorate. E-mail her at jeanlamar2009@gmail.com.

Michael Lampert (Oregon STOY) teaches physics with gifted colleagues at West Salem High in Oregon. He loves art and finds every excuse to place it into the science curriculum. His students constantly amaze him with their joy for learning. He proudly displays their work and photographs, also including those of his three children. E-mail him at mlampert@aol.com.

Diana Leddy (Vermont STOY) earned her MEd in 1999 from Antioch New England Graduate School. Diana has been active in promoting literacy throughout Vermont. She has coauthored several books for teachers, most recently *Writing for Understanding*. Please e-mail her at kdsquest@aol.com.

Janeen Lewis is a freelance writer living in Kentucky with her husband and son. Before her son Andrew was born, she loved learning from her students as a teacher. Lewis has previously been published in *Chicken Soup for the Soul: Power Moms* and *Chicken Soup for the Soul: Count Your Blessings.*

Anna M. Lowther is pursuing writing full-time. She has been published in several paperback fiction anthologies and magazines. She is currently working on a historical fiction novel for tweens and two adult fantasies. She still works with children as a Venture Crew Leader and church music volunteer.

Patricia L. Marini received her Bachelor and Masters of Science, and Sixth Year Professional Diploma in education from Southern Connecticut State University. She teaches in Bridgeport, Connecticut, where she grew up. She believes before you can teach a child, you have to know him. She resides in Connecticut with her husband.

Sara Matson taught in a variety of environments for seven years. After that, she happily retired from teaching to stay home with her daughters and pursue a writing career. She lives with her family in Minnesota.

Leanne Maule-Sims (Georgia STOY), now an educator in North Georgia, earned her Bachelor's degree in English Education from Eastern Michigan University. Her Master's degree is in Technology and her Specialist Degree, from Nova Southeastern University, is in Brain-based Learning. She plans to write books on the art and science of motivating students.

Dan McCarthy (Nebraska STOY) received his BA (1975) and MS in Education (1983) from Kearney State College. He has devoted his thirty-five-year career to teaching mechanical and architectural drafting at Hastings Senior High School. He met his wife during their first year of teaching and they have three grown children. E-mail Dan at dmccarth@esu9.org.

Lisa McCaskill has been teaching for thirteen years. Each year is a fresh start, and there are always new challenges. Lisa enjoys spending time with family and friends, and whenever there's a free moment, she writes stories of faith, hope, and love. Please e-mail her at mrsmccaskill@yahoo.com.

Vickie Mike (New York STOY) received her Bachelor of Arts, with honors, from Brockport State College, her Master of Education from the University of Buffalo, and her Doctor of Education degree from Binghamton University. She teaches Spanish in Horseheads, New York. Vickie enjoys public speaking, art, travel, and golf. Contact her via e-mail at tmike@stny.rr.com.

Celeste M. Miller, a New York City public school teacher, is a Learning Specialist at the Professional Performing Arts School in Manhattan. Following a corporate career, she became a New York City Teaching Fellow, teaching art to students with special needs and earning a Master's degree in Education before joining the staff of PPAS. E-mail her at Celeste17@juno.com.

Diane M Miller received her Bachelor of General Studies from Indiana University in 1995. She works part-time. Diane enjoys quilting, gaming, traveling and playing with her dogs. She is currently working on a mystery for adults and an adventure book for children. Please e-mail her at dmiller2011@tampabay.rr.com.

Kate Lynn Mishara received her Bachelor of Science in Journalism from the University of Colorado at Boulder in 2008. She is currently working toward her teaching license, and looks forward to becoming an elementary school teacher in upcoming months. Kate loves to travel, ski, and spend time with family and friends.

Martha Moore has taught English and Creative Writing in Texas high schools for most of her life. She is an award-winning author of three Young Adult and Middle Grade novels: *Under the Mermaid*

Angel, Angels on the Roof, and *Matchit*. She enjoys inspiring others to tell their own stories.

Amy (Grether) Morrison spent six years teaching Middle School Language Arts in South-Central Los Angeles. Working now as a freelance writer, Amy lives with her husband, Jamie, and their three future middle-schoolers in Spokane, Washington. Contact her via e-mail at amy@word-spring.com.

Anthony J. Mullen (Connecticut STOY, National TOY) received his BA, with honors, from Long Island University, C.W. Post College, and a Master of Education, with distinction, from Mercy College. Anthony teaches at the ARCH School, an alternative high school in Connecticut. Please e-mail him at Archteacher@optonline.net.

Jeanne Muzi (New Jersey STOY) loves teaching first grade at Ben Franklin School in Lawrenceville, NJ. Jeanne enjoys drawing and reading. She wrote and illustrated a children's book called *Sam's Skates*. She lives in Lawrenceville with her husband and two sons.

Lori Neurohr (Wisconsin STOY) received her Bachelor of Arts, with honors, from Lakeland College in Sheboygan, Wisconsin. She received her Masters of reading and language arts from Cardinal Stritch University in Milwaukee, Wisconsin. Lori enjoys reading, traveling, golfing and working with children. Please e-mail her at slkneurohr@yahoo.com.

Gloria L. Noyes (Maine STOY) is a fifth grade teacher in Southern Maine. In the classroom her passion is literacy instruction, teaching citizenship and making her students feel safe, valued, and precious. She is a lifelong learner and is currently working on her doctorate. Please contact her via e-mail at gnoyes@me.com or http://wsdblog.westbrook.k12.me.us/teacheroftheyear.

Derek Olson (Minnesota STOY) lives and teaches 6th grade in

Stillwater, MN. He received his BA from St. Olaf College and his MA from the University of St. Thomas. Derek also enjoys, fishing, hunting, camping, and hanging out with his wonderful wife and children. You can e-mail him at olsonderek@stillwater.k12.mn.us.

Mark Parisi's "off the mark" comic, syndicated since 1987, is distributed by United Media. Mark's humor also graces greeting cards, T-shirts, calendars, magazines, newsletters and books. Check out: offthemark.com. Lynn is his wife/business partner. Their daughter Jen contributes with inspiration (as do three cats and one dog).

James Edward Phillips (Northern Mariana Islands STOY) teaches at Marianas High School on the Pacific island of Saipan. He holds a Master of Science degree, is a PADI scuba diving instructor, and a CPR/First-Aid instructor trainer.

Stephanie Piro lives in New Hampshire with her husband and three cats. She is one of King Features' "Six Chix" (appearing Saturdays). Her single panel, "Fair Game," appears in newspapers and on stephaniepiro.com. She is also an illustrator, a gift designer for her company Strip T's and a part-time librarian. Contact her via e-mail at stephaniepiro@gmail.com.

Kay Conner Pliszka has received numerous school and community awards for her work with teens. Now retired, she is a frequent contributor to Chicken Soup for the Soul. Also, as a motivational speaker, Kay shares her humorous, turbulent and inspirational experiences from teaching. She may be reached via e-mail at kmpliskza@comcast.net.

Sherry Poff teaches high school English in Chattanooga, Tennessee. She writes non-fiction and poetry. Favorite topics are family, faith, the outdoors, and — of course — teaching.

Tim Ramsey has been an educator since 1983. He currently is a school administrator at Garden Lakes School in Arizona. Writing allows him to share his love for children and teaching with others. Tim lives with his wife, daughter and seven cats in Avondale, Arizona. Please contact him via e-mail at tramsey@q.com.

Adrienne C. Reynolds was a teacher for twenty-two years and now works for Broward County Schools as a Testing Specialist. Adrienne enjoys being with her family and volunteering. One of the goals on her "bucket list" is to write a book that will inspire others for generations to come. Please e-mail her at clasywritr@bellsouth.net.

Cindi Rigsbee (North Carolina STOY), an English Language Arts teacher, currently serves as a Literacy Coach and Beginning Teacher District Mentor in Orange County Schools, NC. A National Board Certified Teacher, Cindi was a finalist for National Teacher of the Year. She enjoys writing poetry and blogging, and her book, *Finding Mrs. Warnecke*, published by Jossey-Bass, highlights her journey as a teacher.

Jayde Rossi received her Bachelor of Science degree in Human Services, with honors, from California State University, Fullerton in 2008. She works for the Orangewood Children's Foundation, an organization that focuses on the ongoing needs of children in the foster care system.

Gary Rubinstein has been teaching math, training new teachers, and writing about teaching since 1991. His first book, *Reluctant Disciplinarian*, where a shortened version of this story first appeared, was published in 1999 by Cottonwood Press, Inc. His second book, *Beyond Survival*, will be published in 2010. You can e-mail him at garymrubinstein@gmail.com.

Marcia Rudoff is a memoir writing teacher and newspaper columnist in her hometown of Bainbridge Island, Washington. A freelance writer, her stories have appeared in anthologies, magazines and newspapers.

Personal interests include quality time with family and friends, travel, baseball and chocolate.

Lisa Miller Rychel earned a BA from the University of North Florida. She teaches middle school science in Tampa. Lisa is also a silversmith, and enjoys racing her sailboat with her family. Her heart remains close to her hometown, Wadsworth, Ohio. Please e-mail her at lrychel@tampabay.rr.com.

Michael Jordan Segal, who defied all odds after being shot in the head, is a husband, father, social worker, author (including a CD/Download of twelve stories entitled *Possible*) and inspirational speaker. He's had many stories published in Chicken Soup for the Soul books. To contact Mike or to order his CD, please visit www.InspirationByMike.com.

Robin Sly (Idaho STOY) is a first grade teacher in Boise, Idaho. She received her Bachelor of Arts and Master's degree from Boise State University. She is currently working on her Doctorate in Teacher Leadership. She enjoys reading, traveling and spending time with family.

Linda A. Smerge (Illinois STOY) received her BS in Education, MS in Early Childhood Education, and JD from Northern Illinois University. Currently, she is working on an advanced degree in administration. She has taught pre-kindergarten through 12th grade and enjoys all grade levels due to the relationships she builds with her students.

Sarah Smiley is a syndicated columnist, author and military wife. Her new book, *I'm Just Saying...*, is a collection of columns about being a wife and mother. Learn more about Sarah at www.SarahSmiley.com.

Rebecca Snyder (Pennsylvania STOY) teaches English and serves as Senior High Language Arts Department Head at Greater Latrobe Senior High School in southwestern Pennsylvania. A 1996 graduate of Saint Vincent College, she believes that a teacher's best tools are creativity, passion, and enthusiasm.

Heather Sparks (Oklahoma STOY) received her BS and Master of Education, with honors, from Oklahoma City University in 1995. She teaches sixth and eighth graders at Taft Middle School in Oklahoma City. Heather is the 2008 recipient of the Presidential Award for Excellence in Mathematics Teaching. Visit her website: www.hisparks.com.

Diane Stark is a teacher, a wife and mother of five, and a writer. She loves to write about the important things in life: her family and her faith. Her first book, *Teacher's Devotions to Go*, was released last fall. She can be reached at DianeStark19@yahoo.com.

Nancy Hamilton Sturm has taught high school English in Wichita, KS for twenty-one years. She also helps facilitate the South Central Kansas Writing Project at Wichita State University. Nancy has published several devotional articles and is currently writing a book of scriptural meditations. Please contact Nancy at sconanstuwich@aol.com.

Mark D. Teesdale (Delaware STOY), a graduate of West Chester University and Wilmington University, teaches 4th and 5th grade general music and chorus at Lake Forest Central Elementary School in Felton, DE. Mark also is a Yale Distinguished Music Educator. Please contact him at mdteesdale@lf.k12.de.us.

Quyen Thai moved to the United States from Australia in February 2008. Quyen teaches elementary school in Washington. She enjoys reading, being outdoors, seeing friends and traveling. She plans to write young adult and middle grade novels. Please e-mail her at quyen1979@hotmail.com.

Will Thomas (Maryland STOY) received his BA in Social Studies-Education from the State University of New York at Albany and his

Master's from Bowie State University. Will teaches AP Government in Prince George's County, MD. He coaches the Mock Trial Team and sponsors the Stock Market/Investment Club at Dr. Henry A. Wise Jr. High School.

Deborah Hohn Tonguis (Louisiana STOY) has a BA from Nicholls State University and a Master's in Student Development from Azusa Pacific University. She teaches Social Studies at Mandeville High in Southern Louisiana and enjoys family, LSU baseball, Saints football and painting. She plans to teach undergraduate education students. E-mail: dtonguis@yahoo.com.

Adrienne Townsend received her BA in Secondary Social Studies and Master of Education in Secondary from Texas Christian University in 2007. She teaches high school U.S. History and World Geography in Texas. Adrienne enjoys traveling abroad, reading, and spending time with her family. Please e-mail her at Adrienne.L.Townsend@gmail.com.

Blythe Turner (New Mexico STOY) received her Bachelor of Education and Master of Education at Eastern New Mexico University. She is a second grade bilingual teacher and is currently a doctoral student in the Language, Literacy and Socio-Cultural Studies department at the University of New Mexico.

Susan Waggener (Arkansas STOY) received her Bachelor of Business Administration from the University of Memphis, 1979, summa cum laude, and her Bachelor of Arts in Education and Mathematics from Arkansas State University, 1980. She currently teaches geometry at West Memphis Senior High School.

Barbara Walton-Faria (Rhode Island STOY) teaches science at Thompson Middle School in Newport, RI. She has a BS in Natural Resources and an MS in Secondary Education from the University of Rhode Island. When not teaching she can be found out on the water kayaking, snorkeling, or photographing wildlife.

George A. Watson (Massachusetts STOY) received his BA in Spanish from Boston University and his MA in Spanish from Middlebury College. He teaches Spanish and is Department Head of Foreign Languages at Walpole High School in Massachusetts. George enjoys traveling, photography, bicycling and cooking. He and his wife Janet have two sons.

Rick Weber has a BA in Journalism from Penn State. He has won the Casey Medal for Meritorious Journalism, been honored twice by the AP Sports Editors and contributed to *Chicken Soup for the Soul: The Golf Book*. His first book, *Pink Lips and Fingertips*, was released in 2009. E-mail him at webodespo@yahoo.com.

Deborah Wickerham (Ohio STOY) has been a teacher for thirty-three years. She graduated from Bowling Green State University and the University of Findlay. Teaching is not a job, but a love. Annie Sullivan, Helen Keller's teacher, taught Deb dedication and caring for children. Deb loves history, science, reading and traveling. E-mail her at dwickerham@findlaycityschools.org.

Bob Williams (Alaska STOY) believes that being a teacher is the best job in the world. He holds degrees in Petroleum Engineering, Mathematics Education, and Educational Leadership. He is an independent speaker, educational trainer, and secondary math teacher. He can be contacted at Bob.Williams@matsuk12.us.

Margaret Williams (Missouri STOY) (BS, MAT), a recently retired thirty-eight-year teacher, worked in two St. Louis public high schools and University City High School. She continues to coach the award-winning U-City Mock Trial Teams and is active with West Side MB Church, Delta Sigma Theta, and her grandchildren. Contact her at marwilliams@sbcglobal.net.

Stephanie Scharaga Winnick is a retired elementary school teacher from Long Island, New York. Her love of children motivates her to continue in the field as a substitute teacher. Her passion for reading is evident in book discussion groups. Please e-mail her at winnick37@optonline.net.

Kimberly Worthy (District of Columbia STOY) is an advocate for educational excellence in urban schools, and has served as a middle school social studies and language arts teacher and a curriculum developer. She uses cultural foundations of teaching and a cross-curricular approach. E-mail her at dc2009toy@gmail.com or visit dctoy2009classroombeyond.shutterfly.com.

D. B. Zane has a multiple-subject credential as well as a single-subject credential in social studies. She currently works for the Middle School Parliamentary Debate Program. In her spare time, she enjoys reading and writing.

Meet Our Authors

Jack Canfield is the co-creator of the *Chicken Soup for the Soul* series, which *Time* magazine has called "the publishing phenomenon of the decade." Jack is also the co-author of many other bestselling books.

Jack is the CEO of the Canfield Training Group in Santa Barbara, California, and founder of the Foundation for Self-Esteem in Culver City, California. He has conducted intensive personal and professional development seminars on the principles of success for more than a million people in twenty-three countries, has spoken to hundreds of thousands of people at more than 1,000 corporations, universities, professional conferences and conventions, and has been seen by millions more on national television shows.

Jack has received many awards and honors, including three honorary doctorates and a Guinness World Records Certificate for having seven books from the *Chicken Soup for the Soul* series appearing on the New York Times bestseller list on May 24, 1998.

You can reach Jack at www.jackcanfield.com.

Mark Victor Hansen is the co-founder of Chicken Soup for the Soul, along with Jack Canfield. He is a sought-after keynote speaker, bestselling author, and marketing maven. Mark's powerful messages of possibility, opportunity, and action have created powerful change in thousands of organizations and millions of individuals worldwide.

Mark is a prolific writer with many bestselling books in addition to the *Chicken Soup for the Soul* series. Mark has had a profound influence in the field of human potential through his library of audios, videos, and articles in the areas of big thinking, sales achievement, wealth building, publishing success, and personal and professional development. He is also the founder of the MEGA Seminar Series.

Mark has received numerous awards that honor his entrepreneurial spirit, philanthropic heart, and business acumen. He is a lifetime member of the Horatio Alger Association of Distinguished Americans.

You can reach Mark at www.markvictorhansen.com.

Amy Newmark is the publisher of *Chicken Soup for the Soul*, after a thirty-year career as a writer, speaker, financial analyst, and business executive in the worlds of finance and telecommunications. Amy is a *magna cum laude* graduate of Harvard College, where she majored in Portuguese, minored in French, and traveled extensively. She is also the mother of two children in college and two grown stepchildren who are recent college graduates.

After a long career writing books on telecommunications, voluminous financial reports, business plans, and corporate press releases, Chicken Soup for the Soul is a breath of fresh air for Amy. She has fallen in love with Chicken Soup for the Soul and its life-changing books, and really enjoys putting these books together for Chicken Soup's wonderful readers. She has co-authored more than two dozen *Chicken Soup for the Soul* books.

Reach Amy through the webmaster@chickensoupforthesoul.com.

Thank You!

My heartfelt thanks go out to Tony Mullen, who introduced me to all the 2009 State Teachers of the Year, and also to Jon Quam, who runs that fabulous program and who welcomed me into the company of these award-winning teachers. This was an incredibly exciting project for us at Chicken Soup for the Soul. We felt so privileged to work with all the 2009 State Teachers of the Year, and especially National Teacher of the Year Tony Mullen, who is creative, compassionate, caring, and certainly educates the "whole child" in his capacity as the head of the alternative high school in our town.

I also owe huge thanks to all of our contributors. We know that you pour your hearts and souls into the thousands of stories and poems that you share with us, and ultimately with each other. We appreciate your willingness to open up your lives to other Chicken Soup for the Soul readers.

We can only publish a small percentage of the stories that are submitted, but we read every single one and even the ones that do not appear in the book have an influence on us and on the final manuscript.

I want to thank Chicken Soup for the Soul editor Kristiana Glavin for reading the thousands of stories and poems that were submitted for this book. She helped me narrow down an incredibly high quality group of submissions. You teachers sure know how to write! I also want to thank D'ette Corona, our assistant publisher, who worked with the State Teachers of the Year and all our other contributors to ensure that students' names were changed when necessary and that everyone was happy with their final story. I also want to thank our editor and webmaster Barbara LoMonaco, a former teacher herself, for her expert proofreading assistance.

We owe a very special thanks to our creative director and book producer, Brian Taylor at Pneuma Books, for his brilliant vision for our covers and interiors. Finally, none of this would be possible without the business and creative leadership of our CEO, Bill Rouhana, and our president, Bob Jacobs.

~Amy Newmark
Publisher and Editor-in-Chief

Chicken Soup for the Soul
Improving Your Life Every Day

Real people sharing real stories—for fifteen years. Now, Chicken Soup for the Soul has gone beyond the bookstore to become a world leader in life improvement. Through books, movies, DVDs, online resources and other partnerships, we bring hope, courage, inspiration and love to hundreds of millions of people around the world. Chicken Soup for the Soul's writers and readers belong to a one-of-a-kind global community, sharing advice, support, guidance, comfort, and knowledge.

Chicken Soup for the Soul stories have been translated into more than forty languages and can be found in more than one hundred countries. Every day, millions of people experience a Chicken Soup for the Soul story in a book, magazine, newspaper or online. As we share our life experiences through these stories, we offer hope, comfort and inspiration to one another. The stories travel from person to person, and from country to country, helping to improve lives everywhere.

Chicken Soup
for the Soul®

Share with Us

We all have had Chicken Soup for the Soul moments in our lives. If you would like to share your story or poem with millions of people around the world, go to chickensoup.com and click on "Submit Your Story." You may be able to help another reader, and become a published author at the same time. Some of our past contributors have launched writing and speaking careers from the publication of their stories in our books!

Our submission volume has been increasing steadily—the quality and quantity of your submissions has been fabulous. We only accept story submissions via our website. They are no longer accepted via mail or fax.

To contact us regarding other matters, please send us an e-mail through webmaster@chickensoupforthesoul.com, or fax or write us at:

Chicken Soup for the Soul
P.O. Box 700
Cos Cob, CT 06807-0700
Fax: 203-861-7194

One more note from your friends at Chicken Soup for the Soul: Occasionally, we receive an unsolicited book manuscript from one of our readers, and we would like to respectfully inform you that we do not accept unsolicited manuscripts and we must discard the ones that appear.

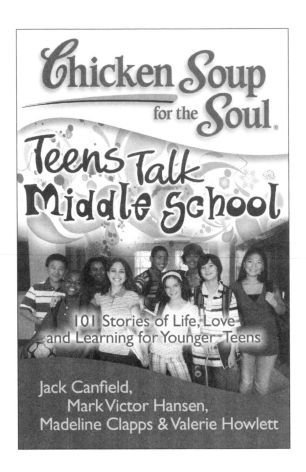

Middle school is a tough time. And this "support group in a book" is specifically geared to those younger teens—the ones still worrying about puberty, cliques, discovering the opposite sex, and figuring out who they are. For ages eleven to fourteen, stories cover regrets, lessons learned, love and "like," popularity, friendship, divorce, illness and death, embarrassing moments, bullying, and finding a passion. Great support and inspiration for middle schoolers.

978-1-935096-26-9

Let your middle schoolers know they are not alone

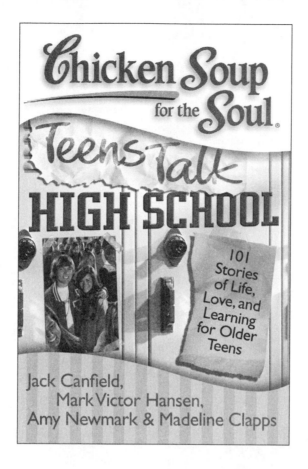

Teens in high school have mainly moved past worrying about puberty and cliques, so this book covers topics of interest to older teens—sports and clubs, driving, curfews, self-image and self-acceptance, dating and sex, family, friends, divorce, illness, death, pregnancy, drinking, failure, and preparing for life after graduation. High school students will find comfort and inspiration in this book, referring to it through all four years of high school, like a portable support group.

978-1-935096-25-2

Help your
high schoolers
navigate those teen years

www.chickensoup.com